SECOND EDITION

PRACTICAL GUIDE TO
CONSOLIDATED RETURNS

JAMES C. WARNER

.CCH

a Wolters Kluwer business

Editorial Staff

Editor . . . . Holly Whorton

Production . . . . Christopher Zwirek

Index . . . . Lynn Brown

Practical Guide to Consolidated Returns was previously published by CCH as *Consolidated Returns Guide*.

This publication is designed to provide accurate and authoritative information in regard to the subject matter covered. It is sold with the understanding that the publisher is not engaged in rendering legal, accounting, or other professional service and that the authors are not offering such advice in this publication. If legal advice or other expert assistance is required, the services of a competent professional person should be sought.

ISBN 978-0-8080-1615-1

No claim is made to original government works; however, within this Product or Publication, the following are subject to CCH's copyright: (1) the gathering, compilation, and arrangement of such government materials; (2) the magnetic translation and digital conversion of data, if applicable; (3) the historical, statutory and other notes and references; and (4) the commentary and other materials.

Printed in the United States of America

To my proud and loving parents,
Henry F. Warner (deceased) and J. Kathryn Warner

To my wife and best friend, Frances Shelburne Warner

To my precious children, Kathryn Pagnotta and Douglas Warner

To my supportive brother and sister, Jack Warner and Jill Harmer

Preface

The principal lesson I have learned from practicing, teaching, and writing about consolidated returns for many years is to "simplify the unsimplifiable." This means explaining things like a teacher: (1) Tell 'em what you are going to say before you say it, say it, and tell 'em what you said, and (2) keep it simple, logical, and concise.

To these ends, the first chapter (and the beginning of each chapter) explains what the book (and each chapter) is about. This generally includes the Internal Revenue Code and more specifically the major "systems" of related consolidated return regulations. Then, each topic in a chapter is discussed at a high level before the chapter (except Chapter 9) ends with a conclusion and frequently asked questions. Each chapter thus points the reader in the right direction without exhausting detail. The volume ends with Practice Tools.

With this *Practical Guide to Consolidated Returns*, readers can easily study the consolidated return regulations, research with an electronic library, and read other books that are designed as research tools—which this book is not. Further, with an understanding of the framework of the consolidated return regulations, readers can gain an insight into the interaction of various provisions that could be lost if 500 pages were devoted to a chapter rather than a much smaller number.

Please send feedback and suggestions for improving this book to james.warner@wal-mart.com.

All information is based on the Internal Revenue Code and Regulations in effect as of December 31, 2006.

James C. Warner

January 2007

About the Author

James C. Warner, CPA, J.D., LL.M, is an accomplished Senior Director, Tax Research for Wal-Mart Stores, Inc.—the world's largest taxpayer. At Wal-Mart, Mr. Warner is the point person for advising the company's Tax Department on federal income tax issues, including consolidated returns. He also trains Tax Department professionals in tax research and persuasive writing.

Before joining Wal-Mart in 2004, Mr. Warner served as Mergers and Acquisitions Segment Leader for Ernst & Young's Online Tax Advisor in Washington, D.C. In that capacity, he reviewed over 500 consolidated return questions submitted by Ernst & Young tax professionals and clients. Mr. Warner also was a finalist for the 2003 Ernst & Young Rosemarie Meschi award for promotion of gender equity.

Before joining Ernst & Young in 1996, Mr. Warner was the lead consolidated return partner for Lee, Toomey & Kent, a tax specialty law firm with a Fortune 500 practice in Washington, D.C. that has since become part of McDermott, Will & Emery. While at Lee, Toomey & Kent, Mr. Warner confidentially reviewed consolidated return regulations for the U.S. Treasury Department before their public release.

Before joining Lee, Toomey & Kent in 1979, Mr. Warner was an attorney-advisor for Judge William Drennen of the U.S. Tax Court and the Interpretative Division of the Chief Counsel's Office of the Internal Revenue Service, both in Washington, D.C.

Mr. Warner graduated first in his class in the LL.M in Taxation program at Georgetown University Law Center, was co-named the outstanding law journal editor at the Ohio State University College of Law, and earned the highest grades of any business student at Grove City College.

This book is the outgrowth of materials Mr. Warner developed for both the consolidated returns course he taught as an adjunct professor at Georgetown University Law Center, a popular one-day consolidated returns seminar he taught for many Tax Executive Institute chapters, and three earlier editions published by CCH and Little Brown.

Mr. Warner co-authored the "Corporate Overview" portfolio (BNA 2005) and wrote "Federal Income Taxation for CPA Candidates" (CPA Study Aids 1982).

Acknowledgments

Despite the single name on the cover, this volume is not the work of just one person. My Lee, Toomey & Kent, Ernst & Young, and Wal-Mart clients contributed with their challenging questions, giving me a base to determine what problems are frequently encountered. Standing at the top of the list of my consolidated return tutors over the years is Andrew Dubroff, the former Treasury Department attorney who wrote much of the current consolidated return regulations and brought me to Ernst & Young. Jerry Mason and Jennifer Shearer at Ernst & Young also provided wisdom on NOL and credit carryovers. The seven responders in the mergers and acquisitions segment of Online Tax Advisor I headed at Ernst & Young—Steven Madsen, Charles Chromow, Jeanne Blackmore, Valerie Williams, Mary Walsh, Michele Burtschi, and Anjanette Frias—also contributed to my knowledge with their expert responses. Holly Whorton, CCH's editor, deserves a pat on the back for her patience and commitment in completing this work.

Courtney Martin, the young star of Wal-Mart's Tax Department, deserves special recognition for drafting the Schedule M-3 piece of Chapter 2. Like all Courtney's work this is excellent.

Like any lawyer, I take full credit for the good aspects of this book and can find someone to blame for any errors.

Contents

Contents in Detail

Chapter 1

Consolidated Returns in General

¶ 101 Overview—Consolidated Returns in General

The purpose of this volume is to provide a concise explanation of the federal income taxation of consolidated groups (i.e., it is a primer rather than a research tool). To make the volume understandable, it addresses situations most commonly encountered. In keeping with the goal of presenting rules of general application, rules relating to special industries, such as oil and gas, thrift, banking, insurance, or mining are ignored. In the same vein, all corporations are C corporations. Having focused on the framework of the consolidated return regulations, the reader should be prepared to address more complex situations with further study of the regulations.

Chapter 2 begins with the treatment of consolidated returns. Chapters 3-6 discuss various "systems" of regulations that are unique to consolidated returns: stock basis, loss limitation, intercompany transaction, and net operating loss and credit limitations. Chapter 7 explores earnings and profits, Chapter 8 examines continuation of the consolidated group, and Chapter 9 provides a checklist of the consolidated return aspects of a subsidiary joining or leaving a consolidated group. Each chapter generally begins with an executive summary and ends with conclusions and frequently asked questions. At the end of the book are a number of Practice Tools, primarily sample elections.

Except as otherwise noted, throughout this volume all corporations file a consolidated return; P, P1, P2, etc. represents the parent of a consolidated subsidiary designated as S, S1, S2, etc. or T. For simplicity, a flat corporate tax rate of 35 percent is assumed.

¶ 115 Treatment of Consolidated Returns

.01 Eligibility for Filing Consolidated Returns

Code Sec. 1501[1] permits an "affiliated group" (as defined by Code Sec. 1504(a)) to elect to file a consolidated return. To qualify as an affiliated group, the group must include a common parent corporation that is an "includible corporation" and at least one other includible corporation in which the parent owns at least 80 percent of the voting power and of the total value of its stock. The affiliated group also includes any other includible corporation if its stock is owned by members of the consolidated group under the same 80-percent-ownership tests. Certain preferred stock described in Code Sec. 1504(a)(4) is not treated as stock for this purpose.

Code Sec. 1504(b) defines an "includible corporation" as any corporation other than certain corporations (such as foreign corporations, insurance companies, and real estate investment trusts (REITs)) that would unnecessarily complicate the consolidated return regulations.

> **Example 1:** P, a large retail company, owns all the stock of S, I, F1, F2, F3, and 99 percent of R. P operates retail stores west of the Mississippi, and S operates retail stores east of the Mississippi. I is a captive insurance company subject to taxation under Code Sec. 801. R is a REIT, which leases the stores to P and S. F1, F2, and F3 operate retail stores in foreign countries.
>
> If P and S elect to file a consolidated return, the P consolidated group would consist of P and S. The P group's consolidated taxable income would be affected by the operations of its other subsidiaries, but the other subsidiaries would not be included in the P group's consolidated return. For example, P's premium payments to I would be deducted on the P group's consolidated return; I, R, F1, F2, and F3's dividends to P would be included in the P group's consolidated return; P and S's lease payments to R would be deducted on the P group's consolidated return; and any other U.S. income, deductions, or credits arising because of F1's, F2's, and F3's operations (e.g., P's subpart F income or section 956 income, or foreign tax credits) would be included on the P group's consolidated return.

If a corporation ceases to be a member of the consolidated group, Code Sec. 1504(a)(3) precludes it from joining the group again for a stated period (approximately five years) unless the IRS waives its right to prevent consolidation.

.02 Advantages and Disadvantages of Filing Consolidated Returns

The principal advantage of filing a consolidated return is the ability to offset the losses of one member against income of another member of the consolidated group. The deferral of intercompany gains also can be an advantage. Finally, intercorporate distributions can be made without taxation although they cause a reduction in the basis of the distributing subsidiary's stock.

---

[1] All references to the Code are to the Internal Revenue Code of 1986, as amended.

The main substantive disadvantage of filing a consolidated return is that losses on the disposition of the stock of a consolidated subsidiary are often disallowed under the loss limitation rules discussed in Chapter 4. These regulations are aimed at preventing stock losses attributable to a subsidiary's recognized built-in gains, but they can be overreaching if the consolidated group did not value those built-in gains when the subsidiary was acquired. The inordinate complexity of the consolidated return regulations can be a disadvantage as well. Other disadvantages are discussed at ¶ 225.

.03 Electing to File a Consolidated Return

An eligible affiliated group exercises its privilege of filing a consolidated return by filing the return by the due date for the common parent's tax return. Each member of the affiliated group during the year of the first consolidated return must consent to the application of the consolidated return regulations. Members consent by joining in the filing of the consolidated return and by filing Form 1122, Authorization and Consent of Subsidiary Corporation To Be Included in a Consolidated Income Tax Return, in the group's first consolidated return year. Consent must occur regardless of the length of time that the member has been affiliated with the consolidated group.

.04 Electronic Filing

Pursuant to Code Sec. 6011(e) and Temp. Reg. §301.6011-5T, corporate income tax returns for corporations that report total assets at the end of the corporation's tax year that equal or exceed $50 million on Schedule L of their Form 1120 must e-file for tax years ending on or after December 31, 2005. This e-filing requirement is extended to corporate income tax returns that report total assets at the end of the corporation's tax year that equal or exceed $10 million on Schedule L of their Form 1120 for tax years ending on or after December 31, 2006.

More precisely, such e-filing is required if such a corporation is required to file at least 250 returns during the calendar year ending with or within its tax year, was required to file a corporate income tax return on Form 1120 for the preceding tax year, and has been in existence for at least one year prior to the due date (excluding extensions) of its corporate income tax return. All members of a controlled group of corporations (as defined in Code Sec. 1563(a)) must e-file their corporate income tax returns if the aggregate number of returns required to be filed by the group is at least 250. For this purpose, a corporation or controlled group of corporations is required to file at least 250 returns, if during the calendar year ending with or within the tax year of the corporation or the controlled group, the corporation or the controlled group is required to file at least 250 returns of any type, including information returns.

The IRS may grant waivers of the e-filing requirements in cases of undue hardship.

¶115.04

.05 Basic Accounting Methods and Periods

In general, every member of the consolidated group must adopt the common parent's tax year, but each member, subject to an anti-avoidance rule, may adopt its own accounting method.

> **Example 2:** P and S in Example 1 would be required to use the same tax year. However, subject to an anti-avoidance rule, they could adopt different accounting methods.

.06 Consolidated Taxable Income

Technically, the separate taxable income of the members are adjusted for the items described in Reg. § 1.1502-11 and Reg. § 1.1502-12, and then added together. Among other special rules, Reg. § 1.1502-28 sets forth rules for the application of Code Sec. 108 and reduction of attributes pursuant to Code Sec. 108(b) when a member of the group realizes discharge of indebtedness income that is excluded from gross income under Code Sec. 108(a). Other specified separately computed consolidated items (e.g., capital gains, Code Sec. 1231 gains or losses, charitable contributions, and net operating losses) then are taken into account.

Each of the consolidated return regulations systems—stock basis (see Chapter 3), loss limitation (see Chapter 4), intercompany transaction (see Chapter 5), and loss and credit limitation utilization (see Chapter 6)—addresses more complicated problems in adjusting the members' separate taxable incomes to determine consolidated taxable income.

.07 Schedule M-3

Effective for tax years ending on or after December 31, 2004, consolidated groups with total assets of $10 million or more are required to file a Schedule M-3, *Net Income (Loss) Reconciliation for Corporations with Total Assets of $10 million or More.*

Schedule M-3 was created as a tool for the IRS to analyze tax return data more efficiency. Specifically, it was intended to help the IRS identify returns with the highest compliance risk, avoid examination of returns with low compliance risk, and improve audit cycle time through increased detail, transparency, and uniformity with regard to reporting book-tax differences. To that end, as explained more fully at ¶ 265, the new Schedule M-3 requires a complete reconciliation from financial accounting net income to taxable income in a standardized and detailed format.

.08 Consolidated Tax Liability

Consolidated tax liability before credits then is computed. Generally, this might include the regular tax imposed by Code Sec. 11, the alternative minimum tax imposed by Code Sec. 55, the accumulated earnings tax imposed by Code Sec. 531, and the personal holding company tax imposed by Code Sec. 541. Each of these taxes, the estimated tax and the credits against tax, are generally computed on a consolidated basis.

¶115.05

¶ 125 Stock Basis System

.01 Regulations at Issue

The consolidated return stock basis system consists of the investment adjustment rules of Reg. § 1.1502-32, the negative stock basis or so-called "excess loss account" rules of Reg. § 1.1502-19, and the disposition-year anti-circular basis rule of Reg. § 1.1502-11(b). The asset consistency rules of Reg. § 1.338-8 also are part of this stock basis system because of their nexus with the investment adjustment rules. Finally, Reg. § 1.1502-30 and Reg. § 1.1502-31 provide special rules for stock basis after certain triangular reorganizations and group structure changes.

.02 Investment Adjustments

The heart of the stock basis system is set forth in the investment adjustment rules of Reg. § 1.1502-32. Those rules adjust the basis that one member in the consolidated group has in another to prevent the subsidiary's change in value (resulting from its taxable income or loss) from being taken into account a second time when the owning member disposes of the subsidiary's stock. Investment adjustments also prevent a subsidiary's tax-exempt income and noncapital, nondeductible expenses from being taxed or deducted when the owning member's subsidiary stock is sold, and they reflect a subsidiary's distributions and the activities of a lower-tier subsidiary. The dividends-received deduction prevents double taxation for affiliated groups that do not file consolidated returns, but the investment adjustment rules prevent double taxation for consolidated groups whether or not prior profits are distributed.

> **Example 3:** P, a holding company, owns all the stock of S, which owns all the stock of S1. P starts with a $100 basis in its S stock, and S starts with a $100 basis in its S1 stock. S1's Year 1 and Year 2 activities are as follows:

S1's Activities

		Year 1	*Year 2*
Taxable income	(1)	+25	0
Tax-exempt income	(2)	0	+30
Federal taxes	(3)	−10	0
Distributions to S	(4)	−15	0

P's and S's investment adjustments to reflect S1's activities are as follows:

P's and S's Investment Adjustments

		Year 0	Year 1	Year 2		Total
Adjustments to P's basis in S stock	(1)		0	0		
	(2)		+15 *	0		
	(3)		0	0		
	(4)		0	0		
	(5)		0 **	+30 ***		
Adjusted basis		**$100**	**+15**	**+30**	**=**	**$145**
Adjustments to S's basis in S1 stock	(1)		+25	0		
	(2)		0	+30		
	(3)		–10	0		
	(4)		–15	0		
Adjusted basis		**$100**	**0**	**+30**	**=**	**$130**

* S's receipt of a $15 distribution from S1 (i.e., tax-exempt income).

** S's net investment adjustment to its S1 stock basis.

*** P's net investment adjustment to its S1 stock basis.

Assuming S and S1 had no unrealized income or deductions, these stock basis adjustments change P's and S's stock basis in S and S1 in precisely the same amounts as the changes in value of S and S1. Thus, if either P sold S or S sold S1 for their assumed values, at the end of Year 1 or Year 2, no gain or loss would be realized. Accordingly, the investment adjustments would serve their purpose of avoiding duplication of S1's previously taxed income and of avoiding indirect taxation of S's tax-exempt income.

.03 Excess Loss Accounts and Their Recapture

When a subsidiary has some debt capital, the resulting leverage may cause negative investment adjustments to exceed the owning member's stock basis, creating negative stock basis. This negative stock basis, called an "excess loss account," even though it may be attributable to causes unrelated to excess losses, is generally (but not always) recaptured as income when the owning member disposes of its subsidiary stock. Reg. § 1.1502-19 addresses when and how negative stock basis is recaptured as income.

> **Example 4:** P forms S with $100, and S borrows $200 from a bank. S loses $300, which is used to offset P's income on the P group's consolidated return, but P never pays S for the tax benefit of its loss. Under the investment adjustment system, S's $300 loss reduces P's $100 starting basis to negative

$200. This is an "excess loss account" that generally would be recovered as income upon the disposition of S.

.04 Disposition-Year Anti-Circular Basis Rule

Generally, the purpose of the anti-circular basis rule of Reg. § 1.1502-11(b) is to prevent the use of a departing consolidated subsidiary's excess deductions and loss carryovers against gain recognized on the disposition of the subsidiary's stock. Without such a rule, the absorption of the excess deductions or loss carryovers would reduce P's basis in its S stock and, in turn, increase P's gain. This in turn would increase the absorption of the excess deductions or loss carryovers that would reduce P's basis in its S stock and, in turn, increase P's gain, and the circle repeats itself. By limiting the availability of the departing member's excess deductions and loss carryovers against P's stock gain, the departing member's tax attributes are preserved for use after it leaves the consolidated group. Similar rules apply when the departing subsidiary is sold at a loss.

> **Example 5:** P starts Year 1 with a $500 basis in its S stock. For Year 1, P has ordinary income of $30 (determined without taking P's gain or loss from the disposition of its S stock into account), and S has an $80 ordinary loss. P sells its S stock for $520 at the close of Year 1. To determine the limitation on the use of S's loss and the effect under Reg. § 1.1502-32 of the absorption of S's loss, P's gain or loss on the disposition of S is not taken into account. P's basis in its S stock is reduced from $500 to $470 (the amount of S's loss absorbed by P) immediately before the disposition. Accordingly, P recognizes a $50 gain from the sale of its S stock, and the group has consolidated taxable income of $50 for Year 1 (P's $30 of ordinary income and $50 gain from the sale of its S stock, less $30 of S's loss).

.05 Asset Consistency Rules

Because the investment adjustment rules prevent a parent of a consolidated subsidiary from recognizing gain on the sale of its subsidiary stock a second time after the subsidiary sells or distributes its assets and recognizes gain, there is an incentive to commit, in the eyes of the Treasury and the IRS, two sins. One is that the parent causes the subsidiary to recognize loss sheltering built-in gain. The loss limitation system discussed in Chapter 4 is designed to prevent this. The other sin is to step up basis of selected subsidiary assets at no cost to the seller, by selling the assets to a buyer and then selling the buyer or an affiliate the subsidiary stock. This incentive exists to the extent of the excess of the value of the subsidiary stock over its parent's basis in the stock. Reg. § 1.338-8 contains complex rules to stop this. Because the benefit of this planning is for the buyer, the penalty is that the buyer takes a carryover basis in the assets acquired.

> **Example 6:** P owns all the stock of S, which A desires to purchase. P has a $600 basis in its S stock. S has a zero basis in its assets. P proposes to sell its S stock to A for $1,500. With a view to stepping up the basis of part of A's assets at no cost to A or the P consolidated group, A instead proposes that it acquire S's capital assets with a zero basis for $900 (S would distribute the

¶125.05

$900 to P) and acquire the S stock for $600 with P (rather than S) paying all the taxes on the $900 gain generated by the sale of assets.

Without the consistency rules, A's objectives could be accomplished. Instead of having a $900 capital gain on the sale of its S stock, it would have a $900 capital gain on the sale of S's assets; P would have a $900 investment adjustment from the gain on the assets that would keep its basis in its S stock at $600 after the distribution of $900 cash. Thus, to the extent of the excess of the value of the subsidiary stock over its basis, the selling group could sell S assets and step up their basis for A's benefit without a tax cost to either A or the selling group.

The consistency rules, however, cause A to take a carryover basis in the acquired assets.

.06 Special Rules

Reg. § 1.1502-30 embraces the rules of Reg. § 1.358-6 for determining the basis of the stock of a company acquired in certain triangular reorganizations except that it permits the basis adjustments to produce an excess loss account where the parties involved were members of a consolidated group following the triangular reorganization.

Reg. § 1.1502-31 authorizes stock basis adjustments after a group structure change, as defined, generally to reflect the change in assets and liabilities of the resulting common parent.

¶ 135 Loss Limitation System

The current loss limitation system consists of Reg. § 1.337(d)-2 for dispositions and deconsolidations of consolidated subsidiaries on or after March 3, 2005, and Reg. § 1.1502-35 generally for stock transfers, deconsolidation of subsidiaries, determinations of worthlessness, and stock dispositions on or after March 10, 2006. Reg. § 1.337(d)-2 assures the taxation of built-in gains, and Reg. § 1.1502-35 prevents a consolidated group from obtaining more than one tax benefit from a single economic loss.

.01 Assuring the Taxation of Built-in Gains

Reg. § 1.337(d)-2 assures the taxation of built-in gains. In 1986, Congress eliminated the statutory provisions that had permitted a corporation to avoid tax on the disposition of an appreciated asset where the transferee or distributee took a stepped-up basis. In connection with the repeal of this so-called General Utilities doctrine, Code Sec. 337(d)(1) authorized the Treasury and the IRS to carry out the purposes of the 1986 legislation. This was to ensure that these purposes could not be circumvented through the use of any law or regulation, including the consolidated return regulations.

Example 7: As an example of circumvention of the repeal of General Utilities before special consolidated return rules were adopted, P buys all the stock of S for $50 on February 1, Year 1, and S becomes a member of the P group. S has two assets. Asset #1 has a basis of $50 and a value of $0, and Asset

#2 has a basis of $0 and a value of $50. S sells Asset #2 during Year 3 for $50 and recognizes a $50 gain. Under the investment adjustment system, P's basis in the S stock increased to $100 as a result of the recognition of the built-in gain. Without a special rule, therefore, if Asset #1 has not changed in value, the P group could sell the S stock for $50 and use the $50 S stock loss to shelter the S asset gain, thereby circumventing the General Utilities repeal.

To this end, Reg. § 1.337(d)-2(a)(1) generally provides that no loss is allowed with respect to the disposition of subsidiary stock by a member of a consolidated group. Also, Reg. § 1.337(d)-2(b)(1) generally requires the basis of a share of subsidiary stock to be reduced to its value immediately before a deconsolidation of the share. An exception to these general rules is found in Reg. § 1.337(d)-2(c)(2), which provides that loss is not disallowed and basis is not reduced to the extent the taxpayer establishes that the loss or basis "is not attributable to the recognition of built-in gain on the disposition of an asset." Reg. § 1.337(d)-2(c)(2) defines the term "built-in gain" as gain that is "attributable, directly or indirectly, in whole or in part, to any excess of value over basis that is reflected, before the disposition of the asset, in the basis of the share, directly or indirectly, in whole or in part."

To mitigate against the valuation difficulties implicit in Reg. § 1.337(d)-2, the IRS will accept the "basis disconformity method" described in Notice 2004-58[2] for determining the extent to which loss or basis is attributable to the recognition of built-in gain on the disposition of an asset for purposes of applying the exception of Reg. § 1.337(d)-2(c)(2).

The basis conformity method disallows loss on a disposition of subsidiary stock and reduces basis (but not below value) on a deconsolidation of subsidiary stock in an amount equal to the lesser of the "gain amount," the "disconformity amount," and the "positive investment adjustment amount."

1. *Gain amount.* For this purpose, the gain amount is the sum of all gains (net of directly related expenses) recognized on asset dispositions of the subsidiary that are allocable to the share while the subsidiary is a member of the group.

2. *Disconformity amount.* The disconformity amount is the excess, if any, of the share's basis over the share's proportionate interest in the subsidiary's "net asset basis." A subsidiary's net asset basis is the excess of (a) the sum of the subsidiary's money, basis in assets (other than stock of consolidated subsidiaries), loss carryforwards that would be carried to a separate return year of the subsidiary under the principles of Reg. § 1.1502-21, and deductions that have been recognized but deferred, over (b) the subsidiary's liabilities that have been taken into account for tax purposes.

3. *Positive investment adjustment amount.* The positive investment adjustment amount is the excess, if any, of the sum of the positive adjustments made to the share under Reg. § 1.1502-32 over the sum of the negative adjustments made to the share under Reg. § 1.1502-32, excluding adjustments for distributions under Reg. § 1.1502-32(b)(2)(iv).

---

[2] 2004-2 CB 520.

Caution: The rules for allowing limited loss disallowance upon disposition and basis reduction upon deconsolidation come into play *only* if a separate statement entitled "section 1.337(d)-2(c) statement" is included with the taxpayer's consolidated return for the year of disposition or deconsolidation. The statement must contain:

- The name and E.I.N. of the subsidiary and
- The amount of the loss not disallowed and the amount of basis not reduced under the regulations.

In other words, the regulations by their terms disallow all stock loss upon disposition of a consolidated subsidiary and reduce stock basis to zero upon disposition of a consolidated subsidiary unless this statement is filed.

.02 Preventing a Consolidated Group from Taking More Than One Loss for a Single Economic Loss

Reg. § 1.1502-35 is designed to prevent a consolidated group from taking more than one loss for a single economic loss. Effective March 9, 2006, Reg. § 1.1502-35 applies when a member of a consolidated group transfers subsidiary stock at a loss as well as when a member holds loss shares of subsidiary stock and the subsidiary ceases to be a member of the group.

The regulations are intended to address at least two types of transactions that may allow a group to obtain more than one tax benefit from a single economic loss. In the first type of transaction, a group absorbs an inside loss (e.g., a loss carryforward, a deferred deduction, or a loss inherent in an asset) of a subsidiary member, and then a member of the group recognizes a loss on a disposition of stock of that subsidiary that duplicates the inside loss.

Example 8: Assume that in Year 1, P forms S with a contribution of $80 in exchange for 80 shares of common stock of S (representing all the outstanding stock of S). In Year 2, P contributes Asset A with a basis of $70 and a value of $20 to S in exchange for an additional 20 shares of S common stock. In Year 3, S sells Asset A and recognizes a $50 loss, which offsets income of P on the group's return. Under the investment adjustment rules of Reg. § 1.1502-32, P's basis in each share of S common stock it holds is reduced by a *pro rata* share of the $50 loss, with the result that the shares acquired in Year 1 have a basis of $40 and the shares acquired in Year 2 have a basis of $60. In Year 4, P sells the shares acquired in Year 2 for $20 and recognizes a $40 loss, which offsets income of P on the group's return.

In this transaction, the group has obtained a total $90 tax benefit from a single $50 loss. Although a taxable disposition of the S common stock acquired in Year 1 would offset the excess tax benefit, the group has various nontaxable options by which to ensure that the excess tax benefit is not reduced. These include retention of the remaining shares of S or the liquidation of S in a Code Sec. 332 liquidation.

Example 9: Assume that in Year 1, P forms S with a contribution of $80 in exchange for 80 shares of the common stock of S. In Year 2, P contributes

Asset A with a basis of $50 and a value of $20 to S in exchange for an additional 20 shares of S common stock. In Year 3, P sells the 20 shares of S common stock that it acquired in Year 2 for $20 and recognizes a $30 loss, which offsets income of P on the group's return. The sale of the 20 shares of S common stock does not result in the deconsolidation of S. In Year 4, S sells Asset A and recognizes a $30 loss, which also offsets income of P on the group return.

In this transaction, the group has obtained the use of two losses from the single economic loss in Asset A. Again, a taxable disposition by P of its remaining S common stock would offset the tax benefit of one of the losses. The group has various nontaxable alternatives by which to ensure that the excess tax benefit is not reduced. These include retention of the remaining shares of S or the liquidation of S under Code Sec. 332.

The complex anti-duplication rules apply to the above examples but do not apply to a taxable disposition of 100 percent of the stock of a consolidated subsidiary. If the reader's consolidated group is in that boat, read no further.

The regulations consist of a basis redetermination rule that attempts to mitigate the effects of the assumptions underlying the investment adjustment rules by reversing certain investment adjustments to take into account the source of certain items of income and loss. In addition, if the subsidiary member remains in the group, the basis redetermination rule equalizes bases in subsidiary stock so that a complex loss suspension rule need not apply.

The loss suspension rule prevents duplication of an economic loss by effectively disallowing a stock loss if the economic loss giving rise to that stock loss is later reflected on the group's return as in the second type of transaction described above. Various anti-abuse rules also must be considered.

¶ 145 Intercompany Transaction System

.01 Regulations at Issue

Reg. § 1.1502-13 provides the intercompany transaction system. The purpose of these rules is to clearly reflect the taxable income (and tax liability) of the consolidated group as a whole by preventing intercompany transactions from creating, accelerating, avoiding, or deferring consolidated taxable income (or consolidated tax liability). Reg. § 1.267(f)-1 (sales of loss property among members of controlled groups) also must be considered.

.02 Property Transactions

The general standard by which this clear reflection policy is measured is that of a single corporation conducting its business through divisions. Separate-entity treatment is preserved, however, for determining the amount and location of each member's items related to an intercompany transaction. For example, a selling member determines its gain or loss on the sale of property to another member on a separate-entity basis, and a buying member takes a cost basis in the property. This allows each party to retain a separate tax history for determining stock basis adjustments, earnings and profits, and other matters.

In general the buying member's accounting method is used to control the timing of both the buying member's and selling member's items (that is, the selling member matches the buying member's timing). When such a "matching rule" will not achieve single-entity treatment, an "acceleration rule" is substituted to determine timing. For example, the selling member accelerates its timing ahead of the buying member when either member leaves the group.

> **Example 10:** S holds raw land with a basis of $70. On January 1 of Year 1, S sells the land to B for $100. On July 1 of Year 3, B sells the land to nonmember X for $110. B reports a $10 gain in Year 3 ($110 amount realized − $100 cost). For each consolidated return year, S takes its intercompany item into account under the matching rule to reflect the difference for the year between B's corresponding item that B would take into account if S and B were divisions of a single corporation and the intercompany transaction were between those divisions (B's "recomputed corresponding item") and B's actual corresponding item taken into account. If S and B were divisions of a single corporation and the intercompany sale were a transfer between divisions, B would succeed to S's $70 basis in the land and would have a $40 gain from the sale to X in Year 3, instead of a $10 gain. Consequently, S takes no gain into account in Years 1 and 2 and takes the entire $30 gain into account in Year 3.

Various rules provide for single entity results, whenever possible, for other attributes (for example, character, source, and status under Code Sec. 382(h) as built-in gain or loss), depending, for example, on the operating timing rule and whether the selling member's and buying member's items offset each other.

A number of other factors should be kept in mind when considering property transactions. In addition to the attributes referred to above, redetermination attributes, holding periods, depreciable property, and exclusion of gain are discussed in Chapter 5.

.03 Other (Nonproperty) Transactions

An intercompany transaction is a transaction between corporations that are members of the same consolidated group immediately after the transaction, and may include nonproperty transactions such as S's performance of services, licensing of technology, rental of property, loan of money to B, and B's payment or accrual of its expenditure for such items. S and B are defined in Chapter 5.

.04 Successor Assets, Persons, and Groups

For purposes of Reg. § 1.1502-13, any reference to an asset includes a reference to any other asset of which the basis is determined, directly or indirectly, in whole or in part, by reference to the basis of the first asset. In general, any reference in Reg. § 1.1502-13 to a person includes, as the context may require, a reference to a predecessor or successor. If the consolidated group ceases to exist because of an acquisition described in Reg. § 1.1502-13(j)(5)(i), the surviving group is treated as the terminating group for purposes of applying Reg. § 1.1502-13 to the intercompany transactions of the terminating group. If a consolidated group terminates because the common parent is the only remaining member, Reg. § 1.1502-13(j)(6) causes the common parent to succeed to the treatment of the terminating group for purposes of applying the intercompany transaction rules so long as it neither becomes a member of an affiliated group filing separate returns, nor becomes a corporation described in Code Sec. 1504(b).

.05 Loss Property, Member Stock, Member Obligations, and Other Rules

Bolstering the "matching and acceleration rules" are special rules for loss property, member stock, member obligations, and other rules.

¶ 155 Loss and Credit Limitation Systems

.01 Regulations at Issue

The loss and credit limitation systems consist of numerous regulations. Reg. § 1.1502-91 through Reg. § 1.1502-96 (consolidated Code Sec. 382 rules for net operating loss (NOL) carryovers), Reg. § 1.1502-21(c) and Reg. § 1.1502-21(f) through Reg. § 1.1502-21(h) (separate return year (SRLY) rules for NOL carryovers and carrybacks), and Reg. § 1.1502-15 (SRLY rules for built-in losses) provide consolidated limitations on the use of NOL carryovers and carrybacks. Under Reg. § 1.1502-98, the rules contained in Reg. § 1.1502-91 through Reg. § 1.1502-96 also apply for purposes of Code Sec. 383, with "appropriate adjustments" to reflect that Code Sec. 383 applies to net capital losses and credits. Reg. § 1.1502-22 provides SRLY rules for net capital loss carryovers similar to those for NOLs. Reg. § 1.1502-3 (consolidated tax credits), Reg. § 1.1502-4 (consolidated foreign tax credit), and Reg. § 1.1502-55 (consolidated minimum tax credit) complete the credit limitation system.

.02 Code Sec. 382 Limitation and Elimination of SRLY Limitation for Most New Loss Members and Loss Subgroups Joining a Consolidated Group

Reg. § 1.1502-21(a) provides that the consolidated NOL deduction for any consolidated return year is the aggregate of the net operating loss carryovers and carrybacks to the year, including any net operating losses of members arising in separate return years carried over or back to the consolidated return year. When a corporation ceases to be a member of a consolidated group, NOL carryovers attributable to the corporation are first carried to the consolidated return year, and only the amount so attributable that is not absorbed by the group in that year is carried to the corporation's first separate return year.

Reg. § 1.1502-91 through Reg. § 1.1502-93 deal with ownership changes of "loss groups" and "loss subgroups," and Reg. § 1.1502-94 deals with ownership changes of "new loss members." An ownership change of a "loss group" would typically occur when a consolidated group with an NOL carryover arising in a consolidated return year of that group (more precisely, a "non-SRLY NOL") is acquired by someone other than a member of another consolidated group. In that event, Code Sec. 382 is applied on a singly-entity basis. That is, whether there is an ownership change is determined with respect to changes in ownership of the common parent of the loss group, and the value of the common parent is used to determine the Code Sec. 382 limitation.

More typically, however, one member of a consolidated group acquires one or more members of another consolidated group with an NOL carryover. Then the

¶155.02

issue is whether there is an ownership change of a "loss subgroup" (defined in Reg. § 1.1502-91 (d) (1)) or a "new loss member" (defined in Reg. § 1.1502-94 (a) (1)). If a loss subgroup is acquired, single entity concepts are used to determine whether there is an ownership change and the amount of the Code Sec. 382 limitation. If a new loss member is acquired, separate-entity concepts are applied.

Example 11: P was formed in Year 1 to provide online tax advice and is owned by 100 individuals, each of whom hold one percent of the outstanding stock. They are unrelated and have owned the stock since P was formed. P formed 16 subsidiaries, one subsidiary for each tax specialty and one subsidiary to develop the needed technology.

The P consolidated group had a $10 million consolidated net operating loss (CNOL) for Year 1, all of which was attributable to its Technology Subsidiary.

At the end of Year 1, P1 expressed an interest in acquiring part or all of P. P1 was owned by Public P1.

What would the Code Sec. 382 limitation be on Technology Subsidiary's $10 million NOL carryover (assume the long-term tax-exempt rate used to compute a Code Sec. 382 limitation is five percent) if one of the following alternative taxable transactions occurred on December 31, Year 1:

    a. P1 purchased the stock of Technology Subsidiary from P for $30 million in cash?

    P1's purchase of the stock of Technology Subsidiary would be an ownership change of a "new loss member." Accordingly, because Public P1, a five-percent shareholder, increases its ownership in Technology Subsidiary by more than 50 percentage points over the lowest percentage of stock of Technology Subsidiary owned by it during the testing period described in Code Sec. 382(i), there is an ownership change. The Code Sec. 382 limitation is five percent of $30 million, or $1.5 million. (As explained in Chapter 6, the SRLY limitation does not apply because of the overlap with Code Sec. 382.) Thus, the P1 consolidated group can use up to $1.5 million of Technology Subsidiary's $10 million NOL carryover against consolidated taxable income without regard to which corporation earns the taxable income. Therefore, assuming the P1 group has sufficient taxable income, it could absorb the NOL carryover in seven years. (See Chapter 6, Example 1(a) for further discussion.)

    b. P1 purchased the stock of P from the P shareholders for $100 million in cash?

    P1's purchase of the stock of P would be an ownership change of a "loss subgroup" and a loss subgroup has an ownership change if the "loss subgroup parent" has an ownership change under Code Sec. 382. Accordingly, because Public P1, a five-percent shareholder, has increased its ownership interest in P by more than 50 percentage points over the lowest percentage of stock owned by it at any time during the

¶155.02

testing period described in Code Sec. 382(i)(3), there is an ownership change. As a result, the "subgroup Code Sec. 382 limitation" is the value of the loss subgroup multiplied by the long-term tax-exempt rate that applies with respect to the ownership change. Here, P1 could use $5 million (five percent of $100 million) of Technology Subsidiary's $10 million NOL carryover each year. (As explained in Chapter 6, the SRLY limitation does not apply because of the overlap with Code Sec. 382.) Thus, the P1 consolidated group can use up to $5 million of Technology Subsidiary's $10 million NOL carryover against consolidated taxable income annually, without regard to which corporation earns the taxable income. Therefore, assuming the P1 group has sufficient taxable income, it could absorb the NOL carryover in two years. (See Chapter 6, Example 1(b) for further discussion.)

.03 SRLY Limitation

Under Reg. § 1.1502-21(c), when the SRLY limitation applies to an NOL, the aggregate of the NOL carryovers and carrybacks of a member arising in separate return limitation years (as defined in Reg. § 1.1502-1(f)) that are included in consolidated NOL deductions may not exceed the consolidated taxable income for all consolidated return years of the consolidated group determined by reference to only the member's taxable income. If previously affiliated members join the consolidated group at the same time as the member with an NOL carryover, the loss corporation and the joining members may constitute an SRLY subgroup, and the SRLY limitation applies to the SRLY subgroup. Similar rules apply to an NOL carryback.

The SRLY limitation is reduced in importance, however, because it is eliminated where there is an overlap with the Code Sec. 382 limitation. However, there are traps for the unwary, because the overlap rule only applies to the members if any Code Sec. 382 loss subgroup is a member of the SRLY subgroup and vice versa. For example, if brother and sister corporations are acquired from another consolidated group, and one or both corporations have an NOL carryover, the SRLY limitation is eliminated only if an election is made under the consolidated Code Sec. 382 regulations to treat the brother and sister corporations as a Code Sec. 382 loss subgroup.

.04 Successive Ownership Changes and Restructuring of Loss Subgroup

After an ownership change of a new loss member or a loss subgroup because of its acquisition by a consolidated group, close attention must be paid to Reg. § 1.1502-94 (new loss member) and Reg. § 1.1502-95 (loss subgroup) if there is a second ownership change or the loss subgroup is restructured. If there are successive ownership changes, the lesser of the two Code Sec. 382 limitations applies. Further, apportionment of a subgroup Code Sec. 382 limitation must be considered if one or more, but not all, members cease to be members of the subgroup. For example, if after the first ownership change of a loss subgroup, not only is there ordinarily a second Code Sec. 382 limitation if the departing member still has part of the NOL carryover it had when it came into the first group, but the first Code Sec. 382 limitation is reduced to zero for the departing member if the common parent of the first consolidated group does not apportion part or all of the first Code Sec. 382 limitation to it.

.05 Miscellaneous Consolidated Return Net Operating Loss Utilization Rules

The consolidated Code Sec. 382 and SRLY rules provide only limited guidance as to how they apply to tax-free acquisitions of new loss members or loss subgroup parents in a Code Sec. 368(a)(1)(A) or Code Sec. 368(a)(1)(C) reorganization.

Two other limitations come into play if, as is normally the case, the new loss member or loss subgroup parent's first tax year after joining the consolidated group is a short tax year. First, if the corporation is acquired in a transaction described in Code Sec. 381(a), use of its NOL carryover for the first tax year of the acquiring consolidated group ending after the acquisition can be offset by the taxable income of the acquiring corporation only to the extent provided by Code Sec. 381(c)(1)(B) (a *pro rata* portion of the acquiring corporation's taxable income for the portion of the year after the date of acquisition). Second, if there is an ownership change of the new loss member or loss subgroup resulting in a Code Sec. 382 limitation or subgroup Code Sec. 382 limitation, the limitation for the short tax year is prorated under Reg. § 1.382-5(c), based on the number of days in the short year bears to 365. Special consolidated return rules apply to built-in gains and losses.

Reg. § 1.1502-21(b)(1) provides ordering rules for determining which of multiple NOL carryovers and carrybacks are absorbed first. Also, Code Sec. 382(l)(2)(B) provides that if losses are carried from the same tax year, losses subject to limitation under Code Sec. 382 are absorbed before losses that are not subject to limitation under Code Sec. 382.

The election to reattribute an NOL carryover of a subsidiary to its common parent under Reg. § 1.1502-20(g) interacts with consolidated Code Sec. 382 and SRLY rules in numerous ways. For example, if the reattributed NOL carryover was subject to a Code Sec. 382 limitation, issues arise regarding whether the common parent or the purchase of the subsidiary inherits the first Code Sec. 382 limitation.

Finally, the use of a departing subsidiary's NOL carryover to offset gain on the disposition of stock of that subsidiary is limited by Reg. § 1.1502-11(b) to prevent a "circular basis" problem. The SRLY limitation is retained for NOL carrybacks to consolidated groups, presumably because Code Sec. 382 does not apply to an NOL carryback.

.06 Net Capital Loss and Credit Utilization System

In general, under Reg. § 1.1502-98, the NOL limitation rules contained in Reg. § 1.1502-91 through Reg. § 1.1502-96 also apply for purposes of Code Sec. 383 with "appropriate adjustments" to reflect that Code Sec. 383 applies to net capital losses and credits. Ordinarily, this means that if the counterpart of a new loss member or a loss subgroup joins a consolidated group in a transaction that results in a change in ownership, and there are pre-change credits but no pre-change losses, the Code Sec. 383 limitation will be 35 percent of the Code Sec. 382 limitation. The successive ownership and apportionment of subgroup Code Sec. 382 limitation principles applicable to NOL utilization also apply to net capital loss and credit utilization. Reg. § 1.1502-15 (built-in losses) and Reg. § 1.1502-22 (regular rules) provide SRLY rules for net capital losses that correspond to the SRLY rules for NOLs. However, under the overlap principles of Reg. § 1.1502-21(g), the SRLY restriction is eliminated in most situations. Reg. § 1.1502-4 eliminates the SRLY restriction for foreign tax credit carryovers (and carrybacks) without regard to an overlap with Code Sec. 383.

¶ 165 Earnings and Profits System

.01 Regulations at Issue

The consolidated return earnings and profits rules are found in Reg. § 1.1502-33 and Reg. § 1.1552-1 and reflect single-entity thinking. The heart of this system consists of rules for tiering up earnings and profits of consolidated subsidiaries, and eliminating those earnings and profits when the subsidiary leaves the group. Other rules address earnings and profits stock basis, allocation of federal income tax liability, a change in structure of the group, and other miscellaneous matters.

.02 Tiering-up of Earnings and Profits

Reg. § 1.1502-33 provides rules for adjusting the earnings and profits of a subsidiary (S) and any member (P) owning S's stock. These rules adjust P's earnings and profits to reflect S's earnings and profits for the period that S is a member of the consolidated group. They duplicate the earnings and profits of lower-tier members in the earnings and profits of higher-tier members, rather than elevate them to the common parent level without duplication at the lower-tiers.

> **Example 12:** P forms S with a $100 contribution. S has $100 of earnings and profits for Year 1 and no earnings and profits for Year 2. During Year 2, S declares and distributes a $50 dividend to P. S's $100 of earnings and profits for Year 1 increases P's earnings and profits for Year 1. P has no additional earnings and profits for Year 2 as a result of the $50 distribution in Year 2 because there is a $50 increase in P's earnings and profits as a result of the receipt of the dividend and a corresponding $50 decrease in S's earnings and profits under Code Sec. 312(a) that is reflected in P's earnings and profits.

.03 Earnings and Profits Stock Basis

For the same reasons that P makes investment adjustments to its stock basis (i.e, to prevent the duplication of gain or loss on the sale of S), P maintains an earnings and profits stock basis that is explained at ¶ 735.

.04 Allocation of Federal Income Tax Liability

The allocation of federal income tax liability for earnings and profits purposes involves both a basic method and, if the consolidated group elects, a complementary method that takes into account the compensation of members for the absorption of their tax attributes. These rules, their effects, and the election procedures for allocation of federal income tax liability are explained at ¶ 745.

¶ 165.04

.05 Changes in Structure of the Group

The common theme running through these earnings and profits rules is to duplicate the earnings and profits of S in P for the period S is a member of the consolidated group. In the same vein, adjustments are made to preserve the duplication of earnings and profits of lower-tier members in higher-tier members following Code Sec. 351 transfers, reverse acquisitions, and certain other changes in structure of the consolidated group.

.06 Elimination of Earnings and Profits upon Deconsolidation

Without special rules, "dividend-stripping" abuses could occur if either S were deconsolidated from P, but P retained S stock, or if the P group were deconsolidated. Separate return dividend distributions from S to P out of earnings and profits accumulated in consolidated return years (which generally would have increased P's S stock basis) generally would not reduce P's S stock basis (except to the extent that Code Sec. 1059 applies). Thus, S's consolidated return year earnings and profits could be distributed, reducing the value of S without a stock basis reduction, thereby creating an artificial loss if the S stock were sold. To prevent this abuse, S's consolidated return year earnings and profits are eliminated upon deconsolidation.

.07 Other Rules

Special rules for intercompany transactions, record-keeping, predecessor, and successor rules also are provided.

¶ 175 Continuation of the Consolidated Group

.01 Regulations at Issue

Continuation of the consolidated group is important for determining when an intercompany transaction or excess loss account is taken into account, when tax liability of a group continues, and other matters. Chapter 8 briefly reviews when, under Reg. § 1.1502-75 or related substance-over-form principles, a consolidated group continues.

.02 Continued Filing Requirement and Election to Discontinue

Although filing a consolidated return for a consolidated group's first tax year is elective, thereafter it is not. If a group wants to discontinue filing a consolidated return after its first year, it must obtain approval of the IRS.

.03 When a Group Remains in Existence

As a general rule, a group remains in existence for a tax year if the common parent remains as the common parent and at least one subsidiary that was affiliated with it at the end of the prior year remains affiliated with it at the beginning of the year, whether or not one or more subsidiaries have ceased to be subsidiaries at any time after the group was formed. This general rule and exceptions for a mere change in identity of the common parent and for the common parent's transfer of assets to a subsidiary are discussed at ¶ 825.

¶165.05

.04 Substance over Form

Applying substance over form, in Rev. Rul. 82-152, the IRS ruled that a group remained in existence when a common parent became a subsidiary of the group, even though the transaction did not literally qualify under the down-stream transaction rules of Reg. § 1.1502-75(d)(2). This ruling indicates that the IRS will apply the group continuation rules in accordance with their single-entity purpose, rather than by their literal language.

.05 Reverse Acquisitions

As discussed at ¶ 845, the consolidated return regulations provide a unique rule for reversing the form of an acquisition of a group where a smaller group acquires a larger group and uses stock as part of its acquisition consideration.

.06 Creation of a Holding Company without Terminating the Consolidated Group

As explained at ¶ 855, the IRS's substance-over-form ruling raises the question of how a holding company parent can be created without terminating the group.

¶ 185 Subsidiary Joining or Leaving the Consolidated Group Checklists

Depending on the form of the transaction and the particular facts, countless consolidated return issues may arise when a subsidiary joins or leaves a consolidated group. In Chapter 9, a selective sample of examples illustrate consolidated return rules commonly encountered. The examples are aimed at providing a review of the concepts discussed throughout this volume.

¶ 195 Practice Tools

At the end of the volume is a checklist of consolidated return statements and elections. Also included are other Practice Tools, primarily sample legal documents for making certain elections.

Chapter 2

Treatment of Consolidated Returns

¶ 201 Overview—Treatment of Consolidated Returns

.01 Eligibility for Filing Consolidated Returns

Code Sec. 1501 permits an "affiliated group" (as defined by Code Sec. 1504(a)) to elect to file a consolidated return. To qualify as an affiliated group, the group must include a common parent corporation that is an "includible corporation" and at least one other includible corporation in which the parent owns at least 80 percent of the voting power and total value of its stock. The affiliated group also includes any other includible corporation if its stock is owned by members of the group under the same 80-percent-ownership tests. Certain preferred stock described in Code Sec. 1504(a)(4) is not treated as stock for this purpose.

Code Sec. 1504(b) defines an *includible corporation* as any corporation other than certain corporations (such as foreign corporations, insurance companies, and REITs) that would unnecessarily complicate the consolidated return regulations.

> **Example 1:** P, a large retail company, owns all the stock of S, I, F1, F2, F3, and 99 percent of R. P operates retail stores west of the Mississippi, and S operates retail stores east of the Mississippi. I is a captive insurance company subject to taxation under Code Sec. 801. R is a REIT, which leases the stores to P and S. F1, F2, and F3 operate retail stores in foreign countries.
>
> If P and S elect to file a consolidated return, the P consolidated group would consist of P and S. The P group's consolidated taxable income would be affected by the operations of its other subsidiaries, but the other subsidiaries

would not be included in the P group's consolidated return. For example, P's premium payments to I would be deducted on the P group's consolidated return; I, R, F1, F2, and F3's dividends to P would be included in the P group's consolidated return; P and S's lease payments to R would be deducted on the P group's consolidated return; and any other U.S. income, deductions, or credits arising because of F1's, F2's, and F3's operations (e.g., P's subpart F income or section 956 income, or foreign tax credits) would be included on the P group's consolidated return.

If a corporation ceases to be a member of the consolidated group, Code Sec. 1504(a)(3) precludes it from rejoining the group again for a stated period (approximately five years), unless the IRS waives its right to prevent consolidation (see ¶ 215).

.02 Advantages and Disadvantages of Filing Consolidated Returns

The principal advantage of filing a consolidated return is the ability to offset the losses of one member against the income of another member of the consolidated group. The deferral of intercompany gains can also be an advantage. Finally, intercorporate distributions can be made without taxation, although they cause a reduction in the basis of the subsidiary stock.

The main substantive disadvantage of filing a consolidated return is that losses on the disposition of the stock of a subsidiary are often disallowed, at least in part, under the loss limitation rules (see Chapter 4). However, the inordinate complexity of the regulations can be a daunting disadvantage as well. Other disadvantages are discussed at ¶ 225.

.03 Electing to File a Consolidated Return

An eligible affiliated group exercises its privilege of filing a consolidated return by filing such return by the due date for the common parent's tax return. Each member of the affiliated group during the year of the first consolidated tax return must consent to the application of the consolidated regulations. Members consent by joining in the filing of a consolidated tax return and by filing Form 1122, Authorization and Consent of Subsidiary Corporation To Be Included in a Consolidated Income Tax Return, in the group's first consolidated return year. Consent must occur regardless of the length of time that the member has been affiliated with the consolidated group (see ¶ 235).

.04 Basic Accounting Methods and Periods

In general, every member of the group must adopt the common parent's tax year, but each member, subject to an anti-avoidance rule, may adopt its own accounting method (see ¶ 245).

.05 Consolidated Taxable Income

Technically, the separate taxable incomes of the members are adjusted for the items described in Reg. § 1.1502-11 and Reg. § 1.1502-12, and then added together. Among other special rules, Reg. § 1.1502-28 sets forth rules for the application of Code Sec. 108 and reduction of attributes pursuant to Code Sec. 108(b) when a member of the group realizes discharge of indebtness income that is excluded from

¶201.02

gross income under Code Sec. 108(a). Other specified separately computed consolidated items (e.g., capital gains, Code Sec. 1231 gains or losses, charitable contributions, and net operating losses) are then taken into account.

Each of the consolidated return regulation systems (stock basis (see Chapter 3), loss limitation (see Chapter 4), intercompany transaction (see Chapter 5), and loss and credit limitation utilization (see Chapter 6)) addresses more complicated problems in adjusting the members' separate taxable incomes to determine consolidated taxable income (see ¶ 255).

.06 Consolidated Tax Liability

Consolidated tax liability before credits is then computed. Generally, this might include the regular tax imposed by Code Sec. 11, the alternative minimum tax imposed by Code Sec. 55, the accumulated earnings tax imposed by Code Sec. 531, and the personal holding company tax imposed by Code Sec. 541. Each of these taxes, the estimated tax and the credits against tax, are generally computed on a consolidated basis (see ¶ 265).

.07 Definitions and Assumptions

Except as otherwise noted, throughout this volume all corporations file a consolidated return; P, P1, P2, etc. represents the parent of a consolidated subsidiary designated as S, S1, S2, etc. or T. In keeping with the goal of this volume to present rules of general application, any rules relating to special industries, such as oil and gas, thrift, banking, insurance, tax-exempts, dual resident corporations, or mining, are ignored (see ¶ 275). In the same vein, all corporations are C corporations. Finally, for simplicity, a flat corporate tax rate of 35 percent is assumed.

¶ 215 Eligibility for Filing Consolidated Returns

Code Sec. 1501 permits an "affiliated group" (as defined by Code Sec. 1504(a)) to elect to file a consolidated return. To qualify as an affiliated group, the group must include a common parent corporation that is an "includible corporation" and at least one other includible corporation in which the parent owns at least 80 percent of the voting power and total value of its stock. The affiliated group also includes any other includible corporation if its stock is owned by members of the group under the same 80-percent-ownership tests. Certain preferred stock described in Code Sec. 1504(a)(4) is not treated as stock for this purpose.[1] Reg. § 1.1504-4 also provides rules regarding the circumstances in which warrants, options, obligations convertible into stock, and other similar interests are treated as exercised for purposes of determining whether a corporation is a member of a consolidated group.

> *Example 2:* As an example of the affiliation requirement, P owns all the stock of S. S owns 70 percent of the stock S1, and P owns 30 percent of the stock of S1. P, S, and S1 all are "includible corporations." P, S, and S1 all are

---

[1] Specifically, the term *stock* does not include any stock that (1) is not entitled to vote; (2) is limited and preferred as to dividends, and does not participate in corporate growth to any significant extent; (3) has redemption and liquidation rights that do not exceed the issue price of such stock (except for a reasonable redemption or liquidation premium); and (4) is not convertible into another class of stock.

members of the affiliated group. This is because P directly owns at least 80 percent of the vote and value of one includible corporation, S; and P and S directly own at least 80 percent of the vote and value of another includible corporation, S1.

Note that there are no constructive ownership rules. To count toward the affiliation requirement, stock must be owned directly. Stock owned by a partnership does not count.[2]

Code Sec. 1504(b) defines an *includible corporation* as any corporation other than certain corporations that would unnecessarily complicate the consolidated return regulations. The excluded corporations include the following:

- Corporations exempt from tax under Code Sec. 501;
- Insurance companies subject to taxation under Code Sec. 801;
- Foreign corporations;
- Corporations with an election under Code Sec. 936 (relating to possession tax credit) in effect for the tax year;
- Regulated investment companies and real estate investment trusts subject to tax under subchapter M or Chapter 1;
- A Domestic International Sales Corporation (DISC) (as defined in Code Sec. 992(a)(1)); and
- An S corporation.

   Example 3: P, a large retail company, owns all the stock of S, I, R, F1, F2, and F3. P operates retail stores west of the Mississippi, and S operates retail stores east of the Mississippi. I is a captive insurance company subject to taxation under Code Sec. 801. R is a REIT, which leases the stores to P and S. F1, F2, and F3 operate retail stores in foreign countries.

   If P and S elect to file a consolidated return, the P consolidated group would consist of P and S. The P group's consolidated taxable income would be affected by the operations of its other subsidiaries, but the other subsidiaries would not be included in the P group's consolidated return. For example, P's premium payments to I would be deducted on the P group's consolidated return; I, R, F1, F2, and F3's dividends to P would be included in the P group's consolidated return; P and S's lease payments to R would be deducted on the P group's consolidated return; and any other U.S. income, deductions, or credits arising because of F1's, F2's, and F3's operations (e.g., P's subpart F income or section 956 income, or foreign tax credits) would be included on the P group's consolidated return.

If an election to file a consolidated return is made, it is binding on all members of the affiliated group.

Special rules permit affiliation of insurance companies,[3] contiguous foreign country subsidiaries,[4] tax-exempt organizations,[5] and for certain amounts derived

---

[2] *See* IRS Letter Ruling 9640010 (June 28, 1996).
[3] *See* Code Sec. 1504(c).
[4] *See* Code Sec. 1504(d).
[5] *See* Code Sec. 1504(e).

from a corporation previously treated as a DISC[6] under the circumstances set forth in the statute.

If a corporation ceases to be a member of the consolidated group, Code Sec. 1504(a)(3) precludes it from rejoining the group again for a stated period (approximately five years), unless the IRS waives its right to prevent reconsolidation.[7]

Code Sec. 1502 authorizes the consolidated return regulations in order that the tax liability of any consolidated group, and each member thereof, will be clearly reflected. Most of the current consolidated return regulations were issued in the 1990s and generally replace regulations promulgated in 1966. To ensure clear reflection of income, the members of the consolidated group under the current regulations are usually, but not always, treated as if they were divisions of a single corporation.

¶ 225 Advantages and Disadvantages of Filing Consolidated Returns

The advantages and disadvantages of filing consolidated returns depend on the alternative under consideration (e.g., an affiliated group filing separate returns, or a "parent" corporation with single member LLCs). The discussion below compares the major differences of filing a consolidated return with an affiliated group filing separate returns (referred to as an "affiliated group").

- A member of a consolidated group can offset its consolidated year losses and credits against the income of other members of the consolidated group, whereas a member of an affiliated group cannot. Score: Consolidated Groups 1; Affiliated Groups 0.

- A parent of a consolidated group increases the basis of a subsidiary to reflect taxable income and tax-exempt income to prevent double taxation or the indirect taxation of tax-exempt income upon a sale of the stock (see Chapter 3). A member of an affiliated group, however, must distribute its earnings and profits to prevent double taxation. Score: Consolidated Groups 2; Affiliated Groups 0.

- A member of a consolidated group can defer taking into account gain on intercompany transactions (see Chapter 5), whereas a member of an affiliated group cannot. Score: Consolidated Groups 3; Affiliated Groups 0.

- A subsidiary of a consolidated group can make a distribution to its parent without taxation without regard to whether the subsidiary has earnings and profits and without regard to the parent's basis in the subsidiary stock (see Chapter 5). By contrast, a member of an affiliated group can make a distribution to its parent without taxation (because of a 100-percent dividends-received deduction under Code Sec. 243) only if the distribution is

---

[6] *See* Code Sec. 1504(f).

[7] Rev. Proc. 2002-32, 2002-1 CB 959 sets forth the procedure for a qualifying corporation to obtain an automatic waiver of the IRS's right to prevent reconsolidation. The common parent of the consolidated group must in- clude the previously deconsolidated member in the consolidated return and attach a statement to the return that includes the information set forth in the revenue procedure. If this procedure cannot be met, then a waiver can be obtained only by obtaining a private letter ruling.

out of affiliated group earnings and profits. Score: Consolidated Groups 4; Affiliated Groups 0.

- A parent in a consolidated group must reduce its basis in its subsidiary for any distribution (see Chapter 4), whereas a parent in an affiliated group must reduce its basis in its subsidiary for a distribution only as provided by Code Sec. 1059. Score: Consolidated Groups 4; Affiliated Groups 1.

- Loss on the disposition of a consolidated subsidiary is disallowed to the extent it is attributable to the recognition of built-in gain on the disposition of an asset (see Chapter 4); whereas basis of an affiliated subsidiary is reduced only for an extraordinary dividend attributable to built-in gain (see Code Sec. 1059(e)(2)). Score: Consolidated Groups 4; Affiliated Groups 2.

- The consolidated return rules are more complex than the affiliated group rules. Score: Consolidated Groups 4; Affiliated Groups 3.

On balance then, it is generally advantageous to file a consolidated return, at least if one hires a competent advisor to deal with its complexities.

¶ 235 Electing to File a Consolidated Return

A group that did not file a consolidated return for the immediately preceding tax year may file a consolidated return in lieu of separate returns for the tax year, provided that each corporation that has been a member during any part of the tax year for which the consolidated return is to be filed consents in the manner provided by the regulations under Code Sec. 1502.[8] If a group wishes to exercise its privilege of filing a consolidated return, such consolidated return must be filed not later than the last day prescribed by law (including extensions of time) for the filing of the common parent's return.[9] Such consolidated return may not be withdrawn after such last day (but the group may change the basis of its return at any time prior to such last day).[10]

The consent of a corporation must be made by such corporation joining in the making of the consolidated return for the year.[11] A corporation will be deemed to have joined in the making of such return for such year if it files a Form 1122 in the manner specified in the regulations.[12]

If a member of the group fails to file Form 1122, the IRS may, under the facts and circumstances, determine that such member has joined in the making of a consolidated return by such group.[13] The following circumstances, among others, will be taken into account in making this determination:

- Whether the income and deductions of the members were included in the consolidated return;

- Whether a separate return was filed by the member for that tax year; and

- Whether the member was included in Form 851, Affiliations Schedule.

---

[8] Reg. § 1.1502-75(a)(1).
[9] Reg. § 1.1502-75(a)(1).
[10] Reg. § 1.1502-75(a)(1).
[11] Reg. § 1.1502-75(b)(1).
[12] Reg. § 1.1502-75(b)(1).
[13] Reg. § 1.1502-75(b)(2).

If the IRS determines that the member has joined in the making of the consolidated return, such member will be treated as if it had filed a Form 1122 for such year.

If any member has failed to join in the making of a consolidated return, then the tax liability of each member of the group must be determined on the basis of separate returns, unless the common parent corporation establishes to the satisfaction of the IRS that the failure of such member to join in the making of the consolidated return was inadvertent, or due to a mistake of law or fact.[14] In such case, the member will be treated as if it had filed a Form 1122 for such year, and thus joined in the making of the consolidated return for such year.

A group that filed (or was required to file) a consolidated return for the immediately preceding tax year is required to file a consolidated return for the tax year, unless it has made an election to discontinue filing consolidated returns as provided in the regulations.[15]

¶ 245 Basic Accounting Methods and Periods

The basic accounting methods and periods rules are a mixture of single entity and separate return concepts.

.01 Tax Year

The consolidated return of a group must be filed on the basis of the common parent's tax year, and each subsidiary must adopt the common parent's annual accounting period for the first consolidated return year for which the subsidiary's income is includible in the consolidated return.[16]

.02 Items Included in the Consolidated Return

A consolidated return must include the common parent's items of income, gain, deduction, loss, and credit for the entire consolidated return year for which it is a member.[17] If the consolidated return includes the items of a corporation for only a portion of its tax year determined without taking the above rule into account, items for the portion of the year not included in the consolidated return must be included in a separate return (including the consolidated return of another group).

.03 Accounting Methods

In contrast to the single tax year rule for a consolidated group, the method of accounting to be used by each member of the group must be determined in accordance with the provisions of Code Sec. 446 as if such member filed a separate return.[18]

However, if one member (B) directly or indirectly acquires an activity of another member (S), or undertakes S's activity, with the principal purpose to avail

---

[14] Reg. § 1.1502-75(b)(3).

[15] Reg. § 1.1502-75(d)(2).

[16] If any member is on a 52–53 week tax year, the basic tax year rule may, with the advance consent of the IRS, be deemed satisfied if the tax years of all members of the group end within the same seven-day period (Reg. § 1.1502-76(a)(1)); any request for such consent must be filed with the Commissioner of Internal Revenue, Washington, DC 20224, not later than the 30th day before the due date (not including extensions of time) for the filing of the consolidated return.

[17] Reg. § 1.1502-76(b)(1).

[18] Reg. § 1.1502-17(a).

the group of an accounting method that would be unavailable (or would be unavailable without securing consent from the IRS if S and B were treated as divisions of a single corporation), B must use the accounting method for the acquired or undertaken activity determined under Reg. § 1.1502-17(c)(2).[19] Under that provision, B must use the method of accounting that would be required if B acquired the activity from S in a transaction to which Code Sec. 381 applied.[20] Thus, the principles of Code Sec. 381(c)(4) and Code Sec. 381(c)(5) apply to resolve any conflicts between the accounting methods of S and B, and the acquired or undertaken activity is treated as having the accounting method used by S. Appropriate adjustments are made to treat all acquisitions or undertakings that are part of the same plan or arrangement as a single acquisition or undertaking.

Special rules are provided in Reg. § 1.1502-18 for inventory adjustments.

¶ 255 Consolidated Taxable Income

"Consolidated taxable income" is the base upon which the federal income tax of a consolidated group is determined. Consolidated taxable income is determined by taking into account the "separate taxable income" of each member of the group, plus six consolidated income or deduction items.[21]

The separate taxable income of a member (including a case when deductions exceed gross income) is computed in accordance with the provisions of the Code covering the determination of taxable income of separate corporations, subject to the following modifications:

- Transactions between members and transactions with respect to stock, bonds, or obligations of members must be reflected according to the provisions of Reg. § 1.1502-13 (see Chapter 5);

- Any deduction that is disallowed under Reg. § 1.1502-15 (relating to built-in deductions) must be taken into account as provided in those sections (see Chapter 6);

- The method of accounting under which such computation is made and the adjustments to be made because of any change in method of accounting must be determined under Reg. § 1.1502-17;

- Inventory adjustments must be made as provided in Reg. § 1.1502-18;

- Any amount included in income under Reg. § 1.1502-19 (relating to excess loss accounts) must be taken into account;

- For rules relating to loss limitation or basis reduction on the disposition or deconsolidation of stock of a subsidiary, see Reg. § 1.337(d)-2 and Reg. § 1.1502-35(f) (see Chapter 4);

- In the computation of the deduction under Code Sec. 167, property does not lose its character as new property as a result of a transfer from one member to another member during a consolidated return year if the transfer occurs after January 4, 1973, and the transfer is an intercompany transaction as

---

[19] Reg. § 1.1502-17(c)(1).
[20] Reg. § 1.1502-17(c)(2).

[21] *See* Reg. § 1.1502-11.

defined in Reg. § 1.1502-13, or the basis of the property in the hands of the transferee is determined (in whole or in part) by reference to its basis in the hands of the transferor;

- The application of Code Sec. 108 and the reduction of attributes pursuant to Code Sec. 108(b) is made pursuant to Reg. § 1.1502-28;

- No net operating loss deduction may be taken into account;

- No capital gains or loss may be taken into account;

- No gains or losses subject to Code Sec. 1231 may be taken into account;

- No deduction under Code Sec. 170 may be taken into account;

- No deductions under Code Sec. 243(a)(1), Code Sec. 244(a), Code Sec. 245, or Code Sec. 247 (relating to deductions with respect to dividends received and dividends paid) may be taken into account; and

- Basis must be determined under Reg. § 1.1502-31, Reg. § 1.1502-32 and Reg. § 1.1502-32T (see Chapter 3), and earnings and profits must be determined under Reg. § 1.1502-33 (see Chapter 7).

After aggregating the separate taxable incomes of the members, the following consolidated items are taken into account:

1. Any consolidated net operating loss deduction (see Reg. § 1.1502-21 and Chapter 6 and the example below for the computation);

2. Any consolidated capital gain net income (see Reg. § 1.1502-22 and the example below for the computation);

3. Any consolidated Code Sec. 1231 net loss (see Reg. § 1.1502-23 and the example below for the computation);

4. Any consolidated charitable contributions deduction (see Reg. § 1.1502-24 for the computation);

5. Any consolidated dividends-received deduction (see Reg. § 1.1502-26 for the computation); and

6. Any consolidated Code Sec. 247 deduction (see Reg. § 1.1502-27 for the computation).

Example 4: For an example of the computation of consolidated taxable income, P owns all the stock of S1, S2, and S3. For Year 1, P generates $600,000 ordinary income for the year, a $100,000 capital loss that is not taken into account in Year 1 under the intercompany transaction rules, and a $500,000 Code Sec. 1231 loss; S1 generates $200,000 ordinary income; S2 generates a $200,000 capital gain and a $400,000 Code Sec. 1231 gain; and S3 generates a $200,000 ordinary loss and a $400,000 capital loss. Consolidated taxable income is $500,000, computed as demonstrated in the following table.

¶255

	P	S1	S2	S3	Consolidated Taxable Income
Separate Taxable Income (Loss)	$600,000	$200,000	$0	($200,000)	$600,000
Capital Gain (Loss)	(100,000) deferred	0	200,000	(400,000)	0
Code Sec. 1231 Gain (Loss)	(500,000)	0	400,000	0	(100,000)
					$500,000

Note that the consolidated capital loss and consolidated Code Sec. 1231 computations mirror separate return computations, except that intercompany gains and losses are deferred and each member's capital gains and losses and Code Sec. 1231 gains and losses are consolidated before determining their effects on consolidated taxable income.[22] Thus, in this example, S3's capital loss offsets S2's capital gain, but the excess amount does not offset consolidated taxable income. Further, P's and S2's Code Sec. 1231 gains and losses are offset to determine their character as capital gain or ordinary loss. Here, because P's Code Sec. 1231 loss exceeds S2's Code Sec. 1231 gain, the excess amount is treated as an ordinary loss in computing consolidated taxable income.

¶ 265 Schedule M-3

Effective for tax years ending on or after December 31, 2004, the IRS replaced Schedule M-1, *Reconciliation or Income (Loss) per Books with Income per Return*, with Schedule M-3, *Net Income (Loss) Reconciliation for Corporations with Total Assets of $10 Million or More*.

.01 Purpose

Schedule M-3 was created as a tool for the IRS to analyze tax return data more efficiently. Specifically, Schedule M-3 is intended to help the IRS identify returns with the highest compliance risk, avoid examination of returns with low compliance risk, and improve audit cycle time through increased detail, transparency, and uniformity with regard to reporting book-tax differences. To that end, the new Schedule M-3 requires a complete reconciliation from financial accounting net income to taxable income in a standardized and detailed format.[23]

---

[22] *See* Reg. § 1.1502-22(a) (consolidated capital gains and losses); Reg. § 1.1502-23(a) (Code Sec. 1231 gains and losses).

[23] Charles Boynton and William Wilson, "A Review of Schedule M-3: The Internal Revenue Service's New Book-Tax Reconciliation Tool," *Petroleum Accounting and Financial Management Journal*, Vol. 25, No. 1 (Spring 2006): 1-16.

.02 Taxpayers Required to File Schedule M-3

For tax years ending on or after December 31, 2004, Schedule M-3 is required only for regular C corporations and U.S. consolidated groups with total assets of $10 million or more.

The IRS added requirements for taxpayers filing Forms 1120PC, 1120 L, 1120S, and 1065 in December 2005, effective for tax years ending on or after December 31, 2006. As a result, the IRS issued Form 8916, *Reconciliation of Schedule M-3 Taxable Income with Tax Return Taxable Income for Mixed Groups*, for consolidated groups containing both Form 1120 and Forms 1120PC and/or 1120L. These forms are beyond the scope of this text.

Taxpayers with total assets under $10 million will continue to use Schedule M-1.

.03 Overview of Schedule M-3

Schedule M-3 is comprised of three parts. Each part provides reconciliations for different aspects of the financial statements and tax returns. Part I reconciles net income as reported in the financial statements to book income per the tax return. Parts II and III reconcile income and expense items as reported in the financial statements to their respective tax return balances. Part I contains both a general questionnaire section and a reconciliation section. Parts II and III are organized as lists of specific transactions with four different columns in which they are classified: the balance per the financial statements, temporary differences arising from the tax treatment of the item, permanent differences arising from the tax treatment of the item, and a total column representing the tax return balance for the item.

For the first year a taxpayer is required to file Schedule M-3, the requirement to complete all four columns is waived, and a taxpayer only needs to designate temporary and permanent differences for each line item. The IRS adopted this rule as a concession to allow taxpayers to test their accounting systems and ensure that the required information can be gathered for future reporting periods.[24]

.04 Part I: Financial Information and Net Income (Loss) Reconciliation

Part I provides specific information about a corporation's financial statements, including information on public filings, net income/loss reported on financial statements, and detail of any adjustments necessary to reconcile financial statement net income to book income per the tax return. These adjustments can include exclusion of income/loss from entities not included in the tax return (nonincludible entities), adjustments to intercompany eliminations between the tax return group (includible entities) and nonincludible entities, any adjustments necessary to reconcile the financial statement reporting period to the tax return reporting period, adjustments to intercompany dividends, and any other adjustments required to reconcile between financial income/loss and book income/loss per the tax return.

---

[24] John O. Everett, Cherie J. Hennig, and William A. Raabe, PRACTICAL GUIDE TO SCHEDULE M-3 COMPLIANCE (Chicago: CCH, 2006), 110.

.05 Part II: Reconciliation of Net Income (Loss) per Income Statement of Includible Corporations with Taxable Income per Return—Income (Loss) Items

Part II provides a reconciliation for various income and gain/loss transactions. Specific line items are provided for transactions identified by the IRS as potential areas of tax shelter activity. Specifically, these items are intended to provide detail for overly broad areas of income or gain/loss and prevent netting of similar items in an attempt to obscure true book-tax differences.[25]

Part II contains 30 lines with eight subparts, for a total of 38 specific line items. Transactions falling into one of the specific line items must be reported as such, regardless of whether a book-tax difference exists for that item. Some transactions, such as reportable transactions or transactions flowing through from a pass-through entity, are reported on designated lines regardless of where they would be otherwise classified if not for these requirements. Further, transactions not falling into one of the specified line items but with associated book-tax differences are reported separately from other transactions without specified lines and without book-tax differences.

Cost of goods sold reconciliation. The IRS has recently announced the addition of Form 8916-A, *Reconciliation of Cost of Goods Sold Reported on Schedule M-3*. This form is required for each entity that files Schedule M-3, and it is referenced as a supporting form in Schedule M-3, Part II, line 17. The form contains 19 line items identified as potential differences between cost of goods sold reported for book and for tax, as well as lines for other items with differences and items with no differences.

.06 Part III: Reconciliation of Net Income (Loss) per Income Statement of Includible Corporations with Taxable Income per Return—Expense/ Deduction Items

Part III provides a reconciliation for various expense or deduction transactions. As in Part II, specific line items are provided for transactions identified by the IRS as potential areas of tax shelter activity.

Part III contains 34 lines for specific items of expense or deduction. The treatment of transactions in Part III is identical to that discussed in Part II.

.07 Schedule M-3 and Consolidated Returns

Special rules exist for consolidated groups and their filing requirements for Schedule M-3. The consolidated group files one complete Schedule M-3, which includes Parts I through III. Additionally, the parent corporation must also file a separate complete Schedule M-3, with Part I reflecting the activity of the group, but Parts II and III representing only its own activity. Further, each subsidiary included in the consolidated group is required to file a separate, partial M-3, which includes only Parts II and III. Finally, a separate, complete Schedule M-3 is necessary to eliminate any differences related to intercompany transactions and to include any

---

[25] *Ibid.*

¶265.05

limitations on deductions, such as charitable contributions or capital loss limitations.

.08 Schedule M-3 and Disclosures

The significant book-tax difference category was removed from the IRS list of Reportable Transactions for any transaction entered into after January 6, 2006. Corporations filing Schedule M-3 are considered to have satisfied the disclosure requirements for this category and are not required to file Form 8886, *Reportable Transaction Disclosure Statement*, for these transactions.

Transactions falling into one of the five remaining categories of reportable transactions must be reported separately on Part II, Line 12 of Schedule M-3. The filing of Schedule M-3 does not satisfy the disclosure requirements for these transactions, and Form 8886 is still required.

¶ 275 Consolidated Tax Liability

Consolidated tax liability, whether it is the regular tax,[26] the estimated tax,[27] the alternative minimum tax,[28] the accumulated earnings tax,[29] or the personal holding company tax,[30] generally is computed on a consolidated basis.

.01 Consolidated Credits

The credits for consolidated groups are out of date. Reg. § 1.1502-3 provides for a consolidated investment credit,[31] but the investment credit was repealed in 1986. Reg. § 1.1502-4 provides for a consolidated foreign tax credit[32] but has not been updated to reflect the "baskets" and other current details of the foreign tax credit. Reg. § 1.41-6 provides for a consolidated research credit.

Most practitioners believe that the most reasonable approach for the general business and other credits is to apply them on a consolidated basis, using the consolidated investment credit and consolidated foreign tax credit as analogues.

For consolidated limitations on credits, see Chapter 6.

¶ 285 Definitions and Assumptions

Except as otherwise noted, throughout this volume all corporations file a consolidated return, and P, P1 or P2, etc. represent the parent of a consolidated subsidiary designated as S, S1, S2, etc. or T. In keeping with the goal of this volume to present rules of general application, any rules relating to special industries such as banking, insurance, oil and gas, tax-exempts, dual resident corporations, or mining, are ignored. In the same vein, all corporations are C corporations. Finally, for simplicity, a flat corporate tax rate of 35 percent is assumed.

---

[26] *See* Reg. § 1.1502-2(a) and Proposed Reg. § 1.1502-2(a)(1)(i).

[27] *See* Reg. § 1.1502-5 and Proposed Reg. § 1.1502-5.

[28] *See* Reg. § 1.1502-55 and Proposed Reg. § 1.1502-55.

[29] *See* Reg. § 1.1502-2(d), Proposed Reg. § 1.1502-2(b)(2) and Reg. § 1.1502-43.

[30] *See* Code Sec. 542(b), Reg. § 1.1502-2(b) (compute on consolidated basis if Code Sec. 542(b)(1) applies), Reg. § 1.1502-2(c) (compute on separate return basis if Code Sec. 542(b)(2) "kick-out" rule applies), Proposed Reg. § 1.1502-2(b)(1) and Proposed Reg. § 1.1502-2(b)(3).

[31] *See* Reg. § 1.1502-3 and Proposed Reg. § 1.1502-3.

[32] *See also* Reg. § 1.1502-9 (consolidated overall foreign losses and separate limitation losses).

¶ 295 Conclusions

Eligibility to elect filing consolidated returns generally is limited to domestic C corporations that are members of an "affiliated group." To qualify as an affiliated group, the group must include a common parent corporation and at least one other corporation in which the parent owns at least 80 percent of the voting power and total value of its stock. The affiliated group also generally includes any other domestic C corporation if its stock is owned by members of the group under the same 80-percent-ownership tests.

The principal advantage of filing a consolidated return is the ability to offset the losses of one member against the income of another member of the consolidated group. By contrast, the main disadvantage of filing a consolidated return is that losses on the disposition of the stock of a subsidiary are often disallowed under loss limitation rules (see Chapter 6) designed to assure the taxation of built-in gains and thus prevent circumvention of the repeal of the General Utilities doctrine.

An eligible affiliated group exercises its privilege of filing a consolidated return by filing such return by the due date for the common parent's tax return. Each member of the affiliated group during the year of the first consolidated tax return must consent to the application of the consolidated return regulations.

In general, every member of the group must adopt the common parent's tax year, but each member, subject to an anti-avoidance rule, may adopt its own accounting method.

Technically, the separate taxable incomes of the members are adjusted for the items described in Reg. § 1.1502-11 and Reg. § 1.1502-12, and then added together. Among other special rules, Reg. § 1.1502-28 sets forth rules for the application of Code Sec. 108 and reduction of attributes pursuant to Code Sec. 108(b), when a member of the group realizes discharge of indebtedness income that is excluded from gross income under Code Sec. 108(a). Other specified separately computed consolidated items (e.g., capital gains, Code Sec. 1231 gains or losses, charitable contributions, and net operating losses) then are taken into account.

Each of the consolidated return regulations systems—stock basis (see Chapter 3), loss limitation (see Chapter 4), intercompany transaction (see Chapter 5), and loss and credit limitation utilization (see Chapter 6)—addresses more complicated problems in adjusting the members' separate taxable incomes to determine consolidated taxable income.

¶ 297 Frequently Asked Questions

Question

What are the five most important traps for the unwary that a tax executive should know about the consolidated return rules?

Answer

    1. As discussed in Chapter 4, the consolidated return regulations disallow loss on the disposition of a consolidated subsidiary, except to the extent the consolidated group shows that the loss was not attributable to the

recognition of built-in gains. This requires an appraisal of the assets of a subsidiary when it is acquired. If such an appraisal is not made, certain assumptions may be made regarding the amount of recognized built-in gains. Finally, *no* loss is allowed unless a statement of allowed loss required by the regulations is filed with the consolidated group's return for the year of disposition.

2. As discussed in Chapter 9, if the P group is unlikely to absorb the NOL carryover of an acquired subsidiary (S), it should consider electing to treat part or all of the loss as having expired immediately before the subsidiary becomes a member of the P group. If no such election is made, P will be required to make a negative basis adjustment to its S stock when the loss expires.

3. As discussed in Chapter 3, when a subsidiary has some debt capital, the resulting leverage may cause negative investment adjustments to exceed the owning member's stock basis, creating negative stock basis. This negative stock basis, called an "excess loss account," is generally recaptured as income when the owning member disposes of its subsidiary stock. This recapture can be avoided, however, if the subsidiary is liquidated under Code Sec. 332 (generally a liquidation of a solvent subsidiary).

4. As discussed in Chapter 6, consolidated loss and credit limitation systems (consolidated versions of Code Secs. 382 and 383) limit the use of NOL and credit carryovers when a new loss member or loss subgroup joins the consolidated group.

5. As discussed in Chapter 9, the common parent may apportion all or part of each element of the consolidated Code Sec. 382 limitation or subgroup Code Sec. 382 limitation. For example, if P acquires L, which owns L1, and L and L1 constitute a loss subgroup, the L subgroup has a subgroup Code Sec. 382 limitation. If P1 acquires L1, any remaining loss carryover of L1 will have no value unless P apportions part of the subgroup Code Sec. 382 limitation to L1.

Chapter 3

Stock Basis System

¶ 301 Overview—Stock Basis System

The consolidated return stock basis system consists of the investment adjustment rules of Reg. § 1.1502-32, the negative stock basis or so-called excess loss account rules of Reg. § 1.1502-19, and the disposition-year anti-circular basis rule of Reg. § 1.1502-11(b). The asset consistency rules of Reg. § 1.338-8 also are part of this stock basis system because of their nexus with the investment adjustment rules. Finally, Reg. § 1.1502-30 and Reg. § 1.1502-31 provide special rules for stock basis after certain triangular reorganizations and group structure changes, respectively.

.01 Investment Adjustments

The heart of the stock basis system is set forth in the investment adjustment rules of Reg. § 1.1502-32. Those rules adjust the basis that one member in the group has in another, to prevent the subsidiary's change in value (resulting from its taxable income or loss) from being taken into account a second time when the owning member disposes of the subsidiary's stock. Investment adjustments also prevent a subsidiary's tax-exempt income and noncapital, nondeductible expenses from indirectly being taxed or deducted when the owning member's subsidiary stock is sold, and reflect a subsidiary's distributions and the activities of a lower-tier consolidated subsidiary. The dividends-received deduction prevents double taxation for affiliated groups that do not file consolidated returns, but the investment adjustment rules prevent double taxation, whether or not prior profits are distributed (see ¶ 315).

.02 Excess Loss Accounts and Their Recapture

When a subsidiary has some debt capital, the resulting leverage may cause negative investment adjustments to exceed the owning member's stock basis, creating negative stock basis. This negative stock basis, called an "excess loss account," even though it may be attributable to causes unrelated to excess losses, is generally (but not always) recaptured as income when the owning member disposes of its subsidiary stock. Reg. § 1.1502-19 addresses when and how negative stock basis is recaptured as income (see ¶ 325).

.03 Disposition-Year Anti-Circular Basis Rule

Generally, the purpose of the anti-circular basis rule is to prevent the use of a departing subsidiary's excess deductions and loss carryovers against gain recognized on the disposition of the subsidiary's stock. Without such a rule, the absorption of the excess deductions or loss carryovers would reduce P's basis in its S stock and, in turn, increase P's gain. This in turn would increase the absorption of the excess deductions or loss carryovers that would reduce P's basis in its S stock, and in turn increase P's gain, and the circle repeats itself. By limiting the availability of the departing member's excess deductions and loss carryovers against P's stock gain, the departing member's tax attributes are preserved for its use after it leaves the group. Similar rules apply when the departing subsidiary is sold at a loss (see ¶ 335).

.04 Asset Consistency Rules

Because the investment adjustment rules prevent a parent of a consolidated subsidiary from recognizing gain on the sale of its subsidiary stock a second time after the subsidiary sells or distributes its assets and recognizes gain, there is an incentive to commit, in the eyes of the Treasury and the IRS, two terrible sins. One is that the parent causes the subsidiary to recognize gain on built-in gain assets (by sale or distribution) and then sells the stock at a loss to offset the gain. The loss limitation system discussed in Chapter 4 is designed to prevent this. The other sin is to step up the basis of selected subsidiary assets at no cost to the seller, by selling the assets to a buyer and then selling the buyer or an affiliate the subsidiary stock. This incentive exists to the extent of the excess of the value of the subsidiary stock over its parent's basis in the stock. Reg. § 1.338-8 contains complex rules designed to stop this. Because the benefit of this planning is for the buyer, the penalty is that the buyer takes a carryover basis in the assets acquired (see ¶ 345).

.05 Special Rules

Reg. § 1.1502-30 embraces the rules of Reg. § 1.358-6 for determining the basis of the stock of a company acquired in certain triangular reorganizations, except that it permits the basis adjustments to produce an excess loss account where the parties involved were members of a consolidated group following the triangular reorganization.

Reg. § 1.1502-31 authorizes stock basis adjustments after a group structure change, as defined, to reflect the change in the assets and liabilities of the resulting common parent (see ¶ 355).

¶301.02

¶ 315 Investment Adjustments

As explained below, four types of investment adjustments to P's S stock basis are possible under Reg. § 1.1502-32(b)(2) when S has no consolidated subsidiaries. Specifically, P's S stock basis is:

1. Increased by S's taxable income or reduced by S's taxable loss;

2. Increased by S's tax-exempt income;

3. Reduced by S's noncapital, nondeductible expenses (including expired loss carryovers); and

4. Reduced by S's distributions to P.

In addition, when S owns stock in another member of the consolidated group, P adjusts the basis of its S stock to duplicate S's investment adjustments to the basis of any lower-tier stock.[1]

.01 No Duplication of Adjustments

The investment adjustment rules are in addition to basis adjustments required by other rules of law, such as Code Sec. 358. Thus, it may be necessary to modify investment adjustments so that they do not duplicate other adjustments.[2]

.02 Taxable Income or Loss

The starting point to adjusting P's S stock basis is a positive investment adjustment for S's taxable income or a negative adjustment for S's taxable loss for the tax period.[3] This prevents S's taxable income (or loss) from being taxed (or deducted) a second time when P disposes of S, to the extent that such items have already been taken into account on the consolidated return.

S's taxable income or loss for this purpose is consolidated taxable income (or loss) determined by including only S's items. Thus, S takes an intercompany gain into account when so required by Reg. § 1.1502-13. For a list of the adjustments to S's separate taxable income in determining consolidated taxable income, see Reg. § 1.1502-12 and Reg. § 1.1502-80.

Year of absorption of losses. S's deductions and losses are taken into account to the extent that they are absorbed by S or any other member of the consolidated group.[4] For this purpose, any S deduction or loss absorbed as a *carryback* in a prior separate or consolidated year is treated as absorbed in the year it arises. By contrast, any S deduction or loss absorbed as a *carryover* to a later year is taken into account in the carryover year.

As explained in ¶ 335, to avoid a circular basis problem, limitations are imposed on the absorption of S's deductions and losses for S's final year in the P group.

---

[1] Reg. § 1.1502-32(a)(3)(iii).
[2] Reg. § 1.1502-32(a)(2).

[3] Reg. § 1.1502-32(b)(2)(i).
[4] Reg. § 1.1502-32(b)(3)(i).

.03 Tax-Exempt Income

Next, a positive adjustment is made for S's tax-exempt income.[5] This prevents the consolidated group from being taxed indirectly on such income when P disposes of S.

S's tax-exempt income is its income and gain that is taken into account but *permanently* excluded from its gross income, and that increases, directly or indirectly, the basis of S's assets (or an equivalent amount). For example, S's receipt of a refund of federal income taxes, dividend income from another member, or tax-exempt interest would generate a positive adjustment. The regulations provide, however, that S's realized gain from redemption of stock of a liquidating subsidiary does not generate an investment adjustment, even though Code Sec. 332 prevents recognition of such gain.

Further, a deduction or loss that permanently offsets S's taxable income or gain and does not reduce, directly or indirectly, the basis of S's assets (or an equivalent amount) is treated as tax-exempt income.[6]

> **Example 1:** As an example of S's receipt of a dividend eligible for the dividends-received deduction (DRD), S receives a $100 dividend from an unaffiliated corporation for which a $70 dividends-received deduction is allowed by Code Sec. 243, without a corresponding stock basis reduction under Code Sec. 1059. P is entitled to increase the basis of its S stock by $100. In addition to a $30 increase for the portion of the dividend that is not offset by the dividends-received deduction, a $70 increase is allowed for the portion of the dividend that is effectively tax-exempt and does not reduce the basis of S's assets.

Special rules apply to S's discharge of indebtedness income.[7] Such income that is excluded from gross income under Code Sec. 108 is treated as tax-exempt income only to the extent that the discharge is applied to reduce tax attributes. S's discharge of indebtedness income is treated as applied to reduce tax attributes only to the extent that such attribute reduction reduces stock basis as a noncapital, nondeductible expense, as described below.

If the amount of the discharge exceeds the amount of the attribute reduction, the excess still is treated as applied to reduce tax attributes to the extent that (1) a loss carryover expired without tax benefit, (2) the expiration was taken into account as a negative adjustment on the ground that it was a noncapital, nondeductible expense, and (3) the loss carryover would have been reduced had it not expired.

> **Example 2:** As an example of a discharge of indebtedness, P forms S on January 1 of Year 1, and S borrows $200 from an unrelated party. During Year 1, S's assets decline in value, and the P group has a $100 consolidated net operating loss when determined by including only S's items. None of the loss is absorbed by the group in Year 1, and S is discharged from $100 of indebtedness at the close of Year 1. Under Code Sec.108(a), S's $100 of

---

[5] Reg. § 1.1502-32(b)(2)(ii).
[6] Reg. § 1.1502-32(b)(3)(ii)(B).
[7] Reg. § 1.1502-32(b)(3)(ii)(C).

indebtedness income is excluded from gross income because of insolvency. Under Code Sec. 108(b), S's $100 net operating loss is reduced to zero at the close of Year 1. The reduction of the net operating loss is treated as a noncapital, nondeductible expense in Year 1 because the net operating loss is permanently disallowed. All $100 of S's discharge of indebtedness income is treated as tax-exempt income in Year 1 because the discharge results in a $100 reduction to S's net operating loss. Consequently, the loss and the cancellation of the indebtedness result in no net adjustment to P's S stock basis.

Basis shifts. An increase in the basis of S's assets is treated as tax-exempt income to the extent that the increase is not otherwise taken into account in determining stock basis, it corresponds to a negative investment adjustment that is taken into account by the group, and it has the effect of a permanent recovery of the reduction.[8]

.04 Noncapital, Nondeductible Expenses (Including Expired Loss Carryovers)

The flip side of the positive adjustment for S's tax-exempt income is a negative adjustment for S's noncapital, nondeductible expenses.[9] S's noncapital, nondeductible expenses are its deductions and losses that are taken into account but *permanently* disallowed or eliminated, and that decrease, directly or indirectly, the basis of S's assets (or an equivalent amount).[10] This prevents the group from indirectly deducting such items when P disposes of S. Examples include S's payment of federal taxes described in Code Sec. 275 and a loss on a distribution to a nonmember not recognized under Code Sec. 311(a).

Expired loss carryovers. Perhaps the most controversial investment adjustment is the negative adjustment for the expiration of any S loss carryover.[11] The treatment of such an expired loss carryover as a noncapital, nondeductible expense reflects a concern that the failure to so reduce P's S stock basis could have the effect of indefinitely extending the carryover period for using such a loss.

> **Planning Note:** Many are surprised to learn that, in general, there is a negative stock basis adjustment for a subsidiary's expired loss carryovers. Often this can be avoided by making an election to waive part or all of a loss carryover when the loss subsidiary comes into the consolidated group.

Transitional relief. In response to taxpayer criticism about the harshness of applying this negative investment adjustment for expired losses retroactively to stock acquired before the effective date of the 1995 regime, no such adjustment is made for expiration of a separate return limitation year (SRLY) loss carryover if S became a member of the consolidated group in a consolidated return year beginning before January 1, 1995.[12]

Waiver of SRLY loss carryovers. The regulations contain a loss waiver rule that allows an acquiring group to waive loss carryovers from separate return

---

[8] Reg. § 1.1502-32(b)(3)(ii)(D).
[9] Reg. § 1.1502-32(b)(2)(iii).
[10] Reg. § 1.1502-32(b)(3)(iii)(A).

[11] Reg. § 1.1502-32(b)(3)(iii)(A).
[12] Reg. § 1.1502-32(h)(4).

¶315.04

limitation years (SRLYs) of an acquired subsidiary.[13] Specifically, the acquiring group may make an irrevocable election to treat all or any portion of the loss carryover as expiring for all federal income tax purposes immediately before the subsidiary becomes a member of the consolidated group. If the subsidiary was a member of another group immediately before it became a member of the consolidated group, the expiration is also treated as occurring immediately after it ceases to be a member of the prior group.

The loss waiver rule consists of three subrules:

- *Qualifying transactions.* If the loss subsidiary becomes a member of the consolidated group in a qualifying cost basis transaction and the loss waiver election is made, the noncapital, nondeductible expense resulting from the deemed expiration does not result in a corresponding stock basis adjustment for any member.[14] A qualifying cost basis transaction is the purchase (i.e., a transaction in which basis is determined under Code Sec. 1012) by members of the acquiring consolidated group (while they are members) in a 12-month period of an amount of the subsidiary's stock satisfying the requirements of Code Sec. 1504(a)(2).

- *Nonqualifying transactions.* If the loss subsidiary becomes a member of the consolidated group other than in a qualifying cost basis transaction and the loss waiver election is made, the basis of its stock that is owned by members immediately after it becomes a member is subject to reduction under the investment adjustment rules to reflect the deemed expiration.[15] However, the reduction occurs immediately before the subsidiary becomes a member, but after it ceases to be a member of any prior group, and it therefore does not result in a corresponding stock basis adjustment for any higher-tier member of the transferring or acquiring consolidated group.

- *Lower-tier rules.* Special rules apply when a chain of corporations is acquired and loss carryovers of a lower-tier member of the chain are waived.[16] These rules result in adjustments within the chain of acquired corporations but do not affect the acquiring group's basis in the stock of the highest-tier member.

The requirements for electing the loss waiver rule are set forth in Reg. § 1.1502-32(b)(4)(iv).

Nondeductible basis recoveries. Any other decrease in the basis of S's assets (or an equivalent amount) may be treated as a noncapital, nondeductible expense to the extent that the decrease is not otherwise taken into account in determining stock basis and is permanently eliminated for purposes of determining S's taxable income or loss.[17] Whether a decrease is so treated is determined by taking into account both the purposes of the Code or regulatory provision resulting in the decrease and the purposes of the investment adjustments.

---

[13] Reg. § 1.1502-32(b)(4)(i).
[14] Reg. § 1.1502-32(b)(4)(ii)(A).
[15] Reg. § 1.1502-32(b)(4)(ii)(B).

[16] Reg. § 1.1502-32(b)(4)(ii)(C).
[17] Reg. § 1.1502-32(b)(3)(iii)(B).

¶315.04

Code Sec. 78 gross-up. Also included as a noncapital, nondeductible expense is the amount of any gross-up for taxes paid by another that S is treated as having paid, such as foreign taxes included in income under Code Sec. 78.

Federal tax liabilities. For investment adjustment purposes, Reg. § 1.1502-32(b)(3)(iv)(D) requires that taxes be taken into account by applying the principles of the group's basic method for allocating taxes for earnings and profits purposes under Code Sec. 1552, but using the complementary percentage method under Reg. § 1.1502-33(d)(3) for compensating a member for the use of its tax attributes, by assuming a 100-percent allocation of any decreased tax liability. See ¶ 745 for a discussion of the percentage complementary method.

Under Reg. § 1.1502-33(d)(3), the percentage complementary method allocates tax liability based on the absorption of tax attributes without taking into account the ability of any member to subsequently absorb its own tax attributes. As applied for investment adjustment purposes, each profit member's allocation under its basic method is increased by 100 percent of the excess, if any, of the following:

- The member's separate return tax liability for the consolidated return year, as determined under the second basic method, over
- The amount allocated to the member under Code Sec. 1552.

Corresponding amounts are allocated as a right to receive payment to each member whose tax attributes are absorbed, in a manner that reasonably reflects the absorption.

> ***Example 3:*** For an example of allocation of federal income taxes: P owns all the stock of S1 and S2. For Year 1, each member's taxable income for purposes of the regulations under Code Sec. 1552 and redetermined as if the members had filed separate returns, is as follows: P: $0, S1: $2,000, and S2: ($1,000). Thus, the P group's consolidated tax liability for Year 1 is $350 (assuming a 35-percent tax rate). For earnings and profits purposes, under the first basic method, all of the group's $350 tax is allocated to S1. For investment adjustment purposes, the P group must use the percentage complementary method for compensating members whose tax attributes are absorbed: S1, the profit member, is allocated another $350 of tax liability because S1 would have had a $700 tax liability under the second basic method, but only $350 is allocated to S1 under the first basic method. Thus, P's S1 stock basis is reduced by a noncapital, nondeductible federal income tax expense of $700. Conversely, because the additional $350 allocated to S1 is attributable to the absorption of S2's losses, P's S2 stock basis is increased by $350 for the deemed income tax refund (i.e., tax-exempt income) to S2.

The significance of this allocation of federal tax liabilities is often reduced, however, because stock basis is further adjusted to reflect any actual tax sharing of the members without regard to their method of allocation. If the allocated obligation is not paid, the amount not paid is generally treated as a distribution, contribution, or both, depending on the relationship between the members.

> ***Example 4:*** For an example of where actual payment varies from the allocated amount: P owns all the stock of S. For Year 1, each member's taxable

income, both for purposes of Code Sec. 1552 and redetermined as if the members had filed separate returns, is as follows: P: $0 and S: $1,000. Under the above-described rules, S is charged with a $350 tax liability for investment adjustment purposes, and P accordingly reduces its S stock basis to reflect this noncapital, nondeductible expense. If S pays the $350 tax liability, there is no further effect on stock basis. If P pays the $350 tax liability, however, (and the parties do not treat the payment as a loan) P is treated as contributing $350 to S, thereby increasing P's S stock basis by $350 (with no net change in P's S stock basis as a result of the allocation and payment of the tax liability). Conversely, if S were to pay a tax liability allocated to P without reimbursement by P, S would be treated as distributing that amount to P.

.05 Distributions

The fourth investment adjustment is a negative adjustment for dividend and return of capital distributions by S to P.[18] It is immaterial whether any dividend so distributed was out of earnings and profits earned in the current year, a prior consolidated return year that built up stock basis, or a pre-consolidation year in which earnings and profits may not have been reflected in P's S stock.

Transitional relief. Because the prior rules did not require a negative adjustment for certain distributions of earnings and profits accumulated when P and S were affiliated but filed a separate return, a transitional rule prevents a negative adjustment for such a distribution made in a consolidated return year beginning before January 1, 1995.[19]

Example 5: In a pre-1995 distribution of affiliation year earnings and profits (E&P), P owned all the stock of S for Years 1–3, and S accumulated $200 of earnings and profits during such affiliation years. Because P and S did not elect to file a consolidated return until Year 4, S's Year 1–3 earnings and profits did not increase P's S stock basis. In Year 4, S distributes its $200 of earnings and profits, accumulated in Years 1–3, to P. Whether P must reduce its S stock basis to reflect S's distribution depends on whether the distribution satisfies the transitional rule. Unless S distributed the $200 in a consolidated return year beginning before January 1, 1995, P must reduce its S stock basis to reflect the distribution.

The deemed dividend and recontribution election of the prior regime was not continued under the current rules. Any such election for a consolidated return year beginning before January 1, 1995, however, is respected.[20] Thus, if the P group made such an election to P's S stock basis to reflect earnings and profits earned when P and S were affiliated but filed separate returns, the current rules will not eliminate that basis increase.

---

[18] Reg. § 1.1502-32(b)(2)(iv).

[19] Reg. § 1.1502-32(h)(3)(ii). More precisely, no negative investment adjustment to reduce P's S stock basis is required as a result of a distribution of earnings and profits accumulated in separate return years, if the distribution did not cause a negative adjustment under the

investment adjustment rules in effect at the time of the distribution. For a discussion of the prior rules, *see* WARNER, CONSOLIDATED RETURNS: STOCK BASIS, LOSS DISALLOWANCE, AND INTERCOMPANY TRANSACTIONS (CCH Tax Trans. Lib., 1992).

[20] Reg. § 1.1502-32(h)(3)(i).

.06 Tiering Up of Adjustments

The last investment adjustment tiers up the investment adjustments made by S to the stock basis of S's consolidated subsidiaries.[21] As illustrated in the following example, a holding company with no operations would make investment adjustments for the receipt of distributions (tax-exempt income) and the tiering up of such lower-tier investment adjustments.

Example 6: To demonstrate a tiering up of adjustments: GP owns all the stock of P, which owns all the stock of S. GP starts with a $100 basis in its P stock, and P starts with a $100 basis in its S stock. S's Year 1 and Year 2 activities are as follows:

S's Activities

		Year 1	Year 2
Taxable income	(1)	+25	0
Tax-exempt income	(2)	0	+30
Federal taxes	(3)	−10	0
Distributions to P	(4)	−15	0

GP's and P's investment adjustments to reflect S's activities are as follows:

GP's and P's Investment Adjustments

		Year 0	Year 1	Year 2		Total
Adjustments to GP's basis in P stock	(1)		0	0		
	(2)		+15 *	0		
	(3)		0	0		
	(4)		0	0		
	(5)		0 **	+30 ***		
Adjusted basis		**$100**	**+15**	**+30**	**=**	**$145**
Adjustments to P's basis in S stock	(1)		+25	0		
	(2)		0	+30		
	(3)		−10	0		
	(4)		−15	0		
Adjusted basis		**$100**	**0**	**+30**	**=**	**$130**

* P's receipt of a $15 distribution from S (which qualifies as tax-exempt income to P).

** P's net investment adjustment to its S stock basis.

*** P's net investment adjustment to its S stock basis.

---

[21] Reg. § 1.1502-32(a)(3)(iii).

Assuming S and P had no unrealized income or deductions, these stock basis adjustments change P's S stock basis and GP's P stock basis in precisely the same amounts as the changes in value of S and P. Thus, if either P sold S or GP sold P for their assumed values (S for $100 at the end of Year 1, or for $130 at the end of Year 2; P for $115 at the end of Year 1, or for $145 at the end of Year 2), no gain or loss would be realized. Thus, the investment adjustments would serve their purpose of avoiding duplication of S's previously recognized income and of avoiding indirect taxation of S's tax-exempt income.

.07 Timing of Adjustments

The investment adjustments are made as of the close of each consolidated return year and "as of any other time . . . if a determination at that time is necessary to determine a tax liability of any person."[22] For example, adjustments are made as of P's sale of its S stock or as necessary if P's interest in S varies during the consolidated return year.

This broad rule permitting adjustments as needed to determine tax liability corrects a former problem under the old regulations: they literally did not require adjustments for a subsidiary in the year it was liquidated.

.08 Allocation of Adjustments

Allocation issues arise if, for example, P owns less than all the S stock, S has minority shareholders who are not members of the P group, P's interest in S varies, S has more than one class of stock, or P has positive basis in one block and negative basis in another block of S common stock.

Distributions. The negative investment adjustment for S's distributions is allocated to the shares of S stock to which the distribution relates.[23] The remainder of the net adjustment for taxable income or loss, tax-exempt income, and noncapital, nondeductible expenses is allocated among the shares of S stock under the rules explained below.

Nonmember shareholders. The remaining net adjustment is allocated *pro rata* among the shares of S stock of the same class, including shares owned by nonmembers. Thus, if P owns 80 percent of S's only class of stock and nonmembers own 20 percent, 80 percent of the adjustments are allocated to P's S stock. The basis of the 20 percent of S's stock owned by nonmembers is not adjusted.

Varying interests. Generally, if P's interest in the S stock is not the same during the entire year, S's taxable income, etc., is apportioned to each relevant segment of the year in accordance with the rules in Reg. § 1.1502-76(b).[24]

> **Example 7:** As an example of varying interests: P acquires 80 percent of S's stock on January 1, Year 1, another 10 percent on July 1, Year 1, and the remaining 10 percent on October 1, Year 1. S earns $100 of taxable income in Year 1, all of which is subject to daily apportionment under Reg. § 1.1502-76(b).

---

[22] Reg. § 1.1502-32(b)(1)(i).
[23] Reg. § 1.1502-32(c)(1).

[24] Reg. § 1.1502-32(b)(1)(ii).

The $100 positive investment adjustment is allocated as follows:

1. $50 is allocated to the period ending June 30, Year 1, for which a $40 positive investment adjustment (80 percent of $50) is allowed for P's S stock.

2. $25 is allocated to the period beginning July 1, Year 1, and ending September 30, Year 1, for which a $22.50 positive investment adjustment (90 percent of $25) is allowed for P's S stock.

3. Finally, $25 is allocated to the period beginning October 1, Year 1, and ending December 31, Year 1, for which a $25 positive investment adjustment (100 percent of $25) is allowed for P's S stock.

Thus, for Year 1, the total positive investment adjustment allocated to P for S's $100 of taxable income is $87.50.

Multiple classes of stock. The premise of the allocation rules for multiple classes of stock is that, because of its similarity to debt, only preference amounts are allocated to S's preferred stock. Residual amounts, after preference dividends, are allocated to common stock. In the same vein, negative adjustments (other than for distributions) are not allocated to preferred stock. Finally, stock basis adjustments must be redetermined whenever necessary to determine the tax liability of any person, for example, when subsequent events demonstrate that a prior allocation to reflect preferred dividends would conflict with the actual rights of shares of preferred and common stock.

Preferred stock. A negative adjustment is made for any distribution made with respect to preferred stock. No negative adjustment is made to preferred stock, however, for S's losses. The only positive investment adjustment with respect to P's S preferred stock is for an amount that reflects preferred dividends.

If the net amount of the investment adjustments for taxable income or loss, tax-exempt income, and noncapital, nondeductible expenditures is positive, then such net amount is allocated first to S preferred stock in an amount equal to the distributions under Code Sec. 301 to which the S preferred stock is entitled, plus all accumulated and unpaid dividends on the S preferred stock during the period S has been a member of the current group and any prior consolidated group to which P and S belonged.[25] If the net amount of such investment adjustments is less than the sum of the allocations required for all classes of S preferred stock, then the net amount is allocated among the various classes of preferred stock to reflect their relative priorities.

Common stock. After allocating distributions to the applicable stock, the net amount of the positive investment adjustments not allocable to preferred stock and all of the net amount of any negative investment adjustments are allocated to S common stock.[26]

[25] Reg. § 1.1502-32(c)(3).

[26] Reg. § 1.1502-32(c)(2). For the allocation of investment adjustments among classes of common stock, *see* Reg. § 1.1502-32(c)(2)(ii).

Example 8: For an example of positive investment adjustments allocated to S preferred stock: On January 1, Year 1, P owns all of S's common stock with a basis of $800, and nonmembers own all of S's preferred stock that was issued for $200. The preferred stock has an annual cumulative preferred dividend of $20 and a liquidation preference of $200. No dividend arrearages exist with respect to the preferred stock. During Year 1, S has $50 of taxable income. No distributions are declared or made by S. The $50 positive adjustment is allocated $20 to the S preferred stock (to reflect the dividend arrearage arising from Year 1) and $30 to the S common stock.

Smoothing adjustments. After a *pro rata* allocation between all owners of S common stock, if one or more shares of S common stock owned by a member has a negative basis, a net positive investment adjustment is allocated first to those shares to the extent necessary to eliminate the negative basis.[27] Similarly, a net negative investment adjustment, apart from distributions, is allocated first to common shares having a positive basis before being allocated to shares having a negative basis.

Reallocation of adjustments. A member's basis in each share of S's preferred and common stock must be redetermined whenever it is necessary to calculate the tax liability of any person.[28] The redetermination is made by reallocating S's net adjustment described in Reg. § 1.1502-32(b)(2)(i) through Reg. § 1.1502-32(b)(2)(iii) (i.e., the investment adjustments without taking into account distributions) for each consolidated return year (or other applicable period) of the group, by taking into account all facts and circumstances affecting allocations as of the redetermination date. For this purpose:

- Amounts may be reallocated from one class of S stock to another class, but not from one share of a class to another share of the same class.

- If there is a change in the equity structure of S (e.g., as the result of S's issuance, redemption, or recapitalization of shares), a cumulative redetermination is made for the period before the change.

- If S becomes a nonmember as a result of a change in equity structure, any reallocation is made only among the shares of S's stock immediately before the change.

- Any reallocation is treated for all purposes after it is made as the original allocation, but the reallocation does not affect any prior period. However, an amount may not be reallocated to the extent that the amount has been used before the reallocation. For this purpose, an amount has been used to the extent that it has been taken into account, directly or indirectly, by any member in determining income, gain, deduction, or loss or in determining the basis of any property that is not subject to the investment adjustment rules (e.g., stock of a corporation that has become a nonmember). For example, if P sells a share of S stock, an amount previously allocated to the share sold cannot be reallocated to another share of S stock, but an amount allocated to another share of S stock can still be reallocated to the sold share

---

[27] Reg. § 1.1502-32(c)(2)(i).   [28] Reg. § 1.1502-32(c)(4).

¶315.08

because the reallocated amount has not been taken into account. Any adjustment reallocated to the sold share may effectively be eliminated, however, because the reallocation was not in effect when the share was previously sold, and P's gain or loss from the sale is not redetermined.

Example 9: As an example of redetermination of allocations: P owns all of S's common and preferred stock. The preferred stock has a $100 annual, cumulative preference as to dividends. For Year 1, S has $200 of taxable income, the first $100 of which is allocated to the preferred stock, and the remaining $100 of which is allocated to the common stock. For Year 2, there are no investment adjustments, and P sells all of its common stock at the close of Year 2. P's basis in S's common stock must be redetermined as of the date of sale of such stock, by reallocating all of the $200 of taxable income to the preferred stock. This is because the common stock is not entitled to any of the $200 of taxable income from Year 1. Thus P's basis in the common stock will reflect no investment adjustments.

Example 10: As an example of reallocation to subsequently issued preferred stock: In January Year 1, S is formed with only common stock outstanding, all of which is owned by P, for an investment of $10. S earns $100 of taxable income in Year 1, all of which is distributed to P on December 31, Year 1. S has no other activities in Year 1. On January 1, Year 2, S issues to a nonmember $1,000 of nonvoting preferred stock that satisfies the requirements of Code Sec. 1504(a)(4). For Year 2, the dividend accruing on S's preferred stock is $110. S earns only $30 of net income for Year 2, none of which is distributed. Initially, all of the $100 positive adjustment for S's $100 of Year 1 income is allocated to the common stock owned by P, and P suffers a negative basis adjustment of $100 for the Year 1 distribution on the S common stock, leaving P with a positive $10 basis in the S common stock. The issuance of $1,000 of preferred stock in Year 2, however, coupled with the fact that S's Year 2 income was $80 less than the dividend that accrued in Year 2 on the S preferred stock, might require the reallocation of $80 of the $100 positive adjustment for S's Year 1 net income from the S common stock to the S preferred stock.[29] In that case, P would be left with a $70 negative basis in the S common stock (beginning basis of $10, minus $100 for the Year 1 distribution, plus $20 for the Year 1 net income).[30]

Treasury and the IRS indicate that, in determining whether all or part of the positive adjustment for S's Year 1 net income should be reallocated to the preferred stock, it is irrelevant whether a dividend is actually paid on the S common stock owned by P in Year 1.[31] It is likely, however, that, under applicable state law, P would not be required to return to S any portion of the $100 dividend paid on the S common stock in Year 1, provided S was not rendered insolvent by the dividend and had sufficient surplus or current earnings to pay the dividend. In that case, the owner of the S preferred stock in substance has no interest in, or right to receive,

---

[29] *See* Reg. § 1.1502-32(c)(5), Example 3(c).

[30] Because the S preferred stock is held by a nonmember, any adjustment allocated to the preferred stock will not be reflected in the adjusted basis of that stock. Reg. § 1.1502-32(c)(1).

[31] Reg. § 1.1502-32(c)(5), Example 3(f).

¶315.08

any of the income earned by S in Year 1. For this reason, the author believes that a reallocation of any portion of the Year 1 income to the S preferred stock is not proper.

.09 Anti-Avoidance Rule

If any person acts with a principal purpose contrary to the purposes of the investment adjustment rules (for example, to avoid the effect of the rules, or to avoid the effect of any other provision of the consolidated return regulations), adjustments are authorized as necessary to carry out the purposes of these rules.[32]

.10 Predecessors and Successors

Any reference in the investment adjustment regulations to a corporation or share includes all predecessors and successors to the corporation or share, as the context may require.[33] A "successor share" is any share of which the adjusted basis is determined, in whole or in part, by reference to the adjusted basis of the predecessor share, and a "successor corporation" is any corporation of which the adjusted basis of the assets is determined, in whole or in part, by reference to the adjusted basis of the assets of its predecessor corporation.

Because the investment adjustment system only adjusts the basis of "subsidiary" stock, it does not address the basis of stock issued by nonmembers. Thus, a "successor share" should not include a share of stock issued by a corporation that is not a subsidiary, and a "successor corporation" generally should not include a corporation that is not a subsidiary. If the basis in a new member's stock is determined in part by reference to the basis of the stock of a former subsidiary, however, and in part by reference to the basis of the stock of a nonmember, then it would seem appropriate to treat the new member as a "successor corporation" and the new member's stock as "successor shares."

.11 Recordkeeping Requirement

Reg. § 1.1502-32(g) requires that investment adjustments be reflected annually on permanent records, including work papers, which will enable the group to identify the amount, allocation, and nature of investment adjustments. Failure to comply with this recordkeeping requirement could result in penalties under Code Sec. 6662.

.12 Effective Dates and Transitional Relief

The current investment adjustment rules apply to determinations of stock basis in consolidated return years beginning on or after January 1, 1995.[34] Thus, if the P group uses the calendar year, the rules apply to P for any disposition of S in 1995 or later years. When applicable, the new rules generally apply retroactively. Indeed, they apply to consolidated return years before 1966, when the prior investment adjustment system first was put into place.

As previously discussed, however, transitional relief was provided in these situations:

---

[32] Reg. § 1.1502-32(e).
[33] Reg. § 1.1502-32(f).

[34] Reg. § 1.1502-32(h).

¶315.09

- *Expired loss carryovers.* If S became a member of a consolidated group in a consolidated return year beginning before January 1, 1995, and had a loss carryover from a separate return limitation year (SRLY) at that time, a special rule exempts the group from treating expiration of the loss carryover as a negative investment adjustment.[35]

- *S's distribution of pre-consolidation affiliation-year earnings and profits.* If S distributed earnings and profits to P in a consolidated return year beginning before January 1, 1995, and the distribution did not require a negative basis adjustment under the rules in effect at the time of the distribution, no negative investment adjustment is required.[36]

- *Deemed dividend elections.* The deemed dividend election of old Reg. § 1.1502-32(f)(2) was not carried over to the new regulations. If a deemed dividend election was made in a consolidated return year beginning before January 1, 1995, however, the deemed distribution and recontribution under the election are respected.[37]

¶ 325 Excess Loss Accounts and Their Recapture

The concept of an excess loss account (i.e., negative stock basis) is unique to consolidated returns. Its creation and recapture are discussed here.

.01 Creation of Negative Stock Basis

When S has debt capital, the resulting leverage may cause P's negative investment adjustments for S's losses to create a negative S stock basis. For this reason, the regulations refer to such a negative stock basis as an "excess loss account." Reg. § 1.1502-19 generally, but not always, requires P to recapture the amount of its negative S stock basis as income or gain (generally as capital gain) when P disposes of its S stock.

Consolidated groups should be aware, however, that negative stock basis subject to recapture can arise for reasons unrelated to S's losses. For example, P's S stock basis is reduced to reflect S's distributions to P. As another example, P may have a negative stock basis under Code Sec. 358 following a Code Sec. 351 transfer by P to S, when the liabilities assumed or taken subject to by S exceed the basis of the assets transferred by P to S. This is because Code Sec. 357(c), which generally requires gain to be recognized on such a transfer, does not apply to an intercompany transaction.[38]

> **Planning Note:** Negative stock basis is eliminated in a Code Sec. 332 liquidation of the subsidiary; however, the subsidiary must be solvent.

.02 Recapture Events

P is treated as disposing of a share of S stock under Reg. § 1.1502-19(c), subject to these exceptions:

---

[35] Reg. § 1.1502-32(h)(4).
[36] Reg. § 1.1502-32(h)(3)(ii).

[37] Reg. § 1.1502-32(h)(3)(i).
[38] Reg. § 1.1502-80(d)(1).

1. *Transfer, cancellation, etc.* When P ceases to own the share, even if no gain or loss is taken into account, or on the occurrence of any event in which P recognizes gain or loss (in whole or in part) with respect to the share.

2. *Deconsolidation.* When

    a. P becomes a nonmember, or a nonmember determines its basis in the share (or any other asset) by reference to P's basis in the share, directly or indirectly, in whole or in part.

    b. S becomes a nonmember, or P's basis in the share is reflected, directly or indirectly, in whole or in part, in the basis of any asset other than member stock.

3. *Worthlessness.* On any day that

    a. substantially all of S's assets are treated as disposed of, abandoned, or destroyed. An asset of S is not considered disposed of or abandoned to the extent that the disposition is in complete liquidation of S or is in exchange for consideration.

    b. an indebtedness of S is discharged *and* any part of the amount discharged is neither included in gross income, nor treated as tax-exempt income under Reg. § 1.1502-32(b)(3)(ii)(C).

    c. a member takes into account a deduction or loss for the uncollectibility of an indebtedness of S, and the deduction or loss is not matched in the same tax year by S's taking a corresponding amount of income or gain from the indebtedness in determining consolidated taxable income.

.03 Recapture Exceptions and Deferral

If P is treated as disposing of its S stock, P generally takes its negative stock basis into account as income or gain from the disposition. Except as discussed below, P's income or gain is subject to any applicable deferral or nonrecognition provision.

> **Planning Note:** Thus, a redemption of P's S stock in a liquidation of S into P under Code Sec. 332 would not cause P to recapture its negative S stock basis.[39] Instead, like positive S stock basis, the negative S stock basis would disappear. In the same vein, if P transferred its S stock to another member of the group in a transaction for which P is entitled to nonrecognition treatment under Code Sec. 351, Code Sec. 354, Code Sec. 355, or Code Sec. 361, P would not recapture its negative stock basis. Instead, in a Code Sec. 351 transfer, for example, P's basis in the stock of the transferee corporation received in the exchange would be reduced by the amount of P's negative stock basis. And, the transferee corporation would carry over P's negative basis in the S stock.

Nonrecognition or deferral inapplicable. If P's disposition results from a deconsolidation of P or S, or worthlessness of S, however, P's income or gain is taken into account notwithstanding any deferral or nonrecognition rules to the contrary.[40]

---

[39] Reg. § 1.1502-19(b)(2)(i). [40] Reg. § 1.1502-19(b)(2)(ii).

¶325.03

Acquisition of group by another group. P would not be considered as having a recapture event as a result of deconsolidation if the disposition results solely from the termination of the group because the group is acquired, if (1) there is a surviving consolidated group and the terminating group ceases to exist as a result of an acquisition of the assets of the common parent in a reorganization described in Code Sec. 381(a)(2) or an acquisition of the stock of the common parent, or (2) the group ceases to exist under the principles of Reg. § 1.1502-75(d)(2) or Reg. § 1.1502-75(d)(3). Instead, the surviving group is treated as continuing the terminating group.[41]

.04 Character of Recapture Gain

P's recapture gain is generally treated as a sale or exchange for purposes of determining the character of the amount realized (i.e., generally P's gain is capital gain).[42] P's recapture gain is treated as ordinary income, however, to the extent, if any, that S is insolvent within the meaning of Code Sec. 108(d)(3) immediately before the disposition. For this purpose, liabilities include certain preferred stock and discharged debts that were treated as tax-exempt income under the investment adjustment rules. The amount treated as ordinary income is reduced to the extent that it exceeds the amount of P's negative stock basis redetermined without taking into account S's distributions to P that resulted in negative investment adjustments.[43]

.05 Smoothing Adjustments

If P has a negative stock basis in shares of S stock, any basis adjustment with respect to other shares of the same class held by P is allocated first to equalize and eliminate the negative stock basis.[44] Prior to 2006, application of the smoothing adjustment rule was sensitive to the form of the transaction.

> **Example 11:** As an example of a smoothing adjustment that depended on the form of the transaction: P owns all the stock of S with an excess loss account of $100 and all the stock of T with a basis of $150, and T merges into S in a reorganization described in Code Sec. 368(a)(1)(D) in which P receives additional shares of S Stock. P's excess loss account in its original shares of S stock was first eliminated. Therefore, P's original shares would have an aggregate basis of $0 and P's new S shares would have an aggregate basis of $50. If, instead, S merged into T in a reorganization under Code Sec. 368(a)(1)(D) in which P received additional shares of T stock, because P did not already have T shares that had an excess loss account, Reg. § 1.1502-19 did not apply. Therefore, P's original shares would have a basis of $150 and P's new T shares would have an excess loss account of $100.

To prevent the smoothing adjustment rule effectively being elective depending on which direction a transaction occurred, in 2006, Temp. Reg. § 1.1502-19T added an additional rule. It provides that if a member would otherwise determine shares of a class of S's stock (a new share) to have an excess loss account and such

---

[41] Reg. § 1.1502-19(c)(3).
[42] Reg. § 1.1502-19(b)(1).

[43] Reg. § 1.1502-19(b)(4).
[44] Reg. § 1.1502-19(d).

member owns one or more other shares of the same class of S's stock, the basis of such other shares is allocated to eliminate and equalize any excess loss account that would otherwise be in the new shares.

> ***Example 12:*** A an example of the new smoothing rule that eliminates the electivity of the rule depending on the direction of the transaction: In the example above in which S merges into T under Code Sec. 368(a)(1)(D) and P receives additional shares of T stock, the basis of P's original T shares will first be applied to eliminate the excess loss account that P would otherwise have in its new shares. Therefore, P will have aggregate basis of $50 in its original T shares and an aggregate basis of $0 in its new T shares.

.06 Anti-Avoidance Rule

If any person acts with a principal purpose contrary to the purposes of the excess loss account rules, to avoid the effect of the rules or to apply those rules to avoid the effect of any other provision of the consolidated return regulations, adjustments are authorized as necessary to carry out the purposes of the rules.[45]

In a change from the prior rules, worthlessness of P's S stock within the meaning of Code Sec. 165(g) is not an event causing P to recapture its negative S stock basis. Instead, S ordinarily will be considered worthless for this purpose only at the time substantially all of S's assets are treated as disposed of, abandoned, or destroyed for federal income tax purposes. However, if S ceases any substantial operations with respect to its assets, but maintains their ownership with a principal purpose to avoid P taking into account its negative S stock basis, the anti-avoidance rule will be used to treat S as worthless, causing P to have a recapture event.[46]

.07 Effective Date

The negative stock basis rules apply to determinations of the basis in stock of a member in consolidated return years beginning on or after January 1, 1995.[47] When applicable, these rules apply retroactively.

¶ 335 Disposition-Year Anti-Circular Basis Rule

Reg. § 1.1502-11(b) limits the use of S's loss in the year P disposes of its S stock and limits the carryover of S's items in the same manner in order to prevent circular basis adjustments that would waste S's loss or loss carryover.

.01 The Circular Basis Problem and Its Solution

The purpose of this limitation is to prevent P's gain from the disposition of its S stock from increasing the absorption of S's deductions and losses, because the increased absorption would reduce P's basis in its S stock under Reg. § 1.1502-32 and, in turn, increase P's gain.[48] The limitation preserves S's deductions and losses for S's use after it leaves the P group.

The amount of S's deductions and losses that may offset P's gain from the disposition of its S stock is determined by tentatively computing the taxable income

---

[45] Reg. § 1.1502-19(e).
[46] Reg. § 1.1502-19(g), Example 6.
[47] Reg. § 1.1502-19(h)(1).
[48] Reg. § 1.1502-11(b)(1).

(or loss) for the year of disposition (and any prior years to which the deductions or losses may be carried) without taking into account P's gain from the disposition.[49] To the extent that S's deductions and losses in the year of disposition cannot offset P's gain because of the limitation, the items are carried to other years under the applicable provisions of the Code and regulations as if they were the only items incurred by S in the year of disposition.[50]

> **Example 13:** As an example of limitation on S's losses for stock gain: P has a $500 basis in its S stock. For Year 1, P has ordinary income of $30 (determined without taking P's gain or loss from the disposition of its S stock into account), and S has an $80 ordinary loss. P sells its S stock for $520 at the close of Year 1. To determine the limitation on the use of S's loss and the effect under Reg. § 1.1502-32 of the absorption of S's loss, P's gain or loss on the disposition of S is not taken into account. P is tentatively treated as having $30 of income, and thus $30 of S's loss is absorbed. P's basis in its S stock is reduced under Reg. § 1.1502-32 from $500 to $470 immediately before the disposition. Accordingly, P recognizes a $50 gain from the sale of its S stock, and the group has consolidated taxable income of $50 for Year 1 (P's $30 of ordinary income and $50 gain from the sale of its S stock, less $30 of S's loss.) S's $50 of limited loss is treated as a separate net operating loss attributable to S and, because S ceases to be a member, the loss is apportioned to S under Reg. § 1.1502-21 and carried to its first separate return year.

The same principles apply to the extent necessary to carry out the purposes of Reg. § 1.1502-11(b) if P recognizes a deduction or loss from disposition of its S stock.[51]

> **Example 14:** As an example of limitation on S's losses for stock loss: P has a $400 basis in its S stock. For Year 1, P has a capital gain of $100 (determined without taking P's gain or loss from the disposition of P's S stock into account), and S has both a $60 capital loss and a $200 ordinary loss. P sells its S stock for $140 at the close of Year 1. To determine the limitation on the use of S's losses, the group's consolidated net operating loss and consolidated net capital loss are determined without taking into account P's loss from the disposition of its S stock. According to Reg. § 1.1502-11(b)(3)(ii), the limitation is necessary to prevent P's S stock loss from affecting the absorption of S's losses and thereby the adjustments to P's S stock basis, which in turn affect P's loss. Consequently, the amount of the limitation on S's losses is determined by tentatively treating the P group as having a $40 net capital gain and a $200 ordinary loss. Thus, P's $100 of capital gain is reduced by S's $60 capital loss and $40 of S's $200 net operating loss. This results in a $160 consolidated net operating loss for Year 1, all of which is attributable to S. Thus, $160 of S's ordinary loss is limited. S departs with a $160 net operating loss carryforward. The absorption of $100 of S's losses reduces P's S stock basis from $400 to $300, producing a loss of $160. (This loss may or may not be allowed. See Chapter 3.)

[49] Reg. § 1.1502-11(b)(2)(i).
[50] Reg. § 1.1502-11(b)(2)(ii).
[51] Reg. § 1.1502-11(b)(3).

.02 Multiple Member Dispositions

The anti-circular basis adjustment limitation also applies to deferred gains or losses restored with respect to S stock and to dispositions of subgroups. There is no limitation, however, on the use of a sister subsidiary's losses against gain recognized on a disposition of a brother subsidiary's stock, or vice versa, even if both subsidiaries' stock is sold in the same year.[52]

¶ 345 Asset Consistency Rules

The consistency rules of Reg. § 1.338-8 generally apply if the purchasing corporation acquires an asset directly from target during the consistency period described in Code Sec. 338(h)(4) and acquires the stock of target (a consolidated subsidiary) in a qualified stock purchase without making a Code Sec. 338 election. Without the consistency rules, a selling consolidated group could sell assets to the purchaser with a stepped up basis, to the extent of the excess of the value of the subsidiary stock over its basis, without cost to the selling group. This is because investment adjustments for the asset gains would shelter the selling group from stock gain. Under the consistency rules, the purchasing corporation generally takes a carryover basis in the asset.

> **Example 15:** As an example of a basic case of consistency rules: P owns all the stock of S, which A desires to purchase. P has a $600 basis in its S stock. S has a zero basis in its assets. P proposes to sell its S stock to A for $1,500. With a view to stepping up the basis of part of A's assets at no cost to A or the P consolidated group, A instead proposes that it acquire S capital assets with a zero basis for $900 (S would distribute the $900 to P) and acquire the S stock for $600 with P (rather than S) paying all the taxes on the $900 gain generated by the sale of the assets. Without the consistency rules, A's objectives could be accomplished. Instead of having a $900 capital gain on the sale of its S stock, it would have a $900 capital gain on the sale of S's assets; P would have a $900 investment adjustment from the gain on the assets that would keep its basis in its S stock at $600 after the distribution of $900 cash. Thus, to the extent of the excess of the value of the subsidiary stock over its basis, the selling group could sell S assets and step up their basis for A's benefit without a tax cost to either A or the selling group.

Under Reg. § 1.338-8(b) and Reg. § 1.338-8(d), however, A must take a zero carryover basis in the acquired assets because:

1. The assets are disposed of during the target "consistency period" (see Code Sec. 338(h)(4));

2. The basis of target stock, as of the target acquisition date, reflects gain from the disposition of the assets; and

3. The assets are owned, immediately after their acquisition and on the target acquisition date, by a corporation that acquires stock of the target in the qualified stock purchase (or by an affiliate of an acquiring corporation).

---

[52] Reg. § 1.1502-11(b)(4).

¶335.02

Numerous protections apply to prevent circumvention of these rules. For example, even intercompany transactions between the seller and its subsidiary before the transaction with the purchasing corporation are considered "arrangements" that can trigger the carryover basis rule.[53] Also, anti-avoidance rules have to be considered.[54]

¶ 355 Special Rules

Some special rules must be kept in mind for stock basis after certain triangular reorganizations and after a group structure change, as noted here.

.01 Stock Basis After Certain Triangular Reorganizations

The general rules for determining the stock basis of a subsidiary acquired in a triangular reorganization are set forth in Reg. § 1.358-6. The model for those rules generally adjusts a controlling corporation's (P's) basis in the stock of its controlled corporation (S or T) as a result of certain triangular reorganizations as if P had acquired the T assets (and any liabilities assumed or to which the T assets were subject) directly from T in a transaction in which P's basis in the T assets was determined under Code Sec. 362(b), and P then had transferred the T assets (and liabilities) to S in a transaction in which P's basis in the S or T stock was adjusted under Code Sec. 358. These regulations provide a limitation that prevents the reductions from producing a net negative basis adjustment to P's basis in its S stock.

Reg. § 1.1502-30 embraces these rules, except that the limitation on net negative basis adjustments does not apply, where P and S or P and T, as applicable, were members of a consolidated group following the triangular reorganization.

> **Example 16:** As an example of net negative basis adjustment: T has assets with an aggregate basis of $60 and fair market value of $100. T's assets are subject to $70 of liabilities. Pursuant to a plan, P forms S with $5 of cash (which S retains), and T merges into S. In the merger, the T shareholders receive P stock worth $30 in exchange for their T stock. The transaction is a reorganization to which Code Sec. 368(a)(2)(D) applies.[55]

Under Reg. § 1.358-6, P adjusts its $5 basis in the S stock as if P had acquired the T assets with a carryover basis under Code Sec. 362 and transferred these assets to S in a transaction to which P determines its basis in the S stock under Code Sec. 358. Under the rules of Reg. § 1.1502-30, the limitation described in Reg. § 1.358-6(c)(1)(ii) does not apply. Thus, P adjusts its basis in the S stock by –$10 (the aggregate adjusted basis of T's assets decreased by the amount of liabilities to which the T assets are subject). Consequently, as a result of the reorganization, P has an excess loss account of $5 in its S stock.

.02 Stock Basis After Group Structure Change

As discussed in Chapter 7, one corporation (P) may succeed to another corporation (T) under the principles of Reg. § 1.1502-75(d)(2) or (3) as the common

---

[53] See Reg. § 1.338-4(f) and Reg. § 1.338-4(f)(4), Example 2.

[54] See Reg. § 1.338-4(j).

[55] Reg. § 1.1502-30(b)(5), Example 1.

parent of a consolidated group in a "group structure change." If this occurs, the basis of members in the stock of the former common parent (or the stock of a successor) is adjusted or determined under Reg. § 1.1502-31. For example, if P owns all the stock of another corporation (S), and T merges into S in a group structure change that is a reorganization described in Code Sec. 368(a)(2)(D) in which P becomes the common parent of the T group, P's basis in S's stock must be adjusted to reflect the change in S's assets and liabilities.

These rules coordinate with the earnings and profits adjustments required under Reg. § 1.1502-33(f)(1), generally conforming the results of transactions in which the T group continues under Reg. § 1.1502-75 with P as the common parent. By preserving in P the relationship between T's earnings and profits and asset basis, these adjustments limit possible distortions under Code Sec. 1502 (e.g., in the deconsolidation rules for earnings and profits under Reg. § 1.1502-33(e), and the continued filing requirements under Reg. § 1.1502-75(a)). These rules apply whether or not T continues to exist after the group structure change.

1. *Asset acquisitions.* If a corporation acquires the former common parent's assets (and any liabilities assumed or to which the assets are subject) in a group structure change, the basis of members in the stock of the acquiring corporation is adjusted immediately after the group structure change to reflect the acquiring corporation's allocable share of the former common parent's net asset basis as determined under Reg. § 1.1502-31(c). Under that provision, the former common parent's net asset basis is the basis it would have in the stock of a newly formed subsidiary, if:

   a. The former common parent transferred its assets (and any liabilities assumed or to which the assets are subject) to the subsidiary in a transaction to which Code Sec. 351 applies;

   b. The former common parent and the subsidiary were members of the same consolidated group (see Reg. § 1.1502-80(d) for the non-application of Code Sec. 357(c) to the transfer); and

   c. The asset basis taken into account is each asset's basis immediately after the group structure change (e.g., taking into account any income or gain recognized in the group structure change and reflected in the asset's basis).

   If T's net asset basis is a negative amount, it reduces P's basis in S's stock and, if the reduction exceeds P's basis in S's stock, the excess is P's excess loss account in S's stock.

2. *Stock acquisitions.* If a corporation acquires stock of the former common parent in a group structure change, the basis of the members in the former common parent's stock immediately after the group structure change (including any stock of the former common parent owned before the group structure change) that is, or would otherwise be, transferred basis property is redetermined in accordance with the results for an asset acquisition described above. For example, if all of T's stock is contributed to P in a group structure change to which Code Sec. 351 applies, P's basis in T's

¶355.02

stock is T's net asset basis, rather than the amount determined under Code Sec. 362. Similarly, if S merges into T in a group structure change described in Code Sec. 368(a)(2)(E) and P acquires all of the T stock, P's basis in T's stock is the basis that P would have in S's stock under Reg. § 1.1502-31 (b)(1) if T had merged into S in a group structure change described in Code Sec. 368(a)(2)(D).

3. *Additional adjustments.* In addition to the foregoing adjustments, the following adjustments are made:

   a. *Consideration not provided by P.* The basis is reduced to reflect the fair market value of any consideration not provided by the member. For example, if S acquires T's assets in a group structure change described in Code Sec. 368(a)(2)(D), and S provides an appreciated asset (e.g., stock of P) as partial consideration in the transaction, P's basis in S's stock is reduced by the fair market value of the asset.

   b. *Allocable share.* (i) Asset acquisitions. If a corporation receives less than all of the former common parent's assets and liabilities in the group structure change, the former common parent's net asset basis taken into account under the above rules is adjusted accordingly.

   (ii) Stock acquisitions. If less than all of the former common parent's stock is subject to the redetermination described above, the percentage of the former common parent's net asset basis taken into account in the redetermination equals the percentage (by fair market value) of the former common parent's stock subject to the redetermination. For example, if P owns less than all of the former common parent's stock immediately after the group structure change and such stock would otherwise be transferred basis property, only an allocable part of the basis determined under these rules is reflected in the shares owned by P (and the amount allocable to shares owned by nonmembers has no effect on the basis of their shares). Alternatively, if P acquired 10 percent of the former common parent's stock in a transaction in which the stock basis was determined by P's cost, and P later acquires the remaining 90 percent of the former common parent's stock in a separate transaction that is described in Reg. § 1.1502-32 (b)(2), P retains its cost basis in its original stock and the basis of P's newly acquired shares reflects only an allocable part of the former common parent's net asset basis.

   c. *Allocation among shares of stock.* The basis determined under these rules is allocated among shares under the principles of Code Sec. 358. For example, if P owns multiple classes of the former common parent's stock immediately after the group structure change, only an allocable part of the basis determined above is reflected in the basis of each share. See Reg. § 1.1502-19(d) for special allocations with respect to excess loss accounts.

   d. *Higher-tier members.* To the extent that the former common parent is owned by members other than the new common parent, the basis of members in the stock of all subsidiaries owning, directly or indirectly, in whole or in part, an interest in the former common parent's assets or liabilities is adjusted in accordance with the above principles. The adjustments are applied in the order of the tiers, from the lowest to the highest.

4. *Waiver of loss carryovers of former common parent.* An irrevocable election may be made to treat all or any portion of a loss carryover attributable to the common parent as expiring for all federal income tax purposes immediately before the group structure change. Thus, if the loss carryover is treated as expiring under the election, it will not result in a negative adjustment to the basis of P's stock under Reg. § 1.1502-32(b).

5. *Examples.* For purposes of the examples below, unless otherwise stated, all corporations have only one class of stock outstanding, the tax year of all persons is the calendar year, all persons use the accrual method of accounting, the facts set forth the only corporate activity, all transactions are between unrelated persons, and tax liabilities are disregarded.

>   ***Example 17:*** *Forward triangular merger.* (i) Facts. P is the common parent of one group and T is the common parent of another. T has assets with an aggregate basis of $60 and a fair market value of $100 and no liabilities. T's shareholders have an aggregate basis of $50 in T's stock. In Year 1, pursuant to a plan, P forms S, and T merges into S with the T shareholders receiving $100 of P stock in exchange for their T stock. The transaction is a reorganization described in Code Sec. 368(a)(2)(D). The transaction is also a reverse acquisition under Reg. § 1.1502-75(d)(3) because the T shareholders, as a result of owning T's stock, own more than 50 percent of the value of P's stock immediately after the transaction. Thus, the transaction is a group structure change under Reg. § 1.1502-33(f)(1), and P's earnings and profits are adjusted to reflect T's earnings and profits immediately before T ceases to be the common parent of the T group.

(ii) Analysis. P's basis in S's stock is adjusted to reflect T's net asset basis. T's net asset basis is $60, the basis T would have in the stock of a subsidiary under Code Sec. 358 if T had transferred all of its assets and liabilities to the subsidiary in a transaction to which Code Sec. 351 applies. Thus, P has a $60 basis in S's stock.

(iii) Pre-existing S. The facts are the same as in paragraph (i) of this example, except that P has owned the stock of S for several years and P has a $50 basis in the S stock before the merger with T. P's $50 basis in S's stock is adjusted to reflect T's net asset basis. Thus, P's basis in S's stock is $110 ($50 plus $60).

(iv) Excess loss account included in former common parent's net asset basis. The facts are the same as in paragraph (i) of this example, except that T has two assets, an operating asset with an $80 basis and $90 fair market value, and stock of a subsidiary with a $20 excess loss account and

$10 fair market value. T's net asset basis is $60 ($80 minus $20). (See Code Secs. 351 and 358 and Reg. § 1.1502-19.) Consequently, P has a $60 basis in S's stock. Under Code Sec. 362 and Reg. § 1.1502-19, S has an $80 basis in the operating asset and a $20 excess loss account in the stock of the subsidiary.

(v) Liabilities in excess of basis. The facts are the same as in paragraph (i) of this example, except that T's assets have a fair market value of $170 (and $60 basis) and are subject to $70 of liabilities. T's net asset basis is negative $10 ($60 minus $70). (See Code Secs. 351 and 358 and Reg. §§ 1.1502-19 and 1.1502-80(d).) Thus, P has a $10 excess loss account in S's stock. Under Code Sec. 362, S has a $60 basis in its assets (which are subject to $70 of liabilities). (Because the liabilities are taken into account in determining net asset basis, the liabilities are not also taken into account as consideration not provided by P.)

(vi) Consideration provided by S. The facts are the same as in paragraph (i) of this example, except that P forms S with a $100 contribution at the beginning of Year 1, and during Year 6, pursuant to a plan, S purchases $100 of P stock, and T merges into S with the T shareholders receiving P stock in exchange for their T stock. P's $100 basis in S's stock is increased by $60 to reflect T's net asset basis. P's basis in S's stock is decreased by $100 (the fair market value of the P stock) because the P stock purchased by S and used in the transaction is consideration not provided by P.

(vii) Appreciated asset provided by S. The facts are the same as in paragraph (i) of this example, except that P has owned the stock of S for several years, and the shareholders of T receive $60 of P stock and an asset of S with a $30 adjusted basis and $40 fair market value. S recognizes a $10 gain from the asset under Code Sec. 1001. P's basis in S's stock is increased by $60 to reflect T's net asset basis. P's basis in S's stock is decreased by $40 (the fair market value of the asset provided by S). In addition, P's basis in S's stock is increased under Reg. § 1.1502-32(b) by S's $10 gain.

(viii) Depreciated asset provided by S. The facts are the same as in paragraph (i) of this example, except that P has owned the stock of S for several years, and the shareholders of T receive $60 of P stock and an asset of S with a $50 adjusted basis and $40 fair market value. S recognizes a $10 loss from the asset under Code Sec. 1001. P's basis in S's stock is increased by $60 to reflect T's net asset basis. P's basis in S's stock is decreased by $40 (the fair market value of the asset provided by S). In addition, S's $10 loss is taken into account under Reg. § 1.1502-32(b) in determining P's basis adjustments under that section.

Example 18: *Stock acquisition.* (i) Facts. P is the common parent of one group and T is the common parent of another. T has assets with an aggregate basis of $60 and fair market value of $100 and no liabilities. T's shareholders have an aggregate basis of $50 in T's stock. Pursuant to a plan, P forms S, and S acquires all of T's stock in exchange for P stock in a transaction described in Code Sec. 368(a)(1)(B). The transaction is also a reverse acquisition under Reg. § 1.1502-75(d)(3). Thus, the transaction is a group structure change under Reg. § 1.1502-33(f)(1), and the earnings and profits of P and S are adjusted to reflect T's earnings and profits immediately before T ceases to be the common parent of the T group.

(ii) Analysis. Although S is not the new common parent of the T group, adjustments must be made to S's basis in T's stock in accordance with the principles of Reg. § 1.1502-31. Although S's basis in T's stock would ordinarily be determined under Code Sec. 362 by reference to the basis of T's shareholders in T's stock immediately before the group structure change, S's basis in T's stock is determined by reference to T's net asset basis. Thus, S's basis in T's stock is $60.

(iii) Higher-tier adjustments. P's basis in S's stock is increased by $60 (to be consistent with the adjustment to S's basis in T's stock).

(iv) Cross ownership. The facts are the same as in paragraph (i) of this example, except S purchased 10 percent of T's stock from an unrelated person for cash. In an unrelated transaction, S acquires the remaining 90 percent of T's stock in exchange for P stock. S's basis in the initial 10 percent of T's stock is not redetermined under this section. However, S's basis in the additional 90 percent of T's stock is redetermined under this section. S's basis in that stock is adjusted to $54 (90 percent of T's net asset basis).

(v) Allocable share. The facts are the same as in paragraph (i) of this example, except that P owns only 90 percent of S's stock immediately after the group structure change. S's basis in T's stock is the same as in paragraph (ii) of this example. P's basis in its S stock is increased by $54 (90 percent of S's $60 adjustment).

> **Example 19:** *Taxable stock acquisition.* (i) Facts. P is the common parent of one group and T is the common parent of another. T has assets with an aggregate basis of $60 and fair market value of $100 and no liabilities. T's shareholders have an aggregate basis of $50 in T's stock. Pursuant to a plan, P acquires all of T's stock in exchange for $70 of P's stock and $30 in a transaction that is a group structure change under Reg. § 1.1502-33(f)(1). P's acquired T stock is not transferred basis property. (Because of P's use of cash, the acquisition is not a transaction described in Code Sec. 368(a)(1)(B).)

(ii) Analysis. The rules of this section do not apply to determine P's basis in T's stock. Therefore, P's basis in T's stock is $100.

6. *Effective dates.* These rules apply to group structure changes that occur after April 26, 2004. However, a group may apply these rules to group structure changes that occurred on or before April 26, 2004, and in consolidated return years beginning on or after January 1, 1995.

For group structure changes that occur on or before April 26, 2004, and in consolidated return years beginning on or after January 1, 1995, with

¶355.02

respect to which the group does not elect to apply the provisions of Reg. § 1.1502-31, see Reg. § 1.1502-31 as contained in the 26 CFR part 1 edition revised as of April 1, 2003. For group structure changes that occur in consolidated return years beginning before January 1, 1995, see Temp. Reg. § 1.1502-31T as contained in the 26 CFR part 1 edition revised as of April 1, 1994.

¶ 365 Conclusions

The consolidated return stock basis system consists of the following regulations:

- The investment adjustment rules of Reg. § 1.1502-32 adjust the basis that one member in the group has in another, to prevent the subsidiary's change in value (resulting from taxable income or loss) from being taken into account a second time when the owning member disposes of the subsidiary stock. The dividends-received deduction prevents double taxation for affiliated groups that do not file consolidated returns, but the investment adjustment rules prevent double taxation, whether or not prior profits are distributed.

- The negative stock basis, or excess loss account rules, of Reg. § 1.1502-19 address when and how negative stock basis is recaptured as income. This negative stock basis occurs when a subsidiary has some debt capital, with the resulting leverage causing negative investment adjustments to exceed the owning member's stock basis.

- Generally, the purpose of the anti-circular basis rule of Reg. § 1.1502-11(b) is to prevent the use of a departing subsidiary's excess deductions and loss carryovers against gain recognized on the disposition of the subsidiary's stock. Without such a rule, the absorption of the excess deductions or loss carryovers would reduce P's basis in its S stock and, in turn, increase P's gain. By limiting the availability of the departing member's excess deductions and loss carryovers against P's stock gain, the department member's tax attributes are preserved after it leaves the group.

- The asset consistency rules of Reg. § 1.338-8 are designed to prevent stepping up the basis of selected subsidiary assets at no cost to the seller (because of the investment adjustment rules), by selling the assets to the buyer and then selling the buyer or an affiliate the subsidiary stock.

- Reg. § 1.1502-30 determines the basis of the stock of a company acquired in certain triangular reorganizations.

- Reg. § 1.1502-31 authorizes stock basis adjustments after a group structure change to reflect the change in the assets and liabilities of the resulting common parent.

¶ 375 Frequently Asked Questions

Question

Do the consolidated return regulations prevent double taxation?

Answer

Yes, as between the members of the consolidated group. The investment adjustment rules adjust the basis that one member has in another, to prevent the subsidiary's change in value (resulting from its taxable income) from being taken into account a second time when the owning member disposes of the subsidiary's stock.

Question

Can recapture of an excess loss account (negative stock basis) be avoided?

Answer

Recapture of an excess loss account can be avoided by liquidating the loss subsidiary into its parent in a Code Sec. 332 liquidation, provided the subsidiary is solvent.

Question

Do the anti-circular basis rules include a trap for the unwary?

Answer

The amount of S's deductions and losses that may offset P's gain from the disposition of its S stock is determined by tentatively computing the taxable income (or loss) for the year of disposition (and any prior years to which the deductions or losses may be carried) without taking into account P's gain from the disposition. To the extent that S's deductions and losses in the year of disposition cannot offset P's gain because of the limitation, the items are carried to other years under the applicable provisions of the Code and regulations as if they were the only items incurred by S in the year of disposition.

Question

Can a parent cause a subsidiary to recognize gain on built-in gain assets (by sale or distribution), increase the basis of the subsidiary stock under the investment adjustment rules to reflect the gain, and then sell the subsidiary stock to the buyer of the built-in gain assets at a loss to offset the gain?

Answer

The asset consistency rules discourage this by causing the buyer to take a carryover basis in the assets so acquired.

¶375

Chapter 4

Loss Limitation System

¶ 401 Overview—Loss Limitation System

The current loss limitation system consists of:

- Reg. § 1.337(d)-2, which assures the taxation of built-in gains for dispositions and deconsolidations of consolidated subsidiaries on or after March 3, 2005 (for dispositions and deconsolidations after March 6, 2002, and before March 3, 2005, see Temp. Reg. § 1.337(d)-2T); and

- Reg. § 1.1502-35, which prevents a consolidated group from obtaining more than one tax benefit from a single economic loss, generally for stock transfers, deconsolidations of consolidated subsidiaries, determinations of worthlessness, and stock dispositions on or after March 10, 2006 (for rules applicable before March 10, 2006, see Temp. Reg. § 1.1502-35T(j)).

For the regulations that apply to earlier dispositions and deconsolidations of consolidated subsidiaries, see the Preambles to T.D. 9187 and T.D. 9254.

The Treasury Department and the IRS continue to study the problem of assuring the taxation of built-in gains and prevention of loss duplication and intend to publish proposed regulations with a single integrated regulation.[1]

.01 Assuring the Taxation of Built-in Gains

Reg. § 1.337(d)-2 assures the taxation of built-in gains. In 1986, Congress eliminated the statutory provisions that had permitted a corporation to avoid tax on the disposition of an appreciated asset where the transferee or distributee took a stepped-up basis. In connection with this repeal of the so-called General Utilities doctrine, Code Sec. 337(d)(1) authorized the Treasury and the IRS to carry out the purposes of the 1986 legislation. This was to ensure that these purposes could not

---

[1] To this end, see Prop. Reg. § 1.1502-36 for proposed rules that would take effect on or after the date the regulations are finalized.

be circumvented through the use of any law or regulation, including the consolidated return regulations.

> ***Example 1:*** As an example of circumvention of the repeal of the General Utilities doctrine before special consolidated return rules were adopted, P buys all the stock of S for $50 on February 1, Year 1, and S becomes a member of the P group. S has two assets. Asset #1 has a basis of $50 and a value of $0, and Asset #2 has a basis of $0 and a value of $50. S sells Asset #2 during Year 3 for $50 and recognizes a $50 gain. Under the investment adjustment system, P's basis in the T stock increased to $100 as a result of the recognition of the built-in gain. Without a special rule, therefore, if Asset #1 has not changed in value, the P group could sell the S stock for $50 and use the $50 S stock loss to shelter the S asset gain, thereby circumventing the General Utilities repeal.

To this end, Reg. § 1.337(d)-2(a)(1) generally provides that no loss is allowed with respect to the disposition of subsidiary stock by a member of a consolidated group. Also, Reg. § 1.337(d)-2(b)(1) generally requires the basis of a share of subsidiary stock to be reduced to its value immediately before a deconsolidation of the share. However, Reg. § 1.337(d)-2(c)(2) provides that loss is not disallowed and basis is not reduced to the extent the taxpayer establishes that the loss or basis "is not attributable to the recognition of built-in gain on the disposition of an asset."

To mitigate against the valuation difficulties implicit in Reg. § 1.337(d)-2, the IRS will accept the "basis disconformity method" described in Notice 2004-58[2] for determining the extent to which loss or basis is attributable to the recognition of built-in gain on the disposition of an asset for purposes of applying the Reg. § 1.337(d)-2(c)(2) exception. As illustrated at ¶ 402, the basis conformity method disallows loss on a disposition of subsidiary stock and reduces basis (but not below value) on a deconsolidation of subsidiary stock in an amount equal to the least of the "gain amount," the "disconformity amount," and the "positive investment adjustment amount."

1. *Gain amount.* For this purpose, the gain amount is the sum of all gains (net of directly related expenses) recognized on asset dispositions of the subsidiary that are allocable to the share while the subsidiary is a member of the group.

2. *Disconformity amount.* The disconformity amount is the excess, if any, of the share's basis over the share's proportionate interest in the subsidiary's "net asset basis." A subsidiary's net asset basis is the excess of (a) the sum of the subsidiary's money, basis in assets (other than stock of consolidated subsidiaries), loss carryforwards that would be carried to a separate return year of the subsidiary under the principles of Reg. § 1.1502-21, and deductions that have been recognized but deferred, over (b) the subsidiary's liabilities that have been taken into account for tax purposes.

3. *Positive investment adjustment amount.* The positive investment adjustment amount is the excess, if any, of the sum of the positive adjustments made to the share under Reg. § 1.1502-32 over the sum of the negative adjust-

---

[2] 2004-2 CB 520.

¶401.01

ments made to the share under Reg. § 1.1502-32, excluding adjustments for distributions under Reg. § 1.1502-32(b)(2)(iv).

Caution: The rules allowing limited loss disallowance upon disposition and basis reduction upon deconsolidation come into play *only* if a separate statement entitled "section 1.337(d)-2(c) statement" is included with the taxpayer's consolidated return for the year of disposition or deconsolidation. The statement must contain:

- The name and E.I.N. of the subsidiary, and

- The amount of the loss not disallowed and the amount of basis not reduced under the regulations.

In other words, the regulations by their terms disallow all stock loss upon disposition of a consolidated subsidiary and reduce stock basis to zero upon disposition of a consolidated subsidiary unless this statement is filed.

.02 Preventing a Consolidated Group from Taking More Than One Loss for a Single Economic Loss

Reg. § 1.1502-35 is designed to prevent a consolidated group from taking more than one loss for a single economic loss. Effective March 9, 2006, Reg. § 1.1502-35 applies when a member of a consolidated group transfers subsidiary stock at a loss as well as when a member holds loss shares of subsidiary stock and the subsidiary ceases to be a member of the group.

The regulations are intended to address at least two types of transactions that may allow a group to obtain more than one tax benefit from a single economic loss. In the first type of transaction, a group absorbs an inside loss (e.g., a loss carryforward, a deferred deduction, or a loss inherent in an asset) of a subsidiary member, and then a member of the group recognizes a loss on a disposition of stock of that subsidiary that duplicates the inside loss. In the second type of transaction, a member of the group recognizes a loss on the disposition of subsidiary member stock that duplicates an inside loss of the subsidiary member, the subsidiary remains a member of the P group, and the group subsequently recognizes the inside loss of that subsidiary member.

The complex anti-duplication rules do not apply to a taxable disposition of 100 percent of the stock of a consolidated subsidiary.

The regulations consist of a basis redetermination rule that attempts to mitigate the effects of the assumptions underlying the investment adjustment rules by reversing certain investment adjustments to take into account the source of certain items of income and loss. In addition, where the subsidiary member remains in the group, the basis redetermination rule equalizes bases in subsidiary stock so that a complex loss suspension rule need not apply.

The loss suspension rule prevents duplication of an economic loss by effectively disallowing a stock loss if the economic loss giving rise to that stock loss is later reflected on the group's return as in the second type of transaction described above. Various anti-abuse rules also must be considered.

¶ 415 Assuring Taxation of Built-in Gains

To assure the taxation of built-in gains, the net result of Reg. § 1.337(d)-2 is that it allows loss on the disposition of a consolidated subsidiary (and basis is not reduced on deconsolidation of such a subsidiary) to the extent the taxpayer establishes that the loss or basis "is not attributable to the recognition of built-in gain, net of directly related expenses,[3] on the dispostion of an asset." Reg. § 1.337(d)-2(c)(2) defines the term "built-in gain" as gain that is "attributable, directly or indirectly, in whole or in part, to any excess of value over basis that is reflected, before the disposition of the asset, in the basis of the share, directly or indirectly, in whole or in part."[4]

To mitigate against the valuation difficulties implicit in Reg. § 1.337(d)-2, the IRS will accept the "basis disconformity method" described in Notice 2004-58[5] for determining the extent to which loss or basis is attributable to the recognition of built-in gain on the disposition of an asset for purposes of applying the exception of Reg. § 1.337(d)-2(c)(2). The basis conformity method disallows loss on a disposition of subsidiary stock and reduces basis (but not below value) on a deconsolidation of subsidiary stock in an amount equal to the least of the "gain amount," the "disconformity amount," and the "positive investment adjustment amount."

1. *Gain amount.* For this purpose, the gain amount is the sum of all gains (net of directly related expenses) recognized on asset dispositions of the subsidiary that are allocable to the share while the subsidiary is a member of the group.

2. *Disconformity amount.* The disconformity amount is the excess, if any, of the share's basis over the share's proportionate interest in the subsidiary's "net asset basis." A subsidiary's net asset basis is the excess of (a) the sum of the subsidiary's money, basis in assets (other than stock of consolidated subsidiaries), loss carryforwards that would be carried to a separate return year of the subsidiary under the principles of Reg. § 1.1502-21, and deductions that have been recognized but deferred, over (b) the subsidiary's liabilities that have been taken into account for tax purposes.

3. *Positive investment adjustment amount.* The positive investment adjustment amount is the excess, if any, of the sum of the positive adjustments made to the share under Reg. § 1.1502-32 over the sum of the negative adjustments made to the share under Reg. § 1.1502-32, excluding adjustments for distributions under Reg. § 1.1502-32(b)(2)(iv).

Caution: The rules for allowing limited loss disallowance upon disposition and basis reduction upon deconsolidation come into play *only* if a separate statement entitled "section 1.337(d)-2(c) statement" is included with the tax-

---

[3] Federal income taxes may be directly related to built-in gain recognized on the disposition of an asset only to the extent of the excess (if any) of the group's income tax liability actually imposed under Subtitle A of the Code for the tax year of the disposition of the asset over the group's income tax liability for the tax year redetermined by not taking into account the built-in gain recognized on the disposition of the asset. Reg. § 1.337(d)-2(c)(2).

[4] A "netting" exception also applies to the general loss disallowance rule. Specifically, the general loss disallow-

ance rule does not apply with respect to the disposition or deconsolidation of stock of a subsidiary, to the extent that, as a consequence of the same plan or arrangement, gain is taken into account by members of the same consolidated group with respect to stock of the same subsidiary having the same material terms. Reg. §§ 1.337(d)-2(a)(4) and (b)(4).

[5] 2004-2 CB 520.

payer's consolidated return for the year of disposition or deconsolidation. The statement must contain:

- The name and E.I.N. of the subsidiary; and
- The amount of the loss not disallowed and the amount of basis not reduced under the regulations.

Example 2: As an example of built-in gain and other items:

Year 0. S has three ordinary assets, Asset #1 with a basis of $0 and a value of $150 (a $150 built-in gain), Asset #2 with a basis of $50 and a value of $0 (a $50 built-in loss), and Asset #3 with a basis of $50 and a value of $200 (a $150 built-in gain). S has no other assets or liabilities. P purchases all the stock of S, and S becomes a member of the P consolidated group. Valuing S based on the after-tax value of its assets, the purchase price and P's starting S stock basis were $262.50 ($350 value less 35 percent of $250 net built-in gain).

Year 1. P contributes Asset #4 with a basis of $25 and a value of $45 and Asset #5 ($100 cash) to S. In Year 1, S earns $100 before a 35-percent federal income tax (FIT).

Year 2. In Year 2, S loses $40 before a 35-percent federal income tax benefit.

Year 3. In Year 3, S has no operating income or loss. On the last day of Year 3, S sells Asset #1 for $190 and recognizes a $190 gain; S sells Asset #2 for $0 and recognizes a $50 loss; S sells Asset #4 for $45 and recognizes a $20 gain. Valuing S based on its earnings, P sells the S stock for $300, recognizing a $230.50 loss before taking into account Reg. § 1.337(d)-2.

To reflect the foregoing, the adjustments to P's stock basis are as follows:

	Stock Basis
Year 0 starting basis	$262.50
Year 1 capital contributions	+125
Year 1 investment adjustments:	
Income $100	
FIT 35% (35)	+65
Year 2 investment adjustments:	
Loss $40	
FIT Benefit 35% 14	−26
Year 3 investment adjustments:	
After-tax gain on Asset #1	+123.5
After-tax loss on Asset #2	−32.50
After-tax gain on Asset #4	+13
Totals	$530.50

Reg. § 1.337(d)-2 Loss Limitation

If the requisite "section 1.337(d)-2(c) statement" is included in P's consolidated return for Year 3, P's allowed stock loss will be as follows:

Tracing. If P traces the value of S's assets upon the acquisition of S and the sale of Assets #1, #2, and #4, it could prove that only $65 of its S stock loss was attributable to recognized built-in gains (BIG) reflected in S stock basis, and thus it would be allowed a $165.50 ($230.50 loss – $65 recognized built-in gains) stock loss as follows:

Asset	Basis on Acquisition of S	FMV on Acquisition of S	Recognized BIG Reflected in S Stock Basis
#1	$0	$150	$150 less 35%=$97.50
#2	50	0	(50) less 35%=$32.50
#4	N/A	N/A	N/A
Net	$50	$150	$100 less 35%=$65

Without tracing. If P cannot trace its S stock loss attributable to recognized built-in gains reflected in its S stock basis, under Notice 2004-58, the IRS will accept the least of the gain amount, the disconformity amount, or the positive investment adjustment amount as the assumed recognized built-in gains. Each of these amounts is computed below and compared to actual recognized built-in gains reflected in S stock basis.

1. Gain Amount

Asset	(1) Adjusted Basis on Sale	(2) Amount Realized on Sale	(1)-(2) Assumed Recognized BIG Reflected in S Stock Basis
#1	$0	$190	$190 less 35%=$123.50
#2	N/A	N/A	N/A
#4	25	45	20 less 35%=13
Total	$25	$235	$210 less 35%=$136.50

Comment: The gain amount would overstate the recognized built-in gains by $71.50 ($136.50 – $65) for three reasons: First, the assumed recognized built-in gain on Asset #1 would be overstated by $40 less 35 percent, or $26, because the gain on Asset #1 exceeds the actual recognized built-in gain by $40. Second, the assumed recognized built-in gain would be overstated by $50 less 35 percent, or $32.50, because the loss on Asset #2 would not be taken into account. Third, the assumed recognized built-in gain would be overstated by $20 less 35 percent, or $13, because Asset #4 was contributed by P to S, rather than owned by S when P acquired S.

¶415

2. Disconformity Gain

	(1) P's Closing S Stock Basis	(2) S's Closing Net Asset Basis	(1)-(2) Assumed Recognized BIG Reflected in S Stock Basis
Purchase	$262.50	$100	$162.50
Year 1 contributions	125	125	0
Operating income and deductions:			
Year 1 100–35%=65	65	65	0
Year 2 (40)–35%=(26)	–26	–26	0
After-tax gains and losses on assets:			
Asset #1 190–35%=123.50	123.50	123.50	0
Asset #2 (50)–35%=32.50	–32.50	–32.50	0
Asset #4 20–35%=13	13	13	0
Totals	$530.50	$368	$162.50

Comment: The disconformity amount would overstate S's recognized built-in gains reflected in S stock basis by $97.50 ($162.50 – $65) because it assumes the excess of P's beginning stock basis over S's beginning S net asset basis is attributable to recognized built-in gains even though Asset #3 was never sold.

3. Positive Investment Adjustment Amount

	(1) Positive Investment Adjustments	(2) Negative Investment Adjustments	(1)-(2) Assumed Recognized BIG Reflected in S Stock Basis
Year 1	$100	–35	
Year 2	14	–40	
Year 3	190	–66.50	
	+17.50	–50	
	+20	–7	
	$341.50	$198.50	$143

Comment: The positive investment adjustment amount would overstate S's recognized gains reflected in S stock basis by $78 ($143–$65) for three

¶415

reasons: First, the assumed recognized built-in gain on Asset #1 would be overstated by $40 less 35 percent, or $26, because the gain on Asset #1 exceeds the actual recognized built-in gain by $40. Second, the assumed recognized built-in gain would be overstated by $20 less 35 percent, or $13, because Asset #3 was contributed by P to S, rather than owned by S when P acquired S. Third, the assumed recognized built-in gain would be overstated by $60 less 35 percent, or $39 because after-tax net operating income is treated as recognized built-in gain.

Conclusion. If P cannot trace S's recognized built-in gains reflected in its S stock basis, the assumed recognized built-in gains would be the gain amount, or $136.50. Thus, $94 of P's $230.50 S stock loss would be allowed.

¶ 425 Preventing a Consolidated Group from Taking More Than One Loss for a Single Economic Loss

Reg. § 1.1502-35 is designed to prevent a consolidated group from taking more than one loss for a single economic loss. Effective March 9, 2006, Reg. § 1.1502-35 applies when a member of a consolidated group transfers subsidiary stock at a loss as well as when a member holds loss shares of subsidiary stock and the subsidiary ceases to be a member of the group.

As illustrated in the following two examples, the regulations are intended to address at least two types of transactions that may allow a group to obtain more than one tax benefit from a single economic loss.

Example 3: Assume that in Year 1, P forms S with a contribution of $80 in exchange for 80 shares of common stock of S (representing all the outstanding stock of S). In Year 2, P contributes Asset A with a basis of $70 and a value of $20 to S in exchange for an additional 20 shares of S common stock. In Year 3, S sells Asset A and recognizes a $50 loss, which offsets income of P on the group's return. Under the investment adjustment rules of Reg. § 1.1502-32, P's basis in each share of S common stock it holds is reduced by a *pro rata* share of the $50 loss, with the result that the shares acquired in Year 1 have a basis of $40 and the shares acquired in Year 2 have a basis of $60. In Year 4, P sells the shares acquired in Year 2 for $20 and recognizes a $40 loss, which offsets income of P on the group's return.

In this transaction, the group has obtained a total $90 tax benefit from a single $50 loss. Although a taxable disposition of the S common stock acquired in Year 1 would offset the excess tax benefit, the group has various nontaxable options by which to ensure that the excess tax benefit is not reduced. These include retention of the remaining shares of S or the liquidation of S in a Code Sec. 332 liquidation.

Example 4: Assume that in Year 1, P forms S with a contribution of $80 in exchange for 80 shares of the common stock of S. In Year 2, P contributes Asset A with a basis of $50 and a value of $20 to S in exchange for an additional 20 shares of S common stock. In Year 3, P sells the 20 shares of S common stock that it acquired in Year 2 for $20 and recognizes a $30 loss, which offsets income of P on the group's return. The sale of the 20 shares of S common stock does not result in the deconsolidation of S. In Year 4, S sells Asset A and recognizes a $30 loss, which also offsets income of P on the group return.

In this transaction, the group has obtained the use of two losses from the single economic loss in Asset A. Again, a taxable disposition by P of its remaining S common stock would offset the tax benefit of one of the losses. The group has various nontaxable alternatives by which to ensure that the excess tax benefit is not reduced. These include retention of the remaining shares of S or the liquidation of S under Code Sec. 332.

The complex anti-duplication rules apply to the above examples but do not apply to a taxable disposition of 100 percent of the stock of a consolidated subsidiary. If the reader's consolidated group is in that boat, read no further.

The regulations consist of a basis redetermination rule that attempts to mitigate the effects of the assumptions underlying the investment adjustment rules by reversing certain investment adjustments to take into account the source of certain items of income and loss. In addition, if the subsidiary member remains in the group, the basis redetermination rule equalizes bases in subsidiary stock so that a complex loss suspension rule need not apply.

The loss suspension rule prevents duplication of an economic loss by effectively disallowing a stock loss if the economic loss giving rise to that stock loss is later reflected on the group's return as in the second type of transaction described above. Various anti-abuse rules also must be considered.

¶ 435 Conclusion

The principal lesson to be learned from this chapter is that loss on the disposition of a consolidated subsidiary is disallowed except to the extent the taxpayer can prove the loss is not attributable to the recognition of built-in gain on the disposition of an asset and an appropriate statement is filed with the taxpayer's consolidated return for the year of disposition of the subsidiary stock.

This burden of proof means that the taxpayer has a difficult choice when it purchases a consolidated subsidiary. Either it incurs what can be an expensive cost of an appraisal of the subsidiary's assets to determine the built-in gains and losses, or it accepts the "basis disconformity" methods of Notice 2004-58 for assuming the amount of recognized built-in gains. Under Notice 2004-58, without proof of the actual recognized built-in gains reflected in P's S stock basis, those gains will be assumed to be the least of the gain amount, the basis disconformity amount, or the positive investment adjustment amount. Each amount is flawed in that it can overstate recognized built-in gains.

The "gain amount" is the sum of all gains (net of directly related expenses) recognized on asset dispositions of the subsidiary that are allocable to the share while the subsidiary is a member of the consolidated group. The gain amount thus can overstate recognized built-in gains because it:

- Treats post-acquisition appreciation of an asset as if it were built-in gain.
- Fails to offset built-in gains by built-in losses.
- Treats post-acquisition contributions of appreciated assets by P to S as if they were built-in gains.

¶435

The "disconformity amount" is the excess, if any, of the share's basis over the share's proportionate interest in the subsidiary's "net asset basis." The disconformity amount thus can overstate recognized built-in gains because, for example, it treats unrealized built-in gains as if they were recognized.

The "positive investment adjustment amount" is the excess, if any, of the sum of the positive adjustments made to the share under Reg. § 1.1502-32 over the sum of the negative adjustments made to the share under Reg. § 1.1502-32, excluding adjustments for distributions. The positive investment adjustment amount thus can overstate recognized built-in gains because it:

- Treats post-acquisition appreciation of an asset as if it were built-in gain.

- Treats post-acquisition contributions of appreciated assets by P to S as if they were built-in gains.

- Treats after-tax net operating income as recognized built-in gains.

¶ 445 Frequently Asked Questions

Question

What are the principal purposes of the loss limitation regulations?

Answer

Reg. § 1.337(d)-2 assures the taxation of built-in gains. Reg. § 1.1502-35 prevents a consolidated group from obtaining more than one tax benefit from a single economic loss.

Question

Does Reg. § 1.337(d)-2 require an appraisal of the assets of a target subsidiary when it is purchased?

Answer

Loss on the disposition of a consolidated subsidiary is disallowed except to the extent the taxpayer can prove the loss is not attributable to the recognition of built-in gain on the disposition of an asset and an appropriate statement is filed with the taxpayer's consolidated return for the year of disposition of the subsidiary stock.

This burden of proof means that the taxpayer incurs what can be an expensive cost of an appraisal of the subsidiary's assets to determine the built-in gains and losses, or it accepts the "basis conformity" methods of Notice 2004-58 for assuming the amount of recognized built-in gains.

Question

Does Reg. § 1.1502-35 apply to the disposition of all the stock of a consolidated subsidiary?

Answer

No. For that reason, it seldom applies.

Chapter 5

Intercompany Transaction System

¶ 501 Overview—Intercompany Transaction System

In 1995, Reg. § 1.1502-13 and others were adopted to replace the prior intercompany transaction system.[1] The purpose of these rules is to clearly reflect the taxable income (and tax liability) of the group as a whole by preventing intercompany transactions from creating, accelerating, avoiding, or deferring consolidated taxable income (or consolidated tax liability).[2]

The general standard by which this clear reflection policy is measured is that of a single corporation conducting its business through divisions. Separate-entity treatment is preserved, however, for determining the *amount* and *location* of each member's items related to an intercompany transaction. For example, a selling member determines its gain or loss on a sale of property to another member on a separate-entity basis, and a buying member takes a cost basis in the property. This allows each party to retain a separate tax history for determining stock basis adjustments, earnings and profits, and other matters.

In general, the buying member's accounting method is used to control the *timing* of both the buying member's and selling member's items (that is, the selling member matches the buying member's timing). When such a "matching rule" will not achieve single-entity treatment, an "acceleration rule" is substituted to deter-

---

[1] This chapter focuses on Reg. § 1.1502-13 (the general intercompany transaction rules) and, to a lesser extent, Reg. § 1.267(f)-1 (sales of loss property among members of controlled groups).

[2] Reg. § 1.1502-13(a)(1).

mine timing. For example, the selling member accelerates its timing ahead of the buying member when either member leaves the group.

Various rules provide for single-entity results, whenever possible, for other *attributes* (for example, character, source, and status under Code Sec. 382(h) as built-in gain or loss), depending, for example, on the operative timing rule and whether the selling member's and buying member's items offset each other.

.01 Property Transactions

A number of factors should be kept in mind when considering property transactions. The amount of selling member's and buying member's items, timing, redetermination of attributes, holding periods, depreciable property, and exclusion of gain are just some of the topics to be addressed (see ¶ 515).

.02 Successor Assets, Persons, and Groups

For purposes of Reg. § 1.1502-13, any reference to an asset includes a reference to any other asset of which the basis is determined, directly or indirectly, in whole or in part, by reference to the basis of the first asset. In general, any reference in Reg. § 1.1502-13 to a person includes, as the context may require, a reference to a predecessor or successor. If the consolidated group ceases to exist because of an acquisition described in Reg. § 1.1502-13(j)(5)(i), the surviving group is treated as the terminating group for purposes of applying Reg. § 1.1502-13 to the intercompany transactions of the terminating group. If a consolidated group terminates because the common parent is the only remaining member, Reg. § 1.1502-13(j)(6) causes the common parent to succeed to the treatment of the terminating group for purposes of applying the intercompany transaction rules so long as it neither becomes a member of an affiliated group filing separate returns, nor becomes a corporation described in Code Sec. 1504(b) (see ¶ 535).

.03 Other (Nonproperty) Transactions

An *intercompany transaction* is a transaction between corporations that are members of the same consolidated group immediately after the transaction, and may include nonproperty transactions such as S's performance of services, licensing of technology, rental of property, loan of money to B, and B's payment or accrual of its expenditure for such items (see ¶ 555). S and B are defined below.

.04 Loss Property, Member Stock, Member Obligations, and Other Rules

Bolstering the "matching and acceleration rules" are special rules for loss property (see ¶ 525), member stock rules (see ¶ 545), member obligations (see ¶ 565), and other rules (see ¶ 575).

.05 Definitions

A transaction is not subject to the current system unless it is an *intercompany transaction*, broadly defined as any kind of transaction between corporations that are members of the consolidated group immediately after the transaction.[3] For example, a transfer of property to a partnership composed entirely of members of

---

[3] Reg. § 1.1502-13(b)(1)(i).

¶501.01

the group is not an intercompany transaction because the partnership cannot be a member of the group. This definition, however, must be read in conjunction with the broad anti-avoidance rule of Reg. § 1.1502-13(h) and Example (4) thereunder. There, Treasury and the IRS indicate that transfers to and from a partnership might be treated as intercompany transactions if undertaken with the principal purpose of avoiding the purposes of the regulations.

Each payment or accrual of interest on a loan is a separate transaction.[4] In addition, an accrual of premium is treated as a separate transaction, or as an offset to interest that is not a separate transaction to the extent required under separate-entity treatment.

The following additional definitions, generally following those used in the regulations, are employed in this chapter.

- The *selling member* (S) is the member transferring property or providing services, and the *buying member* (B) is the member receiving the property or services.[5] The payor of interest or bond premium is B and the payee is S.[6] Unless otherwise noted in this chapter, P is the member owning all the stock in S or B.

- S's income, gain, deduction, and loss, including related costs or expenses, directly or indirectly from an intercompany transaction, are its *intercompany items*.[7]

- B's income, gain, deduction, and loss, directly or indirectly from an intercompany transaction, or from property acquired in an intercompany transaction, are its *corresponding items*.[8] B's corresponding items include any amounts that are permanently disallowed or permanently eliminated.[9]

- The *attributes* of an intercompany item or corresponding item are all of the item's characteristics necessary to determine its effect on taxable income (and tax liability) other than amount, timing, and location.[10] For example, attributes include character, source, treatment as excluded from gross income or as a noncapital, nondeductible amount, and treatment as built-in gain or loss under Code Sec. 382(h) or Code Sec. 384.

¶ 515 Property Transactions

A number of elements to property transactions should be addressed, such as the amount of a selling member's and buying member's items (separate return rules), timing (the general matching rule), the selling member's possible accelerated timing (the acceleration rule), holding periods, and sourcing examples.

.01 *Amount of Selling Member's and Buying Member's Items*

The amount of S's intercompany items and B's corresponding items is determined under separate return principles (subject to other consolidated adjustments).

---

[4] Reg. § 1.1502-13(b)(1)(iii).

[5] *See* Reg. § 1.1502-13(b)(1)(i).

[6] *See* Preamble to CO-11-91, 1994-1 CB 725.

[7] *See* Reg. § 1.1502-13(b)(2)(i) and Reg. § 1.1502-13(b)(2)(ii).

[8] *See* Reg. § 1.1502-13(b)(3)(i).

[9] *See* Reg. § 1.1502-13(b)(3)(ii).

[10] *See* Reg. § 1.1502-13(b)(6).

In other words, S determines its gain or loss from a sale of property to B on a separate-entity basis and B takes a cost basis in the property.[11] Thus, the *amount* and *location* of S's intercompany items and B's corresponding items are determined under separate-entity principles.

.02 Timing—The General Matching Rule

The foundation of the current intercompany transaction system is the general "matching rule" of Reg. §1.1502-13(c). This rule seeks to achieve single-entity treatment for timing by matching S's timing with B's timing. Various subrules, discussed below, apply to equate other attributes of the transaction with the consequences that would have ensued if the transaction had occurred between divisions of a single corporation.

Generally, B takes its corresponding item into account when required to do so under its separate accounting method.[12] To illustrate, for *timing* purposes, B's corresponding item normally is the locomotive that pulls the train, whereas S's intercompany items are the caboose.

In general, under the "matching rule," S "matches" B's timing by taking its intercompany item into account for the same year that B takes its corresponding item into account.[13] Because of the possibility that B may recover its basis in the property in increments, for each consolidated return year, S takes into account the difference between the following:

- The corresponding item that B would take into account if S and B were divisions of a single corporation and the intercompany transaction were between those divisions (B's so-called "recomputed corresponding item");[14] and

- The corresponding item that B actually takes into account under its accounting method.[15]

> **Example 1:** As an example of intercompany gain followed by sale to a nonmember at a gain: S holds raw land with a basis of $70. On January 1 of Year 1, S sells the land to B for $100. On July 1 of Year 3, B sells the land to nonmember X for $110. For each consolidated return year, S takes its intercompany item into account under the matching rule to reflect the difference for the year between B's recomputed corresponding item and B's actual corresponding item taken into account. If S and B were divisions of a single corporation and the intercompany sale were a transfer between divisions, B would succeed to S's $70 basis in the land and would have a $40 gain from the sale to X in Year 3, instead of a $10 gain. Consequently, S takes no gain into account in Years 1 and 2 and takes the entire $30 gain into account in Year 3:

---

[11] Reg. §1.1502-13(a)(2).

[12] Reg. §1.1502-13(c)(2)(i) (the redetermination, however, of the attributes of a corresponding item might affect its timing).

[13] Reg. §1.1502-13(c)(2)(ii).

[14] Reg. §1.1502-13(b)(4). As divisions, S and B are treated as engaging in the transaction; that is, B is treated as actually owning the subject matter of the intercompany transaction and as actually transferring to "division" S the consideration (be it cash, notes, or B stock) actually exchanged for the S property. Reg. §1.1502-13(c)(3).

[15] Reg. §1.1502-13(c)(2)(ii).

B's recomputed gain ($110 – $70)	$40
B's actual gain ($110 – $100)	10
Difference	$30

Example 2: As an example of intercompany gain followed by sale to a nonmember at a loss: The facts are the same as in the last example, except that B sells the land to X for $90 rather than $110. If S and B were divisions of a single corporation and the intercompany sale were a transfer between divisions, B would succeed to S's $70 basis in the land and would have a $20 gain from the sale to X instead of a $10 loss. Thus, S takes its $30 gain into account in Year 3:

B's recomputed gain ($90 – $70)	$20
B's actual loss ($90 – $100)	(10)
Difference	$30

.03 Selling Member's Timing—The Acceleration Exception

The matching rule will not always produce the effect of treating S and B as divisions of a single corporation.[16] At least two such situations were contemplated by Treasury and the IRS:

1. S or B becomes a nonmember,[17] or

2. B's cost basis in property purchased from S is carried over by a nonmember, or a nonmember otherwise reflects, directly or indirectly, any aspect of the intercompany transaction.[18]

Reg. § 1.1502-13(d) requires that S take its intercompany items into account in these and other situations to the extent that S's and B's items cannot be taken into account to produce the effect of treating S and B as divisions of a single corporation. The items are taken into account immediately before it first becomes impossible to achieve this effect. This "acceleration rule" thus takes its name from the fact that it causes S, but only S, to take its intercompany items into account before it would be required to do so under the matching rule. B continues to take its corresponding items into account under its accounting method.[19]

Example 3: As an example of S or B becoming a nonmember after an intercompany transaction: S owns raw land with a basis of $70. On January 1 of Year 1, S sells the land to B for $100. On July 1 of Year 3, P sells 60 percent of S's (or B's) stock to nonmember X and, as a result, S (or B) becomes a nonmember. Under the matching rule, none of S's $30 gain is taken into account in Years 1 through 3 because there is no difference between B's $0 recomputed gain and B's $0 actual gain. Under the acceleration rule, however, S's $30 gain is taken into account in Year 3 immediately before S or B becomes a nonmember. Notwithstanding the acceleration of S's gain, B continues to

---

[16] *See* Reg. § 1.1502-13(d).

[17] Reg. § 1.1502-13(d)(1)(i)(A).

[18] Reg. § 1.1502-13(d)(1)(i)(B).

[19] Reg. § 1.1502-13(d)(2)(ii) (the redetermination, however, of the attributes of a corresponding item under the acceleration rule could affect its timing).

take its corresponding items into account, based on subsequent events, under its accounting method. For purposes of determining the *attributes* of B's corresponding items, however (for example, whether its gain or loss on a subsequent sale of the land is ordinary or capital), S and B continue to be treated as divisions of a single corporation.

Caution: Thus, as part of its due diligence in which X purchases the B stock, X must determine whether any of B's assets were acquired in an intercompany transaction.

Example 4: As an example of a carryover basis transaction after an intercompany transaction: S owns raw land with a basis of $70. On January 1 of Year 1, S sells the land to B for $100. On July 1 of Year 3, B transfers the land to Partnership D for a 10-percent interest in the profits and capital of Partnership D (worth $110), and Code Sec. 721 prevents B from recognizing its $10 gain. B takes a $100 basis in its partnership interest under Code Sec. 722. Partnership D carries over B's $100 basis in the land under Code Sec. 723. Under the matching rule, none of S's $30 gain is taken into account in Years 1 through 3, because there is no difference between B's $0 recomputed gain and B's $0 actual gain. Under the acceleration rule, S's $30 gain is taken into account in Year 3 immediately before the transfer to Partnership D that causes Partnership D to carry over B's $100 stepped-up basis (that is, the event that causes the nonmember partnership to reflect an aspect of the intercompany transaction). Notwithstanding the acceleration of S's gain, B continues to take its corresponding item into account, based on subsequent events relating to its substitute asset, the 10-percent partnership interest, under its accounting method (see ¶ 535 for a discussion of the successor rules).

.04 Redetermination of Attributes—Matching Rule

If the timing of S's intercompany item is determined under the matching rule, the separate-entity *attributes* of S's intercompany items and B's corresponding items generally are redetermined to the extent necessary to produce the same effect on consolidated taxable income (and consolidated tax liability) as if S and B were divisions of a single corporation, and the intercompany transaction were between divisions of a single corporation.[20] Thus, the activities of both corporations might affect the character of both S's intercompany item and B's corresponding item. After stating this general rule, the regulations provide these operating rules for offsetting and nonoffsetting amounts:

Offsetting amounts. To the extent that S's intercompany item and B's corresponding item *offset in amount,* the attributes of B's corresponding item generally control the attributes of S's offsetting intercompany item.[21] For example, if S sells depreciable property to B, B's depreciation deductions (ordinary) will require that the treatment of S's income inclusions under the *timing* rule generally be ordinary. To the extent that this result is inconsistent with treating S and B as divisions of a single corporation, however, the attributes of the offsetting items must be redeter-

---

[20] Reg. § 1.1502-13(c)(1)(i).   [21] Reg. § 1.1502-13(c)(4)(i)(A).

mined in a manner consistent with treating S and B as divisions of a single corporation.[22]

For an illustration of how these rules apply to depreciable property[23] see Example 7.

Nonoffsetting amounts. To the extent that S's intercompany item and B's corresponding item do not offset in amount, the redetermined attributes must be allocated to S's intercompany item and B's corresponding item, using a method that is reasonable in light of all the facts and circumstances, including the purposes of Reg. § 1.1502-13 and any other rule affected by the attributes of S's intercompany item and B's corresponding item.[24] A method of allocation is unreasonable if it is not used consistently by all members of the group from year to year.

> *Example 5:* As an example of S's and B's conflicting attributes under the matching rule: S holds raw land for investment with a basis of $70. On January 1 of Year 1, S sells the land to B for $100. B develops the land as residential real estate and sells developed lots to customers during Year 3 for an aggregate amount of $110. S and B are treated under the matching rule as divisions of a single corporation for purposes of determining the attributes of S's intercompany item and B's corresponding item. Thus, although S held the land for investment, whether the gain is treated as capital gain or ordinary income is based on the activities of both S and B. If B's development activities are dominant (which is doubtless the case under these facts), S's $30 gain and B's $10 gain will be ordinary. If S's investment motive is dominant, however, then S's $30 gain and B's $10 gain will be capital.

The acceleration exception. If the timing of S's intercompany item from a sale, exchange, or distribution of property is determined under the acceleration exception, S's and B's nontiming attributes are redetermined as follows:

1. *S's attributes.* The principles of the matching rule are applied as if B sold the property at the time the item is taken into account, for a cash payment equal to B's adjusted basis in the property (that is, at no net gain or loss), under rules that vary depending on whether the property leaves the group.[25]

   a. If the property is owned by a *member* immediately after S's item is taken into account, B is treated as selling the property to an affiliated corporation that is not a member of the group.

---

[22] Reg. § 1.1502-13(c)(4)(i)(B). As an exception to the exception, however, in the unusual case in which B's corresponding item, determined on a separate-entity basis, is excluded from gross income, is a noncapital, nondeductible amount, or is otherwise permanently disallowed or eliminated (for example, B distributes the property to its shareholders in a transaction in which loss is not recognized under Code Sec. 311(a)), the attributes of B's corresponding item always control the attributes of S's offsetting intercompany item. Reg. § 1.1502-13(c)(4)(i)(B).

[23] Reg. § 1.1502-13(c)(3) provides these additional tidbits: As divisions of a single corporation, (1) S and B are treated as engaging in their actual transaction and owning any actual property involved in the transaction rather than treating the transaction as not occurring (for example, intercompany stock is not disregarded even though divisions would have no such stock); (2) each of S and B is allowed to retain its accounting method for a separate trade or business; and (3) each of S and B is permitted to retain any special status they have under the Code or Regulations (for example, as a bank or life insurance company).

[24] Reg. § 1.1502-13(c)(4)(ii).

[25] Reg. § 1.1502-13(d)(1)(ii)(A).

¶515.04

    b. If the property is owned by a *nonmember* immediately after S's item is taken into account, B is treated as selling the property to that nonmember.[26]

The distinction drawn here on whether the property leaves the group grew out of comments received by Treasury and the IRS that the proposed rules, as applied to depreciable property, were overreaching.

  2. *B's attributes.* The attributes of B's corresponding items continue to be redetermined under the principles of the matching rule, with adjustments that depend on whether S and B continue to join with each other in the filing of consolidated returns.[27]

    a. If S and B continue to *join with each other* in the filing of consolidated returns, the attributes of B's corresponding items (and any applicable holding periods) are redetermined by continuing to treat S and B as divisions of a single corporation.

    b. Once S and B *no longer join with each other* in the filing of consolidated returns, the attributes of B's corresponding items are redetermined as if the S division (but not the B division) were transferred by the single corporation to an unrelated person. Thus, S's activities (and any applicable holding period) continue to affect the attributes of the corresponding items (and any applicable holding period).

    Example 6: As an example of attributes under acceleration rule:

    Timing—S holds raw land for investment with a basis of $70. On January 1 of Year 1, S sells the land to B for $100. B holds the land for sale to customers in the ordinary course of business, and expends substantial resources subdividing, developing, and marketing the land over a two-year period. On July 1 of Year 3, before B has sold any of the land, P sells 60 percent of S's stock to X for $60, and as a result, S becomes a nonmember. The acceleration rule requires S to report its $30 gain immediately before S leaves the group.

    S's attributes—Because the land continues to be held within the group, the attributes of S's gain are redetermined under the principles of the matching rule as if B sold the land to an affiliated corporation that is not a member of the group, for a cash payment equal to B's adjusted basis in the land. Thus, whether S's gain is capital gain or ordinary income depends on the activities of both S and B.

.05 Holding Periods

The holding period (which is not defined as an attribute) of property transferred to B in an intercompany transaction is the aggregate of the holding periods of S and B.[28] If the basis in the property is determined by reference to the basis of other property, however, the property's holding period is determined by reference

---

[26] If the nonmember is related for purposes of any provision of the Code or Regulations to any party to the intercompany transaction (or any related transaction), or to the common parent, the nonmember is treated as related to B for purposes of that provision. Reg. § 1.1502-13(d)(1)(ii)(A).

[27] Reg. § 1.1502-13(d)(2)(i).

[28] Reg. § 1.1502-13(c)(1)(ii).

to the holding period of the other property.[29] For example, if S distributes stock of T to B under Code Sec. 355, B's holding period in the distributed T stock is determined by reference to B's holding period in the S stock, not by reference to S's holding period in the T stock.

.06 Depreciable Property Examples—Depreciation Methods

Code Sec. 168(i)(7) requires B to step into S's shoes for purposes of computing depreciation to the extent that B's cost basis in the property does not exceed S's adjusted basis. If S sells depreciable property to B at a gain, B therefore carries over S's adjusted basis and depreciation method and depreciates its *excess* basis under its own depreciation method.

Matching rule. If S sells depreciable property to B at a gain, as B depreciates its excess basis each year under its own depreciation method, S takes into account an offsetting amount of gain based on B's separately determined depreciation method. This reflects the treatment of S and B as divisions of a single corporation, because the excess basis could not have been created in a transaction between divisions.

Conversely, if S sells depreciable property to B at a loss, as B takes less depreciation each year into account than the group would have reported if S and B were divisions of a single corporation, S takes into account an amount of its intercompany loss equal to the shortfall as an ordinary loss.[30]

If B takes into account gain or loss from a disposition of the property, under the matching rule, S takes the balance of its intercompany gain into account to reflect the difference between B's recomputed amount (as if the intercompany sale were a transfer between divisions of a single corporation) and B's actual amount.

> ***Example 7:*** As an example of the matching rule: On January 1 of Year 1, S buys 10-year recovery property for $100 and depreciates it under the straight-line method. On January 1 of Year 3, when S has a basis of $80 in the property, S sells the property to B for $130. Under Code Sec. 168(i)(7)(B)(ii), B is treated as S for purposes of Code Sec. 168 to the extent that B's $130 basis does not exceed S's $80 adjusted basis at the time of the sale. B's additional $50 basis is treated as new 10-year recovery property for which B elects the straight-line method of recovery. (To simplify the example, the half-year convention is disregarded.) B uses the property in its business in Years 3 and 4. On January 1 of Year 5, B sells the property to nonmember X for $110.

Matching with B's annual depreciation deductions. S claims $10 of depreciation for each of Years 1 and 2 and has an $80 basis at the time of the sale to B. Thus, S had a $50 intercompany gain from its sale to B. For Year 3, B has $10 of depreciation with respect to $80 of its basis (the portion of its $130 basis not exceeding S's adjusted basis). In addition, B has $5 of depreciation with respect to the $50 of its additional basis that exceeds S's adjusted basis.

S's $50 gain is taken into account to reflect the difference for each consolidated return year between B's recomputed depreciation and B's depreciation taken into

---

[29] Reg. § 1.1502-13(c)(1)(ii).   [30] *See* Reg. § 1.267(f)-1(c).

account with respect to the property. For each of Years 3 and 4, B takes $15 of depreciation into account. If the intercompany transaction were a transfer between divisions of a single corporation, B would succeed to S's adjusted basis in the property and take into account only $10 of depreciation for each year. Thus, S takes $5 of gain into account in each of Years 3 and 4 (a total of $10), which is ordinary income to S because it is offset by B's $10 of ordinary deduction.

Matching with B's gain on sale to X. The $40 balance of S's intercompany gain is taken into account in Year 5 as a result of B's sale to X, to reflect the difference between B's $50 recomputed gain ($110 amount realized minus the $60 basis B would have if the intercompany sale were a transfer between divisions of a single corporation) and B's actual $10 gain.

Treating S and B as divisions of a single corporation, $40 of the gain is Code Sec. 1245 ordinary income, and the remaining $10 of the gain is Code Sec. 1231 gain. Under Reg. § 1.1502-13(c)(4)(ii), the $10 of Code Sec. 1231 character may be allocated between S and B. The remaining $40 of Code Sec. 1245 character would then be allocated to S and/or B as appropriate. For example, if the $10 of Code Sec. 1231 character were allocated entirely to S, then the $40 of Code Sec. 1245 character would be allocated $30 to S and $10 to B.

In summary, the attributes of S's gain and B's depreciation must be redetermined to the extent necessary to produce the same effect on consolidated taxable income as if the intercompany transaction were between divisions of a single corporation (that is, the group must have a net depreciation deduction of $10 per annum for four years). In each year following the intercompany sale, $5 of B's $15 corresponding depreciation deduction offsets S's $5 intercompany gain taken into account and, under Reg. § 1.1502-13(c)(4)(i), the attributes of B's corresponding item control the attributes of S's intercompany item. Accordingly, S's intercompany gain that is taken into account as a result of B's extra $10 of depreciation deductions is ordinary income, and the remaining $50 of gain that would have been recognized by the group on the sale to X if S and B had been divisions of a single corporation must be redetermined to be $40 of Code Sec. 1245 ordinary income and $10 of Code Sec. 1231 gain.

The acceleration exception. Under the proposed regulations, upon acceleration of S's gain from an intercompany property transaction, S's attributes were to be determined under the principles of the matching rule "as if B resold the property to a nonmember affiliate." Under that rule, S's gain from the sale of depreciable property would always be treated as ordinary income under Code Sec. 1239. Many who commented to the Treasury and the IRS on these regulations objected to this treatment of S's attributes if the property did not remain in the Code Sec. 1239–controlled group, arguing, for example, that if B leaves the Code Sec. 1239–controlled group while it still owns the property, the rules should treat the property as sold to a person whose relationship to the group is the same as B's relationship to the group after it becomes a nonmember. To reflect these comments, the final regulation states the following:

- As under the proposed rule, *if the property is owned by a member* immediately after the event that causes S's acceleration, B is treated as selling the property to an *affiliated* corporation that is not a member of the group (that is, S's gain is treated as ordinary income under Code Sec. 1239),[31] and

- In contrast to the proposed rule, *if the property is owned by a nonmember* immediately after the event that causes acceleration, B is treated as selling the property to that nonmember. In most cases this will not bring Code Sec. 1239 into play. If the nonmember is related for purposes of any provision of the Code or regulations to any party to the intercompany transaction (or any related transaction) or to the common parent, however, the nonmember is treated as related to B for purposes of that provision. Thus, if the nonmember were related to one of these specified parties within the meaning of Code Sec. 1239, the deemed sale would be treated as being described in Code Sec. 1239.[32]

.07 Sourcing Examples

The Preamble to T.D. 8597 addresses comments that Treasury and the IRS had received regarding the effects of using a single-entity approach to allocate a consolidated group's foreign and U.S. source income.[33]

80/20 companies. One commentator noted that under the single-entity approach, a *pro rata* allocation of the group's foreign and U.S. source income (as illustrated in Example 17 of paragraph (c) of the proposed regulations) could cause a member that qualified under Code Sec. 861(a)(1)(A) as an 80/20 company to lose that status. As a result, the member could be required to withhold federal income tax on interest payments to a foreign lender. As indicated above, the final regulations revise the attribute rules to clarify that a redetermination is made only to the extent that it is necessary to achieve the effect of treating S and B as divisions of a single corporation and to provide that redetermined attributes are allocated to S and B using a method that is reasonable in light of the purposes of Reg. § 1.1502-13 and any other affected rule.

Thus, the group is not required to allocate U.S. and foreign source income on a *pro rata* basis, and a member that qualifies as an 80/20 company under current law generally need not lose that status solely as the result of the allocation from a transaction similar to that described in the example.

Treaties. Commentators also suggested that the *pro rata* allocation methodology of the proposed regulations could be inconsistent with U.S. income tax treaties, which require the United States to treat income that may be taxed by the treaty partner as derived from sources within the treaty partner. As revised, the attribute rules do not require the group to allocate U.S. and foreign source income on a *pro rata* basis. Thus, the regulations will generally be consistent with any source rules contained in U.S. income tax treaties. To the extent, however, that a U.S. income tax treaty provides benefits to a taxpayer, these regulations do not prevent a taxpayer from claiming those benefits.

---

[31] Reg. § 1.1502-13(d)(1)(ii)(A)(2).
[32] Reg. § 1.1502-13(d)(1)(ii)(A)(1).

[33] Preamble to T.D. 8597, 1995-2 CB 147.

For intercompany transaction sourcing examples that depend on whether an independent factory or production price exists, see Reg. § 1.1502-13(c)(7)(ii), Examples (14)(a) and (b).

.08 Exclusion of Gain—Nondeductibility of Loss

The matching rule may disallow an intercompany loss to S or cause an intercompany gain or loss to be excluded or unrecognized. For example, when B has a corresponding deduction or loss and in the tax year it is taken into account it is permanently and explicitly disallowed, pure single-entity treatment would suggest that S should be permitted to *exclude* any related intercompany income or gain to the extent necessary to treat B and S as if they were divisions of a single corporation. The regulations provide for such an exclusion of S's gain in limited circumstances, such as when B's corresponding item is a loss that is realized but not recognized under Code Sec. 311(a), on a distribution to a nonmember.[34]

> **Example 8:** As an example of intercompany gain followed by distribution to nonmember at a loss: S sells land with a basis of $70 to B for $100, and the land is subsequently distributed to a nonmember shareholder of B when the land has a value of $90. B's $10 corresponding loss is not recognized under its accounting method (Code Sec. 311(a)). The permanent disallowance of B's corresponding loss is treated as an accounting event that causes S to match with B. If S and B were divisions of a single corporation and the intercompany sale were a transfer between divisions, B would succeed to S's $70 basis in the land and would have a $20 gain from the distribution instead of an unrecognized $10 loss:
>
> | | |
> |---|---:|
> | B's recomputed gain ($110 – $70) . . . . . . | $40 |
> | B's actual gain ($110 – $100) . . . . | 10 |
> | Difference . . . . | $30 |
>
> Under Reg. § 1.1502-13(c)(4)(i), to the extent that S's and B's items offset in amount, the attributes of B's corresponding item control the attributes of S's intercompany item. Thus, $10 of S's $30 gain is redetermined to be excluded from gross income.

Limitations were imposed on S's exclusion of an intercompany income or gain in the lion's share of other situations.[35] An amount is not treated as permanently and explicitly disallowed for this purpose to the extent that:

1. The Internal Revenue Code or regulations provide that the amount is not recognized under Code Sec. 332, Code Sec. 355(c), etc.;

2. A related amount might be taken into account by B with respect to successor property (such as under Code Sec. 280B);

3. A related amount might be taken into account by another taxpayer (such as under Code Sec. 267(d)); or

---

[34] Reg. § 1.1502-13(c)(6)(ii)(B).

[35] Reg. § 1.1502-13(c)(6)(ii)(A).

¶515.08

4. A related amount might be taken into account as a deduction or loss, including as a carryforward to a later year; or the amount is reflected in the computation of any credit against (or other reduction of) federal income tax.

The foregoing limitations, however, do not apply for purposes of determining whether intercompany loss is deductible.

> *Example 9:* As an example of intercompany member stock loss followed by complete liquidation of member: S sells all the stock of T (another member of the P group) to B for $100. S's basis in the T stock is $150, and S recognizes (but does not take into account) a $50 loss on the intercompany sale. Later, when the T stock is worth $120, T liquidates into B, pursuant to Code Sec. 332.

The permanent and explicit elimination of gain or loss to B on the complete liquidation of T is a corresponding item, because there is no successor property that will permit S to match its intercompany item against B's corresponding item in the future.[36] As such, B's corresponding item is $20 of realized gain that is permanently excluded from income, and its recomputed corresponding item is a $30 loss (amount realized of $120, less the $150 basis in the T stock B would have had if S and B had been divisions of a single corporation) that is permanently eliminated, for a difference of $50. Under the timing rule, S is required to take its $50 intercompany loss into account.

To the extent that B's corresponding item ($20 of realized gain that is permanently eliminated) offsets S's intercompany item ($50 of intercompany loss on the T stock sale), however, the character of B's item as excluded income controls S's intercompany item.[37] That is, $20 of S's $50 loss clearly is not allowed. The remaining $30 of S's $50 loss is redetermined by treating S and B as divisions of a single corporation.[38] As divisions of a single corporation, none of S's loss in the T stock would be recognized on T's complete liquidation because of the application of Code Sec. 332. Accordingly, it would appear that the entire amount of S's $50 intercompany loss is not taken into account under the matching rule.

By contrast, suppose S had recognized a $50 gain on the intercompany sale of T stock to B (say S's basis in the T stock was $50, instead of $150). The timing analysis remains unchanged. B's corresponding item is $20 of realized but permanently eliminated gain, and its recomputed corresponding item is $70 of realized but permanently eliminated gain ($120 amount realized, minus the $50 basis B would have had in the T stock if B and S had been divisions of a single corporation), thereby requiring S to take into account all of the $50 intercompany gain at the time of T's liquidation. Furthermore, under the limitations on gain exclusion discussed above,[39] S's intercompany gain is not excluded.[40]

---

[36] Reg. § 1.1502-13(b)(3)(ii).

[37] Reg. § 1.1502-13(c)(4)(i).

[38] Reg. § 1.1502-13(c)(1)(i) and Reg. § 1.1502-13(c)(4)(ii).

[39] *See* Reg. § 1.1502-13(c)(6)(ii)(A)(1), which provides that an amount is not permanently and explicitly disallowed for purposes of determining the attributes of intercompany gain to the extent that the Code or

regulations (for example, Code Sec. 332 or Code Sec. 355) state that gain or loss is realized but not recognized.

[40] *See also* Reg. § 1.1502-13(f)(5)(i). As discussed at ¶ 445, elective relief from this onerous result to S is available under Reg. § 1.1502-13(f)(5)(ii), if the group is able to reincorporate the assets of T in a new corporation within 12 months after the filing of the consolidated return for the year in which T is completely liquidated,

¶515.08

Caution: Thus, the net result in this fact pattern appears to be that S's intercompany gain is always taken into account, whereas its intercompany loss is never taken into account.

¶ 525 Loss Property

When looking at loss property, it is important to consider Code Sec. 267(f), controlled group versus consolidated group, intercompany losses, deferred loss treated as a Code Sec. 108(b) attribute, a transfer to related person outside the controlled group, and the anti-avoidance rule.

.01 Code Sec. 267(f) in General

Prior to the 1984 amendments to Code Sec. 267, Code Sec. 267(a) disallowed loss on the sale or exchange of property between certain related parties and the disallowed loss was lost forever. Instead, on a subsequent disposition of the property (or substituted basis property) the transferee was allowed merely to reduce its gain.[41] These rules did not apply to an intercompany transaction because two related corporations were not subject to Code Sec. 267.

To prevent tax avoidance on transactions between controlled corporations, Code Sec. 267(b) was amended in 1984 to expand the definition of related parties to include two corporations that are members of the same "controlled group."[42] In addition, Code Sec. 267(f)(2) was added generally to defer, rather than deny, any loss from the sale or exchange of property between members of the same controlled group to which Code Sec. 267(a) applies[43] "until the property is transferred outside the controlled group and there would be recognition of loss under consolidated return principles or until such other time as may be prescribed by regulations."

Reg. § 1.267(f)-1 replaces a prior complex regime for implementing Code Sec. 267(f) by relying more heavily on Reg. § 1.1502-13. As discussed below, losses from sales or exchanges of property between related corporations are taken into account in the same manner as is provided in the *timing* provisions (*not* the *attribute* redetermination provisions) of Reg. § 1.1502-13, except that the provisions are applied to the larger "controlled group." The regulations also require loss disallowance similar to Code Sec. 267(a), when B transfers loss property to a nonmember related party.[44]

(Footnote Continued)

and elects in that return to treat the new corporation as a continuation of T.

[41] Code Sec. 267(d) permitted the related purchaser of the loss property to reduce its gain on a subsequent disposition by the amount of the disallowed loss. This provision provides no benefit if the property is not later sold at a gain or is disposed of in a nonrecognition transaction.

[42] Code Sec. 267(b)(3).

[43] Code Sec. 267(a)(1) does not apply to a loss of the distributing corporation (or the distributee) in the case of a distribution in complete liquidation.

[44] Reg. § 1.267(f)-1(c)(1)(iii) (allowing loss on a transfer to a Code Sec. 267(b) or Code Sec. 707(b)–related party only to the extent of any gain taken into account on the transaction). Reg. § 1.267(f)-1 also has its own anti-avoidance rule (*See* Reg. § 1.267(f)-1(h)). For other special rules, *See* Reg. § 1.267(f)-1(d) (intercompany sales of inventory involving foreign persons), Reg. § 1.267(f)-1(e) (treatment of creditor with respect to a loan in nonfunctional currency), and Reg. § 1.267(f)-1(f) (receivables).

.02 Controlled Group Versus Consolidated Group

A *controlled group* generally is defined to mean a controlled group within the meaning of Code Sec. 1563(a), substituting a "more than 50 percent" of the vote or value control test for the "at-least-80-percent" test of Code Sec. 1563(a) to determine membership in the group.[45] Accordingly, a controlled group differs from a consolidated group primarily in three respects:

1. *Stock ownership test.* To be a member of a controlled group, only more than 50 percent of the vote *or* value of a corporation's stock must be owned, rather than the 80 percent of the vote *and* value required for a consolidated group. Also, unlike Code Sec. 1504(a), which has no constructive ownership rules, detailed attribution rules under Code Sec. 1563(e) apply for purposes of determining stock ownership under Code Sec. 267(f)(1).

2. *Eligible corporations.* Certain corporations may be included in a controlled group that are excluded from a consolidated group. A controlled group, for example, may include a foreign corporation that Code Sec. 1504(b)(3) prevents from being a member of a consolidated group.[46]

3. *Brother-sister corporations.* A controlled group does not require a common parent corporation. For this reason, a controlled group may be composed of brother-sister corporations that would not be included in a consolidated group.

In sum, a controlled group may be much larger than a consolidated group.

.03 Intercompany Losses

A selling member's loss or deduction from an intercompany sale to another member of the controlled group is taken into account under the *timing* principles of Reg. § 1.1502-13, treating the intercompany sale as an intercompany transaction. With certain adjustments, the matching and acceleration rules of Reg. § 1.1502-13 apply on a controlled group basis rather than a consolidated-group basis, and generally affect only the *timing* of a loss or deduction, and not its attributes or the holding period of property.[47]

> **Example 10:** As an example of intercompany loss and deconsolidation of B within a controlled group: P owns all the stock of S and B, and the P group is a consolidated group. S holds land for investment with a basis of $130. On January 1 of Year 1, S sells the land to B for $100. B holds the land for sale to customers in the ordinary course of business. On July 1 of Year 3, P sells 25 percent of B's stock to X. As a result of the sale, B becomes a nonmember of the P consolidated group, but S and B remain members of a controlled group.

---

[45] Code Sec. 267(f)(1).

[46] *See generally* Reg. § 1.267(f)-1(b)(3).

[47] Reg. § 1.267(f)-1(a)(2)(i) (the special rules for member stock and member obligations apply, however, only to the extent that the transaction is also an intercompany transaction to which Reg. § 1.1502-13 applies). Reg. § 1.267(f)-1(a)(2)(ii) (if S's loss would be redetermined to be a noncapital, nondeductible amount under the principles of Reg. § 1.1502-13(c)(1)(i) and Reg. § 1.1502-13(c)(6), Reg. § 1.267(f)-1(c)(1)(iv) will operate to continue to defer S's loss until S and B are no longer in a Code Sec. 267(b) controlled-group relationship. For example, assume S sells land (basis of $130) to B for $100, after which B distributes the land to shareholders who are not related to B under Code Sec. 267(b) and Code Sec. 707(b) in a Code Sec. 311 transaction. S's $30 loss will continue to be deferred until S and B are no longer related even though the *timing* rule of Reg. § 1.1502-13(c)(2) would normally require S's loss to be taken into account).

Assume that if S and B were divisions of a single corporation, the items of S and B from the land would be ordinary by reason of B's activities.

S's sale to B is subject to both Reg. § 1.1502-13 and Reg. § 1.267(f)-1. S's loss is redetermined to be an ordinary loss by reason of B's activities. Because S and B remain in a controlled-group relationship, the loss is not taken into account under the acceleration exception merely because B becomes a nonmember of the consolidated group. Nevertheless, S's loss is redetermined to be an ordinary loss, and the character of the loss is not further redetermined. Thus, the loss continues to be deferred, and will be taken into account as ordinary loss based on subsequent events. If P, instead of selling 25 percent of the B stock to X, sells 60 percent of the S stock and 51 percent of the B stock to X, S and B continue to be in a Code Sec. 267(f)–controlled group relationship to each other by reason of X's ownership of 60 percent of the S stock and 51 percent of the B stock. Thus, the S loss continues to be deferred.[48]

> **Example 11:** As an example of intercompany loss and resale within a controlled group: The facts are the same as in Example 10, except that P owns 75 percent of the stock of X, and B resells the land to X rather than P selling any B stock. The results for S's loss are the same as in Example 10. X is also in a controlled-group relationship, and B's sale to X is a second intercompany sale. Thus, S's loss continues to be deferred and is taken into account as ordinary loss based on subsequent events.

.04 Deferred Loss Treated as a Code Sec. 108(b) Attribute

A loss or deduction not yet taken into account under Code Sec. 267(f) or Reg. § 1.1502-13 is treated as basis described in Code Sec. 108(b), subject to any reduction in the basis of property required under Code Sec. 108(b)(2)(E), even though the selling member actually has no remaining interest in the property.[49]

.05 Transfer to Related Person Outside Controlled Group

To the extent that S's loss or deduction from an intercompany sale is taken into account as a result of B's transfer of the property to a person who is not a member of the controlled group but is a person related to any member, immediately after the transfer, under Code Sec. 267(b) or Code Sec. 707(b), or as a result of S or B becoming a nonmember of the controlled group but continuing to be related to any member of the controlled group under Code Sec. 267(b), the loss or deduction is taken into account but allowed only to the extent of any income or gain taken into account as a result of the transfer.[50] The balance not allowed is treated as a loss referred to in Code Sec. 267(d), if it is from the sale or exchange by B (rather than from a distribution).

> **Example 12:** As an example of an intercompany transaction followed by transfer to related partnership: P owns all the stock of S and B, and the P group is a consolidated group. S owns land with a basis of $130. On January 1 of Year 1, S sells the land to B for $100. On July 1 of Year 3, B transfers the land to a

---

[48] Reg. § 1.267(f)-1(b)(3) and Reg. § 1.267(f)-1(j), Example (1)(d).

[49] Reg. § 1.108-3(a).

[50] Reg. § 1.267(f)-1(c)(1)(iii).

partnership in exchange for a 40-percent interest in capital and profits in a transaction to which Code Sec. 721 applies. P also owns a 25-percent interest in the capital and profits of the partnership. Because the partnership is not a member of the controlled group, but is a related person under Code Sec. 267(b) and Code Sec. 707(b), S's $30 loss is taken into account in Year 3 only to the extent of any income or gain taken into account by B as a result of the transfer to the partnership (which is zero). Any subsequent gain recognized by the partnership with respect to the property is offset or reduced under Code Sec. 267(d), to the extent of the loss disallowed.

.06 Anti-Avoidance Rule

If a transaction is "engaged in or structured with a principal purpose to avoid the purposes [of the Code Sec. 267(f) rules] (including, for example, by avoiding treatment as an intercompany sale or by distorting the timing of losses or deductions), adjustments must be made to carry out the purposes [of the Code Sec. 267(f) rules]."[51]

> **Example 13:** As an example of intercompany sale followed by Code Sec. 351 transfer of S stock to X: P owns all the stock of S and B and files a consolidated return with S and B. In Year 1, S sells raw land with a basis of $130 to B for $100, recognizing a $30 capital loss. The land is not essential to S's business. In Year 3, P transfers all of the S stock to X, a newly formed corporation, in exchange for 10 percent of the X stock. Code Sec. 351(a) applies to this exchange. P has no plan or intention of disposing of the X stock. A principal purpose of the Code Sec. 351(a) exchange is to accelerate S's loss in Year 3 so that it can be used in the consolidated return against $30 of capital gain recognized by P. The IRS would apply the anti-avoidance rule to disallow S's $30 loss (which generally would be taken into account under the acceleration rule), not merely defer it. The disallowed loss is treated as a noncapital, nondeductible expenditure for which P must reduce its basis in the S stock immediately before S is deconsolidated.

Under the prior regulations, S could not restore a loss as a result of its deconsolidation, if the property remained in the group, without regard to a showing of a purpose to accelerate the loss.[52] B, on the other hand, would have been allowed to increase its $100 basis in the land purchased from S by the amount of S's disallowed $30 loss.[53] As a practical matter, however, the severity of the new penalty may make it harder to convince a court that the proscribed avoidance exists.

¶ 535 Successor Assets, Persons, and Groups

For purposes of Reg. § 1.1502-13, any reference to an asset includes a reference to any other asset of which the basis is determined, directly or indirectly, in whole or in part, by reference to the basis of the first asset. In general, any reference in Reg. § 1.1502-13 to a person includes, as the context may require, a reference to a predecessor or successor. If the consolidated group ceases to exist because of an

---

[51] Reg. § 1.267(f)-1(h).
[52] *See* Temporary Reg. § 1.267(f)-1T(c)(6).
[53] *See* Temporary Reg. § 1.267(f)-1T(c)(7)(i).

acquisition, the surviving group is treated as the terminating group for purposes of applying Reg. § 1.1502-13 to the intercompany transactions of the terminating group. If a consolidated group terminates because the common parent is the only remaining member, Reg. § 1.1502-13(j)(6) causes the common parent to succeed to the treatment of the terminating group for purposes of applying the intercompany transaction rules, so long as it neither becomes a member of an affiliated group filing separate returns, nor becomes a corporation described in Code Sec. 1504(b).

.01 Successor Assets

For purposes of Reg. § 1.1502-13, any reference to an asset includes, as the context may require, a reference to any other asset of which the basis is determined, directly or indirectly, in whole or in part, by reference to the basis of the first asset.[54] Under the successor asset rule, if B disposes of property acquired from S in a substituted basis transaction outside the consolidated group, S will not take its deferred gain or loss into account unless the transaction is also a carryover basis transaction. Instead, S will apply the matching or acceleration rule to B's disposition of its successor asset.

> **Example 14:** As an example of intercompany sale followed by a Code Sec. 1031 exchange with nonmember: S holds land for investment with a basis of $70. On January 1 of Year 1, S sells the land to B for $100. B also holds the land for investment. On July 1 of Year 3, B exchanges the land for land owned by nonmember X worth $110 in a transaction to which Code Sec. 1031 applies. B recognizes none of its $10 realized gain and takes a $100 basis in the replacement land.

There is no difference in Year 3 between B's $0 recomputed corresponding item and B's $0 actual corresponding item. Thus, none of S's intercompany gain is taken into account under the matching rule as a result of the like-kind exchange. Instead, S's gain is preserved in the replacement land. Furthermore, because X's basis in the land received from B does not reflect any aspect of the intercompany transaction (X also has a substituted basis in that land under Code Sec. 1031 determined by reference to X's basis in the replacement land), the acceleration rule does not apply. Accordingly, under the successor asset rule of Reg. § 1.1502-13(j)(1), S's intercompany gain is taken into account by reference to the replacement land.

.02 Successor Persons

In general, any reference in Reg. § 1.1502-13 to a person includes, as the context may require, a reference to a predecessor or successor.[55] For this purpose, a predecessor is a transferor of assets to a transferee (the successor) in a transaction:

- To which Code Sec. 381(a) applies;
- In which substantially all of the assets of the transferor are transferred to members in a complete liquidation;

---

[54] Reg. § 1.1502-13(j)(1).   [55] Reg. § 1.1502-13(j)(2)(i).

¶535.01

- In which the successor's basis in the assets is determined (directly or indirectly, in whole or in part) by reference to the basis of the transferor, but the transferee is a successor only with respect to the assets of which the basis is so determined; or

- That is an intercompany transaction, but only with respect to assets that are being accounted for by the transferor in a prior intercompany transaction.

If the assets of a predecessor are acquired by a successor member, the successor succeeds to, and takes into account, the predecessor's intercompany items. If two or more successor members acquire assets of the predecessor, the successors take into account the predecessor's intercompany items in a manner that is consistently applied and reasonably carries out the purposes of the intercompany transaction regulations and applicable provisions of law.[56]

> ***Example 15:*** As an example of back-to-back intercompany transactions: S holds land for investment with a basis of $70. On January 1 of Year 1, S sells the land to M for $90. M also holds the land for investment. On July 1 of Year 3, M sells the land for $100 to B, and B holds the land for sale to customers in the ordinary course of business. During Year 5, B sells all of the land to customers for $105.

S's sale of the land to M, and M's sale of the land to B are both intercompany transactions. S is the selling member and M is the buying member in the first intercompany transaction, and M is the selling member and B is the buying member in the second intercompany transaction. Under Reg. § 1.1502-13(j)(2)(i)(D), B is treated as the successor to M for purposes of taking S's intercompany gain into account.

S, M, and B are treated as divisions of a single corporation for purposes of determining the timing of their items from the intercompany transactions. Thus, S's $20 gain and M's $10 gain are both taken into account in Year 5 to reflect the difference between B's $5 gain taken into account with respect to the land and the $35 recomputed gain (the gain that B would have taken into account if the intercompany sales had been transfers between divisions of a single corporation, and B succeeded to S's $70 basis).

The attributes of the intercompany items and corresponding items of S, M, and B are also determined by treating S, M, and B as divisions of a single corporation.[57]

> ***Example 16:*** As an example of liquidation of S or B into another member: On January 1 of Year 1, S sells land with a $70 basis to B for $100. On July 1 of Year 3, B liquidates into P under Code Sec. 332, and P carries over B's $100 basis in the land under Code Sec. 334(b)(1). P is treated as a successor to B. Thus, S will apply the matching and acceleration rules by treating P as B's replacement. If, instead of B liquidating into P, S liquidated into P under Code Sec. 332, then P would be treated as a successor to S. Thus, P would succeed

---

[56] Reg. § 1.1502-13(j)(2)(i).
[57] *See* Reg. § 1.1502-13(j)(4) (if a member's intercompany item or corresponding item affects the accounting of more than one transaction, appropriate adjustments are made to treat all the intercompany transactions as transactions between divisions of a single corporation).

¶535.02

to and take into account, under the matching and acceleration rules, S's intercompany gain.

.03 Successor Groups

If the consolidated group of which S and B are members ceases to exist because of an acquisition described in Reg. § 1.1502-13(j)(5)(i) (for example, X purchases all of the stock of P, the common parent of the terminating group, and a consolidated return is filed by X for the year that includes X's acquisition of P), the surviving group is treated as the terminating group for purposes of applying Reg. § 1.1502-13 to the intercompany transactions of the terminating group.[58]

Such an acquisition will result in such a transfer of S's deferred gain or loss to the surviving group if the acquisition is by a member of another consolidated group of either the assets of the common parent of the terminating group in a reorganization described in Code Sec. 381(a)(2), or the stock of the common parent of the terminating group.[59] Similar principles apply to an acquisition by a member of the terminating group of the stock or assets of a nonmember if the acquisition is treated as a "reverse acquisition" under Reg. § 1.1502-75(d)(3) because the shareholders of the nominal acquired corporation own more than 50 percent by value of the stock of the nominal acquiring corporation immediately after the acquisition (i.e., the minnow swallows the whale).[60]

.04 Common Parent Only Remaining Member

If a consolidated group terminates because the common parent is the only remaining member, Reg. § 1.1502-13(j)(6) causes the common parent to succeed to the treatment of the terminating group for purposes of applying the intercompany transaction rules, so long as it neither becomes a member of an affiliated group filing separate returns nor becomes a corporation described in Code Sec. 1504(b).

¶ 545 Member Stock

Double taxation may continue to be a rude awakening for consolidated groups that fail to consider the effects of intercompany member stock transactions. Other miscellaneous member stock rules need to be considered as well.

.01 Intercompany Transactions Causing Double Taxation

Given the single-entity policy underlying most of the consolidated return regulations, consolidated groups are frequently surprised to learn that S's intercompany gain on a sale or distribution of member stock will be taken into account when, for example, the transferred member later is liquidated into B under Code Sec. 332 or is spun off to P under Code Sec. 355, or the transferred member's assets are treated as sold by way of a Code Sec. 338(h)(10) election. In effect, double-taxation of the outside and inside gain arises because the outside stock gain becomes locked in by the intercompany transaction before the transferred member's assets are sold (that is, outside gain is taken into account before inside gain).

---

[58] Reg. § 1.1502-13(j)(5)(ii).
[59] Reg. § 1.1502-13(j)(5)(i)(A).
[60] Reg. § 1.1502-13(j)(5)(i)(B).

The investment adjustments under Reg. § 1.1502-32 prevent such double taxation only when the inside gain is taken into account before the outside gain.

Example 17: As an example of a Code Sec. 332 liquidation: S owns all the stock of T, with a $10 basis and $100 value, and T's assets have a $10 basis and $100 value. On January 1 of Year 1, S sells all of T's stock to B for $100. On July 1 of Year 3, when T's assets are still worth $100, T distributes all of its assets to B pursuant to a complete liquidation to which Code Sec. 332 applies. Under Code Sec. 334(b)(1), B takes a $10 basis in T's assets. In Year 5, B sells the former T assets for $100 and recognizes $90 of gain. As discussed in ¶ 415, B's unrecognized gain or loss under Code Sec. 332 is a corresponding item for purposes of applying the matching rule. In Year 3 when T liquidates, B has zero gain or loss because B has a $100 basis in the T stock and receives a $100 distribution with respect to its T stock. Treating S and B as divisions of a single corporation, the recomputed corresponding gain would have been $90 of permanently eliminated gain under Code Sec. 332 because B would have succeeded to S's $10 basis in the stock. Thus, under the matching rule, S's $90 intercompany gain is taken into account in Year 3 as a result of the liquidation. Under Reg. § 1.1502-13(c)(1)(i), the attributes of S's gain and B's corresponding item are redetermined as if S and B were divisions of a single corporation. Although S's gain ordinarily would be redetermined to be treated as excluded from gross income to reflect the nonrecognition of B's gain under Code Sec. 332, under Reg. § 1.1502-13(c)(6)(ii), S's gain remains capital gain because B's unrecognized gain under Code Sec. 332 is not permanently and explicitly *disallowed* under the Code.

In effect, the intercompany sale of the T stock locked in S's $90 T stock gain so that it is taken into account as a result of the Code Sec. 332 liquidation before T's assets are sold. As a consequence, B's sale of T's former assets for $100 causes double taxation of the same $90 gain.

Limited relief. This double-taxation issue arose under the prior regulations as well. As described below, only limited relief is provided by the current regulations. Treasury's and the IRS's "one bad apple spoils the bushel" defense against commentators' criticism of this relief is set forth in the Preamble to T.D. 8597:

> As more fully explained in Notice 94-49, the location of items within a group is a core principle underlying the operation of these regulations, which like the prior regulations, adopt a deferred sale approach, not a carryover basis approach. Taking intercompany gain into account in the event of a subsequent nonrecognition transaction is necessary to prevent the transfer and liquidation of subsidiaries from being used to affect consolidated taxable income or tax liability by changing the location of items within a group (a result that would be equivalent to a carryover basis system). For example, assume that S has an asset with a zero basis and a $100 value. The group would like to shift this built-in gain to B. To do so, S could transfer the asset to T, a newly formed subsidiary. After the transfer, S has a zero basis in the T stock under section 358, and T has a zero basis in the asset under section 362. S then sells the T stock to B for $100 and realizes a $100 gain, which is not taken into account. T later liquidates into B, which receives the asset with a zero basis under section 334. If the transaction is not recharacterized as a direct transfer of assets or is not subject to adjustment under section 482, and S's gain on the sale of the T stock is treated as tax-

¶545.01

exempt (or if it is indefinitely deferred), the series of transactions has the effect of a transfer of the asset by S to B in a carryover basis transaction.

For the foregoing reasons, Treasury and the IRS provided only limited relief, permitting the group merely to defer S's T stock gain, provided the group elects and takes steps to treat the liquidation of T as a liquidation-reincorporation transaction that qualifies as a reorganization under Code Sec. 368.[61] To qualify, B must transfer T's assets to a new member (new T) pursuant to a written plan, a copy of which is attached to a timely filed original return (including extensions) for the year of T's liquidation, and the transfer must be completed within 12 months of the filing of that return.[62] The requirements for the election statement are set forth in Reg. § 1.1502-13(f)(5)(ii)(E).

If the election were made in the last example, T should be treated as having transferred its assets to new T under Code Sec. 368(a)(1)(D). As a result, new T would carry over T's $10 basis in its assets under Code Sec. 362(b), and B would avoid recognition of gain under Code Sec. 354. This relief defers S's T stock gain because B's stock in new T would be a successor asset to B's stock in T (see Reg. § 1.1502-13(j)(1) and Code Sec. 358), and S would take its $90 gain into account based on subsequent events relating to the new T stock.[63]

Downstream mergers. Reg. § 1.1502-13(f)(5)(ii)(B)(3) applies similar principles if B's basis in its T stock is eliminated in a transaction comparable to a Code Sec. 332 liquidation, such as a downstream merger under Code Sec. 368(a)(1)(A). That is, S's intercompany gain on a sale of the T stock to B is not taken into account solely as a result of the merger if T (as the successor to B) timely forms new T with substantially all of T's former assets, and the election is made.

Code Sec. 338(h)(10) transactions. An alternative form of relief from double taxation is available if, after S sells T stock at a gain to B, T's Code Sec. 332 liquidation is deemed to occur as a result of a qualified stock purchase of T that the corporate purchaser and B elect under Code Sec. 338(h)(10) to treat as a sale of assets and a liquidation. If the relief is elected, B is treated as recognizing as a corresponding item any loss or deduction it would recognize (determined after adjusting stock basis under Reg. § 1.1503-32) if Code Sec. 331, rather than Code Sec. 332, applied to the deemed liquidation. For all other federal income tax purposes, the deemed liquidation remains subject to Code Sec. 332.

The amount of B's deemed Code Sec. 331 loss for T is limited by Reg. § 1.1502-13(f)(5)(ii)(C)(2). The loss cannot exceed the amount of S's intercompany

---

[61] If S has both intercompany gain and intercompany loss attributable to stock of the same corporation having the same material terms, refer to the netting rule of Reg. § 1.1502-13(f)(5)(i).

[62] Reg. § 1.1502-13(f)(5)(ii)(B)(2).

[63] A group may elect to accelerate the effective date of the relief provisions of Reg. § 1.1502-13, if stock transferred from S to B is later transferred in one of several prescribed transactions on or after July 12, 1995. (It is immaterial whether the stock transfer between S and B occurred prior to July 12, 1995.) These subsequent transactions include (1) a cancellation or redemption of the stock (such as in a Code Sec. 332 liquidation); (2) a deemed cancellation in a liquidation pursuant to a Code Sec. 338(h)(10) election; (3) a distribution (such as under Code Sec. 355); or (4) an exchange for stock of a member (determined immediately after the exchange) in a transaction that would cause S's gain or loss from the transfer to be taken into account under prior law. Reg. § 1.1502-13(l)(3)(iii) prescribes the time and manner for making the election. If the election is made, Reg. § 1.1502-13 applies to determine the timing and attributes of S's and B's gain or loss from stock with respect to all of these "stock elimination" transactions.

¶545.01

gain that is in excess of S's intercompany loss for shares of T stock having the same material terms as the shares giving rise to S's intercompany gain, and the amount of loss cannot exceed the net amount of loss that would be taken into account if Code Sec. 331 applied to all T shares.

    Example 18: As an example of a Code Sec. 338(h)(10) transaction: S owns all the stock of T, with a $10 basis and $100 value. T's assets, all capital assets with holding periods of more than one year, have a $10 basis and $100 value. On January 1 of Year 1, S sells all of T's stock to B for $100. On July 1 of Year 3, when T's assets are still worth $100, T sells all the stock of T to nonmember corporation X for $100 (for which a Code Sec. 338(h)(10) election is made), and T has no liabilities. T timely elects the relief provided by Reg. § 1.1502-13(f)(5)(ii)(C)(1). In Year 3, T recognizes a $90 long-term capital gain on the deemed sale of its assets to X. Under Reg. § 1.1502-32, B increases its $100 cost basis in the T stock to $190, to reflect T's taxable income for the year. In Year 3, when T is deemed to liquidate, B has $90 of deemed recognized loss under Code Sec. 331 because B has a $190 basis in the T stock and receives a $100 distribution with respect to its T stock. Treating S and B as divisions of a single corporation, the recomputed corresponding item would have been zero gain or loss because B would have succeeded to S's $10 basis in the stock, and increased it by $90 to reflect T's recognized gain. Thus, under the matching rule, S's $90 intercompany gain is taken into account in Year 3 as a result of the liquidation and offsets B's $90 corresponding loss. The net result is that T's gain is taxed to the group only once.

Asset sale and liquidation. Reg. § 1.1502-13(f)(5)(ii)(C)(3) applies similar principles if, after S sells T stock at a gain to B, T transfers all of its assets to a nonmember and completely liquidates in a transaction comparable to a Code Sec. 338(h)(10) transaction.

Code Sec. 355 distributions. If B distributes member stock in an intercompany transaction to which Code Sec. 355 applies, the redetermination of the basis of the member stock under Code Sec. 358 causes S's intercompany gain or loss to be taken into account under the matching rule, because B's gain or loss in the member stock is permanently eliminated under Code Sec. 355(c). If an election is made, however, B's distribution is treated as subject to Code Sec. 301 and Code Sec. 311.[64] B's gain or loss in the member stock is not eliminated; hence, matching remains possible based on subsequent events involving the member stock. The price of avoiding taking S's gain into account on the distribution is that, in the case of a split-off that otherwise is treated as a sale or exchange to B under Code Sec. 302(a), B's gain or loss from the distribution also will be taken into account.

.02 Miscellaneous Member Stock Rules

    The intercompany transaction regulations also include a number of special rules relating to member stock.

---

[64] Reg. § 1.1502-13(f)(5)(ii)(D).

Modification of Code Sec. 165(g). In keeping with the symmetry between the treatment of negative stock basis and positive stock basis, Reg. § 1.1502-80(c) provides that positive stock basis of a member is not treated as worthless under Code Sec. 165 before the stock is treated as worthless under the same principles used to determine recapture of negative stock basis under Reg. § 1.1502-19(c)(1)(iii).

Code Sec. 301 distributions. A nonliquidating distribution of property by a member of a consolidated group (DS) to an owning member (PB) brings into play a host of intercompany transaction rules.

- *Treatment of DS.* DS wears two hats when it distributes property within the consolidated group. DS is both a distributing corporation and a selling corporation. DS recognizes gain or loss on a distribution to PB whether the property is gain property or loss property (that is, Code Sec. 311(a) is repealed for all intercompany distributions). If the fair market value of the property (other than an obligation of DS) DS distributes to PB exceeds its adjusted basis, DS recognizes gain as if the property were sold at its fair market value.[65] By virtue of Reg. § 1.1502-13(f)(2)(iii), the principles of Code Sec. 311(b) apply to DS's loss, as well as gain, from an intercompany distribution of property. Thus, either DS's loss or its gain is taken into account under the matching rule, for example, if the property is subsequently sold to a nonmember. Code Sec. 311 (a) continues, however, to prevent recognition of loss on a distribution to a nonmember.

- *Treatment of PB.* Likewise, PB plays two roles when it receives property in an intercompany distribution. PB is both a distributee corporation and a buying corporation. The amount of the intercompany distribution is not included in the gross income of PB, provided that there is a corresponding negative adjustment reflected in PB's basis in its DS stock.[66] This is true without regard to whether the distribution would be a dividend (because DS has sufficient earnings and profits), a return of capital (because DS has insufficient earnings and profits but PB has sufficient basis in its DS stock), or gain (because the distribution exceeds PB's basis in its DS stock) under Code Sec. 301. A distribution in excess of PB's DS stock basis results in a negative basis, subject to later recapture under Reg. § 1.1502-19.

- *Entitlement rule.* An intercompany distribution is treated as taken into account when the shareholding member becomes entitled to it (generally on the record date).[67] For this purpose, PB is treated as entitled to a distribution no later than the time the distribution is taken into account under the Internal Revenue Code.

- *DS's obligations.* In keeping with Reg. § 1.301-1(d)(1)(ii), the IRS has ruled that the amount of a distribution of an obligation of DS (and PB's basis in such obligation) equals the obligation's value.[68]

---

[65] Code Sec. 311(b)(1).
[66] Reg. § 1.1502-13(f)(2)(ii).

[67] Reg. § 1.1502-13(f)(2)(iv).
[68] IRS Letter Ruling 8922056 (March 7, 1989).

¶545.02

Amount and basis of in-kind distributions. Prior to the 1988 amendment of Code Sec. 301, the amount and basis of property distributed to a domestic corporation under separate return rules was the lesser of the fair market value of the property or the adjusted basis (in the hands of the distributing corporation) of the property received, increased in the amount of gain recognized to the distributing corporation. The consolidated return regulations modified this treatment to provide that the amount and basis of any distribution of property other than money was the adjusted basis of the property, increased by any gain recognized by the distributing corporation on the distribution.

Code Sec. 301 was amended in 1988 to provide that the amount and basis of property distributed to any distributee is the fair market value of the property. This reflected the amendment of Code Sec. 311 requiring a distributing corporation to recognize gain, but not loss, on a distribution of property, thereby making the special consolidated return rule deadwood as applied to gain property. At some point it was realized that this change was not deadwood as applied to loss property (because the separate return rules stepped down the basis even though no loss was recognized). That is, in a consolidated return context, if basis were stepped *down* to fair market value as a result of an intercompany distribution, while at the same time Code Sec. 311(a) prevented the distributing member from recognizing the loss, then the loss would be permanently eliminated even though the property has not left the group. This, of course, contravenes the single-entity principle underlying Code Sec. 1502. To address this point, the legislative history of the 1988 amendment indicated that "certain portions of section 301 are repealed as deadwood . . . [footnote 31]." Footnote 31 provided, "[t]his change is made solely as deadwood and is not intended to alter the consequences of a distribution under the consolidated return regulations or any other provision of law or regulations."[69]

If the legislative history for the 1988 change in Code Sec. 301 was correct, reflecting the fact that no loss was recognized under Code Sec. 311(a) on an intercompany distribution, the amount and basis of property DS distributed to PB continued to be DS's adjusted basis in the property so that the basis was not stepped down to its fair market value and the loss was preserved. An example in Reg. § 1.1502-20(e)(3) reflected this interpretation.

As described above, new Reg. § 1.1502-13 resolves this conflict between statute and legislative history by turning off Code Sec. 311(a) and allowing DS to recognize loss, as well as gain, on an intercompany distribution. Thus, the amount and basis of property received in an intercompany distribution will be its fair market value, whether the property is gain or loss property.

Inapplicability of Code Sec. 304. In 1987, Code Sec. 304(b)(4) was enacted to combat the argument that an anomaly in the application of Code Sec. 304 to sales of stock between consolidated brother and sister corporations enabled the consolidated group to dispose of unwanted appreciated assets of a recently acquired member without recognition of gain.[70] Because of the complexity of the remedy for

---

[69] S. Rep. No. 445, at 62 (1988) (Report to the Technical Corrections Act of 1988).

[70] *See* L. Axelrod, Excess Loss Accounts and Other Consolidated Return Gallimaufry, 36 Tax Notes 729 (1987).

this transaction, Congress delegated to Treasury and the IRS the authority to make "appropriate adjustments" to the adjusted basis of any intragroup stock and to earnings and profits of any member to carry out the purposes of Code Sec. 304.

Treasury and the IRS concluded, however, that the purposes of Code Sec. 304(b)(4) could be realized and the complex basis and earnings and profits adjustments avoided if Code Sec. 304 were not applied to a sale of stock by one member of a consolidated group to another. To this end, Reg. § 1.1502-80(b) prevents Code Sec. 304 from applying to any acquisition of stock in an intercompany transaction.

Intercompany Code Sec. 351 transfers. Unlike the prior intercompany transaction system, which did not apply to a Code Sec. 351 transfer in which gain was not recognized, the current system applies to an intercompany Code Sec. 351 transfer, whether or not gain is recognized. As a consequence, S's activities may affect the attributes of B's corresponding items even if S has no intercompany item. (Because of the aggregation of stock under Reg. § 1.1502-34, Code Sec. 351 also might apply to an exchange between members that would not apply if separate return rules alone were applied.[71])

> *Example 19:* As an example of intercompany Code Sec. 351 transfer–no boot: S holds land with a $70 basis and a $100 fair market value for sale to customers in the ordinary course of business. On January 1 of Year 1, S transfers the land to B in exchange for all of the stock of B in a transaction to which Code Sec. 351 applies. S has no gain or loss under Code Sec. 351 (a), and its basis in the B stock is $70 under Code Sec. 358. Under Code Sec. 362(a), B's basis in the land is $70. B holds the land for investment. On July 1 of Year 3, B sells the land to nonmember X for $100. Assume that if S and B were divisions of a single corporation, B's gain from the sale would be ordinary income because of S's activities. S is treated as transferring the land in exchange for B's stock even though, if S and B were divisions of a single corporation, S could not own stock of B.[72] S has no intercompany item, but B's $30 gain from its sale of the land to X is a corresponding item because the land was acquired in an intercompany transaction. B's $30 gain is ordinary income that is taken into account under B's method of accounting.

> *Example 20:* As an example of intercompany Code Sec. 351 transfer– boot: The facts are the same as in the last example, except that S receives $10 cash in addition to the B stock in the transfer. S recognizes $10 of gain under Code Sec. 351(b), and its basis in the B stock is $70 under Code Sec. 358. Under Code Sec. 362(a), B's basis in the land is $80. S takes its $10 intercompany gain into account in Year 3 to reflect the $10 difference between B's $30 recomputed gain and B's $20 actual gain. Both S's $10 gain and B's $20 gain are ordinary income.

Inapplicability of Code Sec. 357(c). If the sum of the amount of liabilities assumed and taken subject to by the transferee corporation in a Code Sec. 351

---

[71] *See* Rev. Rul. 89-46, 1989-1 CB 272.

[72] Reg. § 1.1502-13(c)(3) and Reg. § 1.1502-13(c)(7)(ii), Example (3).

transfer (or in a Code Sec. 361 transfer pursuant to a "D" reorganization) exceeds the total adjusted basis of the property transferred pursuant to the exchange, under separate return rules Code Sec. 357(c) treats such excess as gain. Reg. § 1.1502-80(d)(1), however, prevents Code Sec. 357(c) from applying in an intercompany transaction, provided that there is no plan or arrangement to deconsolidate either the transferor or the transferee. Instead, under Code Sec. 358 the basis of the stock received in the transferee would have a negative basis, subject to recapture under Reg. § 1.1502-19.

Boot in Code Sec. 368 reorganizations. When P exchanges its stock in one consolidated subsidiary for stock and other property in another consolidated subsidiary pursuant to a reorganization of the subsidiaries described in Code Sec. 368, under Code Sec. 354 and Code Sec. 356, P recognizes its realized gain up to the amount of the other property (boot) received. To determine whether the gain recognized is a dividend or capital gain, the dividend equivalency standards of Code Sec. 302 are used. Specifically, after *D.E. Clark,*[73] the boot is treated as if received by P in a postreorganization redemption of P's stock in the acquiring corporation. When P actually or constructively owns all the stock of the acquiring corporation before and after the deemed redemption, for example, all of the boot is dividend equivalent. Code Sec. 356(a)(2), however, limits dividend treatment to the amount of P's "ratable share of the [accumulated] earnings and profits of the corporation." When, as in an intercompany transaction, both parties to the reorganization were commonly controlled by P, even before *Clark* the IRS's view was that the amount of the dividend is measured by the acquiring corporation's accumulated earnings and profits immediately after the reorganization, including those inherited from the acquired corporation under Code Sec. 381(c)(2).[74]

P's receipt of boot raised the following issues under the prior consolidated return regulations:

- Is P's disposition of its stock in the acquired corporation an intercompany transaction if the acquired corporation is no longer a member of the same group immediately after the transaction?

- If P is the selling member in an intercompany transaction, is the character of P's recognized gain as capital gain or dividend determined at the time of the transaction, or when the gain is restored? When is the deferred gain restored?

- If the Code Sec. 356 income would be a dividend under the normal Code Sec. 356(a)(2) rules and would be measured by the acquired corporation's consolidated earnings and profits for which P received a positive adjustment to the acquired corporation's stock under the investment basis adjustment system, would a negative basis adjustment to the acquiring corporation's stock be appropriate under the investment adjustment rules to reflect the "boot" dividend under Code Sec. 356(a)(2)?[75]

---

[73] *D.E. Clark*, SCt, 1989-1 USTC ¶ 9230, 489 US 726, 109 SCt 1455.

[74] *See* Rev. Rul. 70-240, 1970-1 CB 81.

[75] *See* Rev. Rul. 72-498, 1972-2 CB 516 (portion of "boot" dividend sourced to post-1965 earnings and profits reflected in P's basis in acquired corporation's stock was capital gain, not an eliminated dividend, presumably be-

¶545.02

Although there was no policy reason for not deferring any capital gain recognized in an intercompany transaction, the technical analysis supporting such treatment was not readily apparent.

Reg. § 1.1502-13 addresses these issues. Boot received as part of an intercompany reorganization that results in the application of Code Sec. 356 is treated as received in a separate transaction immediately *after* the transaction, provided that a party to the transaction does not become a member or nonmember as part of the same plan or arrangement.[76]

Boot in Code Sec. 355 distributions. Similar principles are applied to boot received as part of an intercompany transaction to which Code Sec. 355 would apply but for the receipt of the boot, except that the separate transaction is treated as occurring immediately *before* the transaction.

Issuer's acquisition of its own stock. If a member acquires its own stock, or an option to buy its own stock, in an intercompany transaction, the member's basis in that stock or option is eliminated.[77] Accordingly, S's intercompany items from the stock or options are taken into account if B acquires the stock or options in an intercompany transaction (unless, for example, B acquires the stock in exchange for successor property within the meaning of Reg. § 1.1502-13(j)(1) in a nonrecognition transaction).[78]

Transactions in common parent stock. Several rules apply to transactions with respect to the common parent's stock.

1. First, a distribution with respect to a member's stock is excluded from the distributee member's income only if, and to the extent that, a negative stock basis adjustment is required under the investment adjustment rules to the distributee's basis in the distributing member's stock.[79] Thus, because no negative basis adjustment is required for a distribution with respect to the stock of the common parent, any dividend received by a member with respect to common parent stock is not excluded from the distributee's income. Instead, the distributee is required to look to the dividends-received deduction rules of Reg. § 1.1502-26(b) for relief from double taxation. Reg. § 1.1502-26(b) currently provides that no dividends-received deduction is allowed with respect to dividends received by one member from another only to the extent not included in gross income under Reg. § 1.1502-13(f)(2).

   Example 21: As an example of dividend on common parent stock: S purchases 100 shares of P common stock in an open market transaction. Shortly after this purchase, P declares and pays a $10 dividend to S with

---

(Footnote Continued)

cause a negative adjustment for this dividend would not be required).

[76] Reg. § 1.1502-13(f)(3).

[77] Reg. § 1.1502-13(f)(4).

[78] For example, suppose S owns B common stock that has a basis of $70 and fair market value of $100. If that common stock is exchanged in a recapitalization de-

scribed in Reg. § 368(a)(1)(E) for B preferred stock that is worth $100, then S's $30 gain is not taken into account because the B preferred stock, having a Code Sec. 358 basis of $70, is successor property that permits S's $30 gain to be taken into account based on future events involving the B preferred stock.

[79] Reg. § 1.1502-13(f)(2)(ii).

¶545.02

respect to these shares. Because S is not required under Reg. § 1.1502-32(b)(2)(iv) to reduce its basis in the P shares by the amount of the $10 dividend, the dividend is not excluded from S's income. Suppose, however, the dividend is sourced under Code Sec. 316 to earnings and profits of P attributable to one or more tax years on each day that P and S are affiliated; in that case, S is entitled to a 100-percent dividends-received deduction for the $10 dividend under Code Sec. 243(b). Also, assuming the dividend is *not* attributable to earnings and profits that either (1) were earned during a period S was not a member of the P group, or (2) are derived from gain on property that accrued economically during the period the corporation holding the property was not a member of the P group,[80] the dividend will be a "qualifying dividend" for which S is not required to reduce its basis in its P stock under Code Sec. 1059(a).[81] Thus, as a general rule, the 100-percent dividends-received deduction allowed under Code Sec. 243(b) will provide S with the same benefit S would have had if the P dividend had been excluded under the consolidated return rule.

2. Second, the regulations radically alter the federal income tax consequences to S on a disposition of common parent P's stock:

   a. The principal rule is that no loss is allowed to S on a sale or other disposition of P stock. The disallowed loss, however, is nonetheless treated as a noncapital, nondeductible expense for which a negative adjustment to the S stock is required under Reg. § 1.1502-32.[82]

   b. To buttress the principal loss disallowance rule, a second rule provides that any deconsolidation of the P stock (whether through a deconsolidation of S or a transfer of the P stock outside the group in a nonrecognition transaction, such as a transfer to a partnership in a Code Sec. 721 exchange or a transfer to an unrelated corporation in a Code Sec. 351 exchange) requires a reduction in the basis of the P stock to the fair market value of the stock immediately before the deconsolidation. This basis reduction also is treated as a noncapital, nondeductible expense for which a negative adjustment to the basis of the S stock is required under Reg. § 1.1502-32.[83]

   c. Finally, a third rule affords S nonrecognition treatment in connection with *gain* on a sale of the P stock outside the group, provided (1) that S received the P stock from P in a Code Sec. 351 exchange or a contribution to capital; (2) that as part of the same plan, the P stock is disposed immediately outside the group; (3) that no nonmember receives a substituted basis in the stock; (4) that the P stock is not exchanged for P stock; and (5) that neither P nor S becomes or ceases to be a member of the group as part of the same plan.[84]

---

[80] *See* Code Sec. 1059(e)(2)(B).
[81] Code Sec. 1059(e)(2)(A).
[82] Code Sec. 1059(e)(2)(B).
[83] Reg. § 1.1502-13(f)(6)(i)(B).

[84] Reg. § 1.1502-13(f)(6)(ii). According to the Preamble to T.D. 8883, 2000-23 IRB 1154, Reg. § 1.1032-3 made Reg. § 1.1502-13(f)(6)(ii) superfluous because there should be no cases that would be subject to recast under the consolidated return regulation, but in which a member would "otherwise recognize gain" as required by the consoli-

¶ 555 Other (Nonproperty) Transactions

An *intercompany transaction* is a transaction between corporations that are members of the same consolidated group immediately after the transaction, and may include nonproperty transactions such as S's performance of services, licensing of technology, rental of property, loan of money to B, and B's payment or accrual of its expenditure for such items.[85]

.01 Timing of Selling Member's and Buying Member's Items

The general matching rule and the acceleration exception govern nonproperty transactions as well as property transactions. Again, the timing of B's corresponding item provides the starting point for applying these rules. Under the matching rule, B generally takes its corresponding item into account under its accounting method, and S takes its intercompany item into account to reflect the difference for the year between B's recomputed corresponding item (as if S and B were divisions of a single corporation) and B's corresponding item taken into account.[86] If an event occurs making it impossible to achieve single-entity treatment under the matching rule, however, S accelerates the timing of its intercompany item, and takes it into account immediately before such event (and before B takes its corresponding item into account under its own accounting method).

.02 Other Attributes—Matching Rule

Under the matching rule, the separate-entity attributes of S's intercompany items and B's corresponding items are generally redetermined to the extent necessary to produce the same effect on consolidated taxable income (and consolidated tax liability) as if S and B were divisions of a single corporation, and as if the intercompany transaction were between divisions (except that the attributes of B's corresponding items govern to the extent that they offset S's intercompany items). The specific attribute rules for nonproperty transactions, which vary depending on whether S's and B's items offset in amount, are the same as those for property transactions described in ¶ 515.

> **Example 22:** As an example of performance of services: S designs and constructs a machine for use in B's business. During Year 1, S incurs $80 of expenses (for example, for employees and equipment) and charges B $100 for its services. B capitalizes its $100 cost for the machine under Code Sec. 263 and takes into account $10 of cost recovery deductions in each of Years 2 through 11. Under its separate method of accounting, S would take its income and expenses into account in Year 1. If S and B were divisions of a single corporation, the costs incurred would be capitalized.

Amounts. S's $100 of income and $80 of related expenses are both included in determining its intercompany income of $20. B's $10 of cost recovery deductions each year are its corresponding items.

(Footnote Continued)

dated return regulation. Accordingly, the effective date paragraph of the consolidated return regulation was modified to limit the applicability of the consolidated return regulation to periods before the effective date of Reg. § 1.1032-3.

[85] Reg. § 1.1502-13(b)(1)(i).

[86] Reg. § 1.1502-13(c)(2).

Timing. B takes its $10 cost recovery deduction each year under its method of accounting. In Year 1, S takes into account $80 of its income and the $80 of expenses. In each of Years 2 through 11, S takes $2 of its $20 intercompany income into account to reflect the annual $2 difference between B's $8 of recomputed cost-recovery deductions (based on the $80 basis B would have if S and B were divisions of a single corporation and B's basis were determined by reference to S's $80 of expenses) and B's $10 of cost-recovery deductions taken into account.

Other attributes. Because S's $80 income inclusion and $80 of expenses for Year 1 and B's cost-recovery deductions are ordinary on a separate return basis, it is not necessary to redetermine the character of those items. For Years 2 through 11, B's $2 of excess annual depreciation deduction offsets S's $2 annual income inclusion, and hence requires the treatment of that intercompany item as ordinary.[87]

Example 23: As an example of rental of property: B operates a ranch that requires grazing land for its cattle. B owns undeveloped land adjoining B's ranch. On January 1 of Year 1, S leases grazing rights to B for Year 1. B's $100 rent expense is deductible for Year 1 under its separate method of accounting.

Amounts. S's $100 of rental income is its intercompany item. B's $100 of rent expense is its corresponding item.

Timing. B takes its $100 rent expense into account in Year 1 under its method of accounting. S takes its $100 of income into account in Year 1 to reflect the $100 difference between B's $0 recomputed rental deduction and B's $100 rental deduction taken into account.

Other attributes. Because S's income is offset by B's ordinary deductions, both items are ordinary.

The acceleration exception. If S's intercompany item is accelerated and is not from a property transaction, S's attributes are determined on a separate-entity basis,[88] B's attributes are redetermined under the same rules as for property transactions.

¶ 565 Member Obligations

The general matching rule of Reg. § 1.1502-13(c) and the acceleration rule of Reg. § 1.1502-13(d) apply to the payment or accrual of interest, original issue discount, or premium under Code Sec. 171.[89] Reg. § 1.1502-13(g) imposes additional special deemed satisfaction and reissuance rules that are among the most complex provisions of the consolidated return regulations. These provisions apply to an "intercompany obligation," simply defined as an obligation between members, but only for the period during which both parties are members.[90]

---

[87] *See* Reg. § 1.1502-13(c)(7)(ii), Example 7.
[88] *See* Reg. § 1.1502-13(d)(1)(ii)(B).

[89] *See* Reg. § 1.1502-13(b)(1), Reg. § 1.1502-13(g)(1), and Reg. § 1.1502-13(g)(5), Example 1.
[90] Reg. § 1.1502-13(g)(2)(ii).

.01 General Deemed Satisfaction and Reissuance Rule

Generally, if a member realizes an amount (other than zero) of income, gain, deduction, or loss, directly or indirectly, from the assignment or extinguishment of all or part of its remaining *rights or obligations* under an intercompany obligation, the intercompany obligation is treated for all federal income tax purposes as satisfied, and, if it remains outstanding, reissued.[91] Similar principles apply if an intercompany obligation becomes an obligation that is not an intercompany obligation.[92] Numerous special rules apply to determine the amount satisfied (e.g., the obligation's fair market value or its stated amount)[93] and to the reissuance.[94] Perhaps the most important of these is that any gain or loss from an intercompany obligation is not subject to Code Sec. 108(a), Code Sec. 354, or Code Sec. 1091.[95] Among other exceptions, these rules do not apply to the amount realized from the "conversion" of an obligation into stock of the obligor (i.e., they do not apply to debt that is convertible by its terms)[96] and they generally do not apply if treating the obligation as satisfied and reissued will not have a significant effect on any person's federal income tax liability for any year.[97]

Because of the complexity of the regulations, an example is worth a thousand words. The following are the two simple examples from the regulations illustrating the general deemed satisfaction and reissuance rule:

> **Example 24:** [98]
>
> *Intercompany debt becomes nonintercompany debt.*
>
> (a) *Facts.* On January 1 of Year 1, B borrows $100 from S in return for B's note providing for $10 of interest annually at the end of each year, and repayment of $100 at the end of Year 20. As of January 1 of Year 3, B has paid the interest accruing under the note and S sells B's note to X for $70, reflecting a change in the value of the note as a result of increases in prevailing market interest rates. B is never insolvent within the meaning of Code Sec. 108(d)(3).
>
> (b) *Deemed satisfaction.* Under Reg. § 1.1502-13(g)(3), B's note is treated as satisfied for $70 immediately before S's sale to X. As a result of the deemed satisfaction of the obligation for less than its adjusted issue price, B takes into account $30 of discharge of indebtedness income under Code Sec. 61(a)(12). On a separate entity basis, S's $30 loss would be a capital loss under Code Sec. 1271(a)(1). Under the matching rule, however, the attributes of S's intercompany item and B's corresponding item must be redetermined to produce the same effect as if the transaction had occurred between divisions of a single corporation. B's corresponding item completely offsets S's intercompany item in amount. Accordingly, under Reg. § 1.1502-13(c)(4)(i), the attributes of B's $30 of discharge of indebtedness income control the attributes of S's loss. Thus, S's loss is treated as ordinary loss.
>
> (c) *Deemed reissuance.* Under Reg. § 1.1502-13(g)(3), B is also treated as reissuing directly to X, a new note with a $70 issue price and a $100 stated redemption price at maturity. The new note is not an intercompany obligation, it has a $70 issue price and $100 stated redemption price at maturity, and the $30 of original

---

[91] Reg. § 1.1502-13(g)(3)(i)(A).
[92] Reg. § 1.1502-13(g)(3)(i)(A).
[93] Reg. § 1.1502-13(g)(3)(ii).
[94] Reg. § 1.1502-13(g)(3)(iii).

[95] Reg. § 1.1502-13(g)(3)(ii)(B)(2).
[96] Reg. § 1.1502-13(g)(3)(i)(B)(3).
[97] Reg. § 1.1502-13(g)(3)(i)(B)(4).
[98] Reg. § 1.1502-13(g)(5), Example 2.

issue discount will be taken into account by B and X under Code Sec. 163(e) and Code Sec. 1272.

(d) *Creditor deconsolidation.* The facts are the same as in paragraph (a) of this Example, except that P sells S's stock to X (rather than S's selling the note of B). Under Reg. § 1.1502-13(g)(3), the note is treated as satisfied by B for its $70 fair market value immediately before S becomes a nonmember, and B is treated as reissuing a new note to S immediately after S becomes a nonmember. The results for S's $30 of loss and B's discharge of indebtedness income are the same as in paragraph (b) of this Example. The new note is not an intercompany obligation, it has a $70 issue price and $100 stated redemption price at maturity, and the $30 of original issue discount will be taken into account by B and S under Code Sec. 163(e) and Code Sec. 1272.

(e) *Debtor deconsolidation.* The facts are the same as in paragraph (a) of this Example, except that P sells B's stock to X (rather than S's selling the note of B). The results are the same as in paragraph (d) of this Example.

(f) *Appreciated note.* The facts are the same as in paragraph (a) of this Example, except that S sells B's note to X for $130 (rather than $70), reflecting a decline in prevailing market interest rates. Under Reg. § 1.1502-13(g)(3), B's note is treated as satisfied for $130 immediately before S's sale of note to X. Under Reg. § 1.163-7(c), B takes into account $30 of repurchase premium. On a separate entity basis, S's $30 gain would be a capital gain under Code Sec. 1271(a)(1), and B's $30 premium deduction would be an ordinary deduction. Under the matching rule, however, the attributes of S's intercompany item and B's corresponding item must be redetermined to produce the same effect as if the transaction had occurred between divisions of a single corporation. Under Reg. § 1.1502-13(c)(4)(i), the attributes of B's corresponding premium deduction control the attributes of S's intercompany gain. Accordingly, S's gain is treated as ordinary income. B is also treated as reissuing a new note directly to X, which is not an intercompany obligation. The new note has a $130 issue price and a $100 stated redemption price at maturity. Under Reg. § 1.61-12(c), B's $30 premium income under the new note is taken into account over the life of the new note.

Example 25: [99]

Loss or bad debt deduction with respect to intercompany debt.

(a) *Facts.* On January 1 of Year 1, B borrows $100 from S in return for B's note providing for $10 of interest annually at the end of each year, and repayment of $100 at the end of Year 5. In Year 3, S sells B's note to P for $60. B is never insolvent within the meaning of Code Sec. 108(d)(3). Assume B's note is not a security within the meaning of Code Sec. 165(g)(2).

(b) *Deemed satisfaction and reissuance.* Under Reg. § 1.1502-13(g)(3), B is treated as satisfying its note for $60 immediately before the sale, and reissuing a new note directly to P with a $60 issue price and a $100 stated redemption price at maturity. On a separate entity basis, S's $40 loss would be a capital loss, and B's $40 of income would be ordinary income. Under the matching rule, however, the attributes of S's intercompany item and B's corresponding item must be redetermined to produce the same effect as if the transaction had occurred between divisions of a single corporation. Under Reg. § 1.1502-13(c)(4)(i), the attributes of B's corresponding discharge of indebtedness income control the attributes of S's intercompany loss. Accordingly, S's loss is treated as ordinary loss.

---

[99] Reg. § 1.1502-13(g)(5), Example 3.

(c) *Partial bad debt deduction.* The facts are the same as in paragraph (a) of this Example, except that S claims a $40 partial bad debt deduction under Code Sec. 166(a)(2) (rather than selling the note to P). The results are the same as in paragraph (b) of this Example. B's note is treated as satisfied and reissued with a $60 issue price. S's $40 intercompany deduction and B's $40 corresponding income are both ordinary.

(d) *Insolvent debtor.* The facts are the same as in paragraph (a) of this Example, except that B is insolvent with the meaning of Code Sec. 108(d)(3) at the time that S sells the note to P. On a separate entity basis, S's $40 loss would be capital, B's $40 income would be excluded from gross income under Code Sec. 108(a), and B would reduce attributes under Code Sec. 108(b) or Code Sec. 1017. However, under Reg. § 1.1502-13(g)(3)(ii)(B), Code Sec. 108(a) does not apply to B's income to characterize it as excluded from gross income. Accordingly, the attributes of S's intercompany loss and B's corresponding income are redetermined in the same manner as in paragraph (b) of this Example.

These "simple" examples from the regulations are helpful in resolving more complex examples. Consider the following:

Example 26: Distribution of intercompany obligation. P keeps track of cash for the P group. In Year 1, S, a cash cow, loaned P $400 million in exchange for a P note. In Year 5, S distributes its P note to P when the value of the note is $380 million.

The deemed satisfaction and reissuance rule causes the P note to be deemed satisfied by P for $380 million immediately before the distribution of the note to P. Thus, P recognizes $20 million of discharge of indebtedness income, and S recognizes a $20 million loss. Under the rules discussed in the second example of the regulations set forth above, both the income and the loss are ordinary. Then, S is treated as distributing to P the $380 million of retirement proceeds.

Example 27: Contribution to capital of debtor. P is the parent of two first tier subsidiaries, S1 and S2. P's original stock basis in S2 was $250. P also loaned S2 $400, and S1 loaned S2 $350. Having lost almost everything, S2 had a net operating loss of $1,000, all of which was absorbed by other members of the P group. Thus, P's S2 stock basis was reduced under the investment adjustment rules of Reg. § 1.1502-32 to an excess loss account (ELA) of $750. S2 is now insolvent as a result of the intercompany debt owed to both P and S1—it has only minimal assets. The group plans to dissolve S2, but prior to doing so, the intercompany debt owed by S2 to both P and S1 will be canceled.

Although canceling S2's $400 debt to P immediately before the dissolution probably would be disregarded as a circular flow of funds under Rev. Rul. 68-602, 1968-2 CB 135, S1's cancellation of the $350 loan to S2 is not circular. Because S2 has only minimal assets, S1 must cancel the $350 loan if P is to avoid becoming responsible for the debt. Although S1's cancellation might be viewed as for the benefit of P, because the debt has little or no value, S1's cancellation of the debt probably should be viewed as writing it off rather than disposing of its creditor's interest indirectly through P.

¶565.01

So viewed, S1's cancellation of the debt should be governed by Reg. § 1.1502-13(g)(5), Example 3 [Example 25 above]. In keeping with that Example, S2 should be treated as satisfying the $350 debt for its $0 fair market value immediately before the cancellation, and Code Sec. 108(a) should not apply. Thus, S2 should have $350 of discharge of indebtedness income, and (because the character of S2's income controls the character of S1's deduction), S1 should have a $350 ordinary deduction. Under the investment adjustment rules of Reg. § 1.1502-32, this decreases P's S2 ELA to $400, and decreases P's S1 stock basis by $350.

This leaves P with a $400 creditor's interest and $400 ELA in S2. As described above, P's contribution of its $400 creditor's interest to S2 probably would be ignored under Rev. Rul. 68-602. Then upon the dissolution of S2 into P, Reg. § 1.1502-13(g)(3) should apply again. Under that regulation, P's $400 debt should be deemed satisfied for its $0 fair market value immediately before the dissolution. Under the same analysis as above, Sub 2 should have $400 of discharge of indebtedness income, and P should have a $400 ordinary deduction. This would eliminate P's S2 ELA to zero.

After the "marking to market" of the intercompany obligation there is no value left to effect the dissolution of S2.

Indeed, because the general deemed satisfaction and reissuance rule comes into play whenever either the debtor or creditor *realizes* an amount (other than zero) on an intercompany obligation, an intercompany obligation is effectively "marked to market" with offsetting income to the debtor and deduction or loss to the creditor immediately before almost any intercompany transaction involving the intercompany obligation.

.02 Deemed Satisfaction and Reissuance of Obligations Becoming Intercompany Obligations

The regulations contain a second deemed satisfaction and reissuance rule for nonintercompany obligations becoming intercompany obligations.[100] Under this rule, if an obligation that is not an intercompany obligation becomes an intercompany obligation:

1. Code Sec. 108(e)(4) does not apply. (Note: Unlike the general deemed satisfaction and reissuance rule, Code Sec. 108(a) generally can apply if the debtor member is insolvent.)

2. The debt is treated for all Federal income tax purposes, immediately *after* it becomes an intercompany debt, as satisfied and a new debt issued to the holder (with a new holding period) in an amount determined under principles of Reg. § 1.108-2(f).

3. The attributes of all items taken into account from the satisfaction are determined on a separate entity basis, rather than by treating S and B as divisions of a single corporation.

---

[100] Reg. § 1.1502-13(g)(4).

4. Any intercompany gain or loss taken into account is treated as not subject to Code Sec. 354 or Code Sec. 1091.

5. Solely for purposes of Reg. § 1.1502-32(b)(4) and the effect of any election under that provision, any loss taken into account under this rule by a corporation that becomes a member as a result of the transaction in which the obligation becomes an intercompany obligation is treated as a loss carryover from a separate return limitation year, and therefore the loss can be waived before entry into the group.

Like the general deemed satisfaction and reissuance rule, this second rule does not apply if treating the obligation as satisfied and reissued will not have a significant effect on any person's Federal income tax liability for any year.[101]

Again, the regulations provide an important example to illustrate the application of this second deemed satisfaction and reissuance rule:

> **Example 28:** [102]
>
> *Nonintercompany debt becomes intercompany debt.*
>
> (a) *Facts.* On January 1 of Year 1, B borrows $100 from X in return for B's note providing for $10 of interest annually at the end of each year, and repayment of $100 at the end of Year 5. As of January 1 of Year 3, B has fully performed its obligations, but the note's fair market value is $70. On January 1 of Year 3, P buys all of X's stock. B is solvent within the meaning of Code Sec. 108(d)(3).
>
> (b) *Deemed satisfied and reissuance.* Under Reg. § 1.1501-13(g)(4), B is treated as satisfying its indebtedness for $70 (determined under the principles of Reg. § 1.108-2(f)(2)) immediately after X becomes a member. Both X's $30 capital loss under Code Sec. 1271(a)(1) and B's $30 of discharge of indebtedness income under Code Sec. 61(a)(12) are taken into account in determining consolidated taxable income for Year 3. Under Reg. § 1.1502-13(g)(4)(ii)(C), the attributes of items resulting from the satisfaction are determined on a separate entity basis. But see section Code Sec. 382 and Reg. § 1.1502-15 (as appropriate). B is also treated as reissuing a new note. The new note is an intercompany obligation, it has a $70 issue price and $100 stated redemption price at maturity, and the $30 of original issue discount will be taken into account by B and X in the same manner as provided in paragraph (c) of Example 1 of Reg. § 1.1502-13(g)(5).
>
> (c) *Election to file consolidated returns.* Assume instead that B borrows $100 from S during Year 1, but the P group does not file consolidated returns until Year 3. Under Reg. § 1.1502-13(g)(4), B's indebtedness is treated as satisfied and a new note reissued immediately after the debt becomes intercompany debt. The satisfaction and reissuance are deemed to occur on January 1 of Year 3, for the fair market value of the note (determined under the principles of Reg. § 1.108-2(f)(2) at that time.)

The interaction of the two deemed satisfaction and reissuance rules is illustrated in this final example:

> **Example 29:** *Distribution of obligation that becomes an intercompany obligation and subsequent contribution of obligation to debtor.* Foreign Holdings owns all the stock of U.S. Parent and Foreign Sister. U.S. Parent owns all the stock of U.S. Sub. U.S. Parent and U.S. Sub file a consolidated return. Foreign

---

[101] Reg. § 1.1502-13(g)(4)(i)(B)(2).   [102] Reg. § 1.1502-13(g)(5), Example 4.

¶565.02

Sister holds a note of U.S. Sub that was originally issued for $20 million, but that is now worth only $3 million. Foreign Sister will cancel the note at the direction of Foreign Parent. U.S. Sub is insolvent, within the meaning of Code Sec. 108(d)(3), by more than $17 million. U.S. Sub has no tax attributes to reduce.

Assume the U.S. Sub note should be treated as first distributed by Foreign Sister to Foreign Holdings, then contributed by Foreign Holdings to U.S. Parent, and finally contributed by U.S. Parent to U.S. Sub. Assume also that, upon the distribution of the U.S. Sub note by Foreign Sister to Foreign Holdings, Foreign Holdings takes a $3 million basis in the note under Code Sec. 301(d).

Under the second deemed satisfaction and reissuance rule, the U.S. Sub note is "marked to market" immediately after the note is contributed by Foreign Holdings to U.S. Parent. Because U.S. Parent inherits Foreign Holdings' $3 million basis under Code Sec. 362, it has no loss from the marking. Because of its insolvency, U.S. Sub excludes from gross income under Code Sec. 108(a) the $17 million of discharge of indebtedness income that it recognizes. Because U.S. Sub has no tax attributes to reduce, U.S. Parent does not increase its basis in U.S. Sub stock as a result of the discharge of indebtedness.[103]

U.S. Sub is deemed to reissue a new note to U.S. Parent with a $3 million issue price. U.S. Parent's subsequent contribution of the new note to U.S. Sub should not be subject to the general deemed satisfaction and reissuance rule because a deemed satisfaction for $3 million would not have a significant effect on any person's federal income tax liability for any year. Thus, the only effect of the cancellation of the note is that U.S. Parent increases its basis of its U.S. Sub stock by $3 million.

¶ 575 Other Rules

Some other rules to keep in mind include timing rules as a method of accounting, an anti-avoidance rule, an election to deconsolidate and request to report intercompany gains on separate-entity basis, and effective date rules.

.01 Timing Rules as a Method of Accounting

The timing rules of Reg. § 1.1502-13 are treated as a method of accounting, to be applied by each member in addition to the member's other methods of accounting, and control, if there is an inconsistency with such other methods.[104] For example, if S sells property to B in exchange for B's note, the timing rules of Reg. § 1.1502-13 apply to S instead of the accrual method or installment sale rules.

A member's ability to change its manner of applying the intercompany transaction regulations is subject to the generally applicable rules for accounting method

---

[103] For a risk that the IRS would require other members of the U.S. Parent group to reduce their tax attributes, *see* Field Service Advice 199912007, December 14, 1998, and Chief Counsel Advice 200149008, August 10, 2001; query how the investment adjustment rules should apply if the IRS were to prevail.

[104] Reg. § 1.1502-13(a)(3)(i) and Reg. § 1.446-1(c)(2)(iii).

changes. To reduce potential administrative burdens, Reg. §1.1502-13(a)(3)(ii) generally provides automatic consent under Code Sec. 446(e) to the extent to which changes in method are required solely by reason of the timing rules of Reg. §1.1502-13 applying to a member for the first time (as a result of the effective date of the regulations or a member entering a group) or no longer applying to a member (because of a member leaving a group). The changes under this automatic consent will generally be effected on a cut-off basis.[105] For example, for a member joining a group, the new method (that is, application of Reg. §1.1502-13) will apply to intercompany transactions occurring on or after the first day of the consolidated return year for which the change is effective.

.02 Anti-Avoidance Rule

If a transaction is entered into or structured with a primary purpose of avoiding the purposes of Reg. §1.1502-13 (for example, attempting to avoid intercompany transaction treatment), the regulations authorize the IRS to make adjustments so that the purposes of Reg. §1.1502-13 will indeed be carried out.[106] According to Reg. §1.1502-13(a)(1), the general purpose of Reg. §1.1502-13 is to provide rules to clearly reflect the taxable income (and tax liability) of the group as a whole by preventing intercompany transactions from creating, accelerating, avoiding, or deferring consolidated taxable income (or consolidated tax liability). As illustrated in the examples set forth in the regulations, Treasury and the IRS interpret this anti-avoidance rule quite broadly.

.03 Election to Deconsolidate and Request to Report Intercompany Gains on Separate-Entity Basis

Reg. §1.1502-75(c)(ii) authorizes the Commissioner to grant all groups, or groups in a particular class, permission to discontinue filing consolidated returns if any provision of the Code or regulations has been amended and the amendment could have a substantial adverse effect relative to the filing of separate returns.

Reg. §1.1502-13(e)(3) continues the procedure whereby the common parent may request consent from the IRS to report intercompany transactions on a separate-entity basis. Any such consent, however, does not apply to losses.[107] The rules for obtaining this consent are set forth in Rev. Proc. 97-49, 1997-43 IRB 22.

.04 Effective Dates

Unlike the investment adjustment rules, which apply retroactively for purposes of determining the adjustments to a member's stock in connection with stock transactions occurring in consolidated return years beginning after January 1, 1995, the intercompany transaction rules are prospective, generally applying only to a transaction occurring in a year beginning on or after July 11, 1995.[108] Numerous special rules apply that need to be considered.

Example 30: As an example of the meaning of a transaction under the effective date rules: S sold property to B in 1994 and recognized a gain that was

---

[105] Reg. §1.1502-13(a)(3)(ii)(B).
[106] Reg. §1.1502-13(h)(1).

[107] *See* Reg. §1.267(f)-1(a)(2)(iii).
[108] Reg. §1.1502-13(1)(1).

deferred under the prior intercompany transaction system. Do the old or current rules govern when S takes its deferred gain into account?

Reg. § 1.1502-13(l)(1) contains an example that provides that if S's and B's items from S's sale of property to B occur in a consolidated return year beginning before July 12, 1995, they are taken into account under prior law, even though B may dispose of the property in a consolidated return year beginning on or after July 12, 1995.

¶ 585 Conclusions

Reg. § 1.1502-13 embodies the intercompany transaction system with respect to intercompany property and nonproperty transactions as well as Reg. § 1.267(f)-1 with respect to sales of loss property among members of the controlled group.

The purpose of Reg. § 1.1502-13 is to clearly reflect the taxable income (and tax liability) of the group as a whole by preventing intercompany transactions from creating, accelerating, avoiding, or deferring consolidated taxable income (or consolidated tax liability).

The general standard by which this clear reflection of income policy is measured is that of a single corporation conducting its business through divisions. For property transactions, this is accomplished by matching the timing of both the buying member's and selling member's items. Specifically, the buying member's accounting method is used to control the timing of both the buying member's and selling member's items. When such a "matching" rule will not achieve single-entity treatment, an "acceleration rule" is substituted to determine timing.

Separate-entity treatment is preserved, however, for determining the amount and location of each member's items related to an intercompany transaction. For example, a selling member determines its gain or loss on a sale of property to another member on a separate-entity basis, and a buying member takes a cost basis in the property. This allows each party to retain a separate tax history for determining stock basis adjustments, earnings and profits, and other matters.

Various rules provide for single-entity results, whenever possible, for other attributes (for example, character, source, and status under Code Sec. 382(h) as built-in gain or loss), depending, for example, on the operative timing rule and whether the selling member's and buying member's items offset each other.

Losses from sales or exchanges of property between related corporations are taken into account in the same manner as is provided in the timing provisions (not the attribute redetermination provisions) of Reg. § 1.1502-13, except that the provisions are applied to a larger "controlled group." The regulations also require loss disallowance similar to Code Sec. 267(a), when B transfers loss property to a nonmember related party.

Other special rules apply to member stock and member obligations.

¶ 595 Frequently Asked Questions

Question

How is single-entity treatment achieved on intercompany transactions?

Answer

Generally under a "matching rule," S matches B's *timing* by taking its intercompany item into account for the same year that B takes its corresponding item into account. Because of the possibility that B may recover its basis in the property in increments, for each consolidated return year, S takes into account the difference between the following:

- The corresponding item that B would take into account if S and B were divisions of a single corporation and the intercompany transaction were between those divisions; and

- The corresponding item that B actually takes into account under its accounting method.

Question

What traps for the unwary in the intercompany transaction rules should a tax executive be apprised of?

Answer

Given the single-entity policy underlying most of the consolidated return regulations, consolidated groups are frequently surprised to learn that S's intercompany gain on a sale or distribution of member stock will be taken into account when, for example, the transferred member later is liquidated into B under Code Sec. 332 or is spun off to P under Code Sec. 355, or the transferred member's assets are treated as sold by way of a Code Sec. 338(h)(10) election. In effect, double-taxation of the outside and inside gain arises because the outside stock gain becomes locked in by the intercompany transaction before the transferred member's assets are sold (that is, outside gain is taken into account before inside gain). As discussed at ¶ 545.01, only limited relief is available to prevent such double taxation. Therefore, be wary.

Reg. § 1.1502-80 also contains a number of special rules that should not be overlooked. For example, it repeals Code Sec. 304 and Code Sec. 357(c) for intercompany transactions.

Chapter 6

Loss and Credit Limitation Systems

¶ 601 Overview—Loss and Credit Limitation Systems

Reg. § 1.1502-91 through Reg. § 1.1502-96 (consolidated Code Sec. 382 rules for net operating loss (NOL) carryovers) and Reg. § 1.1502-21(c) and Reg. § 1.1502-21(f) through Reg. § 1.1502-21(h) (separate return limitation year (SRLY) rules for NOL carryovers and carrybacks) and Reg. § 1.1502-15 (SRLY rules for built-in losses) were adopted in 1999 to replace the prior consolidated limitations on use of NOL carryovers and carrybacks.[1] Similar rules, discussed at ¶ 645, were adopted in 2000 to govern credits. Because the consolidated return loss and credit limitation systems defy summarization in their entirety, this chapter is by necessity selective. Although these rules are inordinately complex, not all the rules are commonly encountered. To make the study of this subject a manageable task, this chapter focuses on the framework of the loss and credit limitation systems and assumes away a number of complexities that are not often encountered. Specifically, the focus is on loss and credit corporations and related affiliates that leave one consolidated group and join another consolidated group in a transaction that constitutes an ownership change under the consolidated return Code Sec. 382

---

[1] The new consolidated Code Sec. 382 rules are generally effective for any testing date on or after June 25, 1999 (Reg. § 1.1502-99(a)). Reg. § 1.1502-94 through Reg. § 1.1502-96 also apply to a corporation that becomes a member of a group or ceases to be a member of a group (or loss subgroup) on any date on or after June 25, 1999 (Reg. § 1.1502-99(a)). Reg. § 1.1502-21 generally applies to tax years for which the due date (without extensions) of the consolidated return is after June 25, 1999 (Reg. § 1.1502-21(h)(1)). Reg. § 1.1502-15 generally applies to built-in losses recognized in tax years for which the due date (without extensions) of the consolidated return is after August 25, 1999 (Reg. § 1.1502-15(h)(1)). Numerous special effective dates also must be considered.

rules.[2] However, in ¶ 635, commonly encountered situations are addressed, namely tax-free asset acquisitions of a new loss member or new loss subgroup parent, for which the regulations curiously provide virtually no guidance. After learning the framework provided in this chapter, the reader should be able to tackle fact patterns with other variables.

.01 Code Sec. 382 Limitation and Elimination of Separate Return Limitation Year (SRLY) Limitation for Most New Loss Members and Loss Subgroups Joining a Consolidated Group

Reg. § 1.1502-21(a) provides that the consolidated net operating loss (NOL) deduction for any consolidated return year is the aggregate of the net operating loss carryovers and carrybacks to the year, including any net operating losses of members arising in separate return years carried over or back to the consolidated return year. When a corporation ceases to be a member of a consolidated group, NOL carryovers attributable to the corporation are first carried to the consolidated return year, and only the amount so attributable that is not absorbed by the group in that year is carried to the corporation's first separate return year.

Reg. § 1.1502-91 through Reg. § 1.1502-93 deal with ownership changes of "loss groups" and "loss subgroups," and Reg. § 1.1502-94 deals with ownership changes of "new loss members." An ownership change of a "loss group" would typically occur when a consolidated group with an NOL carryover arising in a consolidated return year of that group (more precisely, a "non-SRLY NOL") is acquired by someone other than a member of another consolidated group.[3] In that event, Code Sec. 382 is applied on a single-entity basis. That is, whether there is an ownership change is determined with respect to changes in ownership of the common parent of the loss group, and the value of the common parent is used to determine the Code Sec. 382 limitation.

More typically, however, one member of a consolidated group acquires one or more members of another consolidated group with an NOL carryover. Then the issue is whether there is an ownership change of a "loss subgroup" (defined in Reg. § 1.1502-91(d)(1)) or a "new loss member" (defined in Reg. § 1.1502-94(a)(1)).[4] If a loss subgroup is acquired, single-entity concepts are used to determine whether there is an ownership change and the amount of the Code Sec. 382 limitation. If a new loss member is acquired, separate-entity concepts are applied. These definitions and concepts are illustrated in ¶ 615.

---

[2] The discussion and the examples in this chapter generally assume, unless otherwise stated, that (1) each corporation is a member of a consolidated group; (2) each consolidated group and each acquired corporation files its return on a calendar year basis; (3) any acquisition occurs on the last day of the tax year of all parties; (4) each acquisition is of 100 percent of the acquired corporation's stock or assets; (5) each acquisition results in an ownership change; (6) the acquired corporation and its affiliates have no net unrealized built-in gain or loss; (7) no corporation has minority shareholders; (8) each corporation is owned directly or indirectly only by public groups; (9) the new loss member or loss subgroup has only one loss or credit carryover; (10) the larger corpora-

tion always acquires the smaller corporation so there is no reverse acquisition; (11) no ownership change of a loss group occurs as a result of the fold-in rules of Reg. § 1.1502-96(a); (12) any contributions to capital that literally violate the anti-stuffing rule of Code Sec. 382(l)(1) would not result in a reduction in the Code Sec. 382 limitation because they are protected by the legislative history set forth in H.R. CONF. REP. NO. 841, at 189 (1986) (see footnote 24 at ¶ 615); and (13) neither Code Sec. 269, Code Sec. 384, nor any anti-avoidance rules would apply.

[3] See Reg. § 1.1502-92(b)(2), Example 1.

[4] See Reg. § 1.1502-92(b)(2), Example 4(ii) and Reg. § 1.1502-95(d)(3), Examples 3 and 4.

.02 SRLY Limitation

Under Reg. § 1.1502-21(c), when the SRLY limitation applies to an NOL, the aggregate of the NOL carryovers and carrybacks of a member arising in separate return limitation years (as defined in Reg. § 1.1502-1(f)) that are included in consolidated NOL deductions may not exceed the consolidated taxable income for all consolidated return years of the consolidated group determined by reference to only the member's taxable income. If previously affiliated members join the consolidated group at the same time as the member with an NOL carryover, the loss corporation and the joining members may constitute a SRLY subgroup, and the SRLY limitation applies to the SRLY subgroup. Similar rules apply to an NOL carryback.

Regulations issued in 1999 generally eliminate the SRLY limitation for tax years for which the due date (without extensions) of the consolidated return is after June 25, 1999, where there is an overlap with the Code Sec. 382 limitation (even if the new loss member or loss subgroup was acquired before the effective date of the SRLY regulations). However, there are traps for the unwary, because the overlap rule only applies if the members of any Code Sec. 382 loss subgroup are members of the SRLY subgroup and vice versa. For example, if brother and sister corporations are acquired from another consolidated group, and one or both corporations have an NOL carryover, the SRLY limitation is eliminated only if an election is made under the consolidated Code Sec. 382 regulations to treat the brother and sister corporations as a Code Sec. 382 loss subgroup. This is illustrated at ¶ 625, Example 1.

.03 Successive Ownership Changes and Restructuring of Loss Subgroup

After an ownership change of a new loss member or a loss subgroup because of its acquisition by a consolidated group, close attention must be paid to Reg. § 1.1502-94 (new loss member) and Reg. § 1.1502-95 (loss subgroup) if there is a second ownership change or the loss subgroup is restructured. If there are successive ownership changes, the lesser of the two Code Sec. 382 limitations applies. Further, apportionment of a subgroup Code Sec. 382 limitation must be considered if one or more, but not all, members cease to be members of the subgroup. For example, if, after the first ownership change of a loss subgroup, the stock of a member of a loss subgroup is purchased by a second consolidated group, not only is there ordinarily a second Code Sec. 382 limitation if the departing member still has part of the NOL carryover it had when it came into the first group, but the first Code Sec. 382 limitation is reduced to zero for the departing member if the common parent of the first consolidated group does not apportion part or all of the first Code Sec. 382 limitation to it. These traps for the unwary are illustrated at ¶ 625.

.04 Miscellaneous Consolidated Return Net Operating Loss (NOL) Utilization Rules

The consolidated Code Sec. 382 and SRLY rules provide only limited guidance as to how they apply to tax-free acquisitions of new loss members or loss subgroup parents in a Code Sec. 368(a)(1)(A) or Code Sec. 368(a)(1)(C) reorganization.

¶601.04

Two other limitations come into play if, as is normally the case, the new loss member or loss subgroup parent's first tax year after joining the consolidated group is a short tax year. First, if the corporation is acquired in a transaction described in Code Sec. 381(a), use of its NOL carryover for the first tax year of the acquiring consolidated group ending after the acquisition can be offset by the taxable income of the acquiring corporation only to the extent provided by Code Sec. 381(c)(1)(B) (a *pro rata* portion of the acquiring corporation's taxable income for the portion of the year after the date of acquisition). Second, if there is an ownership change of the new loss member or loss subgroup resulting in a Code Sec. 382 limitation or subgroup Code Sec. 382 limitation, the limitation for the short tax year is prorated under Reg. § 1.382-5(c) based on the number of days in the short year bears to 365. The consolidated return Code Sec. 382 and SRLY rules for built-in gains and losses are briefly explained at ¶ 635.

Reg. § 1.1502-21(b)(1) provides ordering rules for determining which of multiple NOL carryovers and carrybacks are absorbed first. Also, Code Sec. 382(l)(2)(B) provides that if losses are carried from the same tax year, losses subject to limitation under Code Sec. 382 are absorbed before losses that are not subject to limitation under Code Sec. 382.

The election to reattribute an NOL carryover of a subsidiary to its common parent under Reg. § 1.1502-20(g) interacts with the consolidated Code Sec. 382 and SRLY rules in numerous ways. For example, if the reattributed NOL carryover was subject to a Code Sec. 382 limitation, issues arise regarding whether the common parent or the purchaser of the subsidiary inherits the first Code Sec. 382 limitation.

As discussed at ¶ 335, the use of a departing subsidiary's NOL carryover to offset gain on the disposition of the stock of that subsidiary is limited by Reg. § 1.1502-11(b) to prevent a "circular basis" problem. The SRLY limitation is retained for NOL carrybacks to consolidated groups, presumably because Code Sec. 382 does not apply to an NOL carryback. The rules listed above are discussed in more detail at ¶ 635.

.05 Net Capital Loss and Credit Utilization System

A brief summary of the separate return Code Sec. 383 rules and consolidated Code Sec. 383 and SRLY rules for net capital loss carryovers and carrybacks, excess foreign tax credit carryovers, business credit carryovers, and minimum tax credit carryovers is provided at ¶ 645. In general, under Reg. § 1.1502-98, the NOL limitation rules contained in Reg. § 1.1502-91 through Reg. § 1.1502-96 also apply for purposes of Code Sec. 383 with "appropriate adjustments" to reflect that Code Sec. 383 applies to net capital losses and credits. Ordinarily, this means that if the counterpart of a new loss member or a loss subgroup joins a consolidated group in a transaction that results in a change in ownership, and there are pre-change credits but no pre-change losses, the Code Sec. 383 credit limitation will be 35 percent of the Code Sec. 382 limitation. The successive ownership and apportionment of subgroup Code Sec. 382 limitation principles applicable to NOL utilization also apply to net capital loss and credit utilization. Reg. § 1.1502-15 (built-in losses) and Reg. § 1.1502-22 (regular rules) provide SRLY rules for net capital losses that

¶601.05

correspond to the SRLY rules for net operating losses. Reg. § 1.1502-3 and Reg. § 1.1502-55, issued in May 2000, retain the SRLY limitation of prior temporary regulations for business credit carryovers and for minimum tax credit carryovers. However, the overlap principles of Reg. § 1.1502-21(g) are adopted for consolidated return years for which the return is due (without extensions) after May 25, 2000. Thus, the SRLY restriction is eliminated in most situations for calendar consolidated groups effective in 2000. As under the prior temporary regulations, Reg. § 1.1502-4 eliminates the SRLY restriction for foreign tax credit carryovers (and carrybacks) without regard to an overlap with Code Sec. 383 (see ¶ 645).

¶ 615 Code Sec. 382 Limitation and Elimination of Separate Return Limitation Year (SRLY) Limitation for Most New Loss Members and Loss Subgroups Joining a Consolidated Group

Different rules under Code Sec. 382 must be considered, depending on whether the return is separate or consolidated.

.01 Separate Return Code Sec. 382 Rules

If a corporation filing a separate return with an net operating loss (NOL) carryover (a "loss corporation") has more than a 50-percentage point change (measured by value) in its stock ownership by its 5-percent shareholders[5] during a "testing period" of generally 3 years (an "ownership change"), the amount of the loss corporation's taxable income for a post-change year that may be offset by the NOL carryover arising before the ownership change is subject to an annual limitation.[6] The "Code Sec. 382 limitation" is the value of the corporation's stock immediately before the ownership change, multiplied by the long-term tax-exempt rate in effect at the time of the change (as published in the Internal Revenue Bulletin).[7] Code Sec. 382 was enacted to prevent trafficking in loss carryovers; a purchaser of a loss corporation may only use the loss corporation's pre-change NOL carryover to the extent of the income that the loss corporation would have generated if its assets were sold and the proceeds invested in long-term tax-exempt bonds. Thus, if all the stock of a loss corporation with a $1,000 NOL carryover were purchased by parties unrelated to the selling shareholders for $10,000, the purchase would result in an ownership change. If the applicable long-term tax-exempt rate were 5 percent, the Code Sec. 382 limitation would be $500. Accordingly, if the loss corporation has sufficient taxable income, it would take two years to absorb the pre-change loss carryover. In addition, the loss carryover is eliminated if the loss corporation fails to satisfy a continuity of business enterprise requirement for two years following an ownership change.[8]

---

[5] The complex rules for determining 5-percent shareholders are beyond the scope of this volume. In general, ownership of the stock is attributed through any higher-tier entities to the ultimate individual beneficial owners of the loss corporation. An important concept is that a group of direct shareholders, each of whom owns less than 5 percent of the loss corporation's stock (a "public group"), is treated as a separate 5-percent shareholder.

[6] Code Sec. 382(a), Code Sec. 382(b), and Code Sec. 382(g).

[7] Code Sec. 382(b)(1), Code Sec. 382(e), and Code Sec. 382(f).

[8] Code Sec. 382(c)(1); however, the Code Sec. 382 limitation shall not be less than the sum of any increase in such limitation for recognized built-in gains for such year, and is also increased for gain recognized by reason of a Code Sec. 338 election, plus any increase in such limitation for amounts that are carried forward to such year (Code Sec. 382(c)(2)).

The Code Sec. 382 limitation is prorated for short tax years.[9] An unused Code Sec. 382 limitation carries over to succeeding years.[10] If there are successive ownership changes, a second Code Sec. 382 limitation can only reduce, not increase, the Code Sec. 382 limitation.[11]

The Code Sec. 382 limitation applies to certain built-in losses recognized within five years after the ownership change.[12] Similarly, the loss corporation is permitted to increase the Code Sec. 382 limitation by certain built-in gains recognized within five years after the ownership change.[13] See ¶ 635 for a more complete discussion.

Special rules are provided for, among other things, midyear ownership changes,[14] capital contributions as part of a plan to avoid or increase the Code Sec. 382 limitation,[15] order of absorption of Code Sec. 382 limited losses and other losses,[16] constructive ownership and other operating matters relating to ownership of stock,[17] a scale-back of loss limitation if a loss corporation's passive assets exceed one-third of value (net of debt),[18] and ownership changes of loss corporations under the jurisdiction of the court in a Title 11 or similar case.[19] The regulations also include important rules for determining when an option is treated as exercised.[20]

.02 Consolidated Code Sec. 382 Rules [21]

The most commonly encountered consolidated Code Sec. 382 regulations are best discussed in the context of an example.

> **Example 1:** As an example of an ownership change of a new loss member or loss subgroup: P, a Delaware corporation, was formed in Year 1 to provide online tax advice and is owned by 100 individuals, each of whom hold 1 percent of the outstanding stock. They are unrelated and have owned the stock since P was formed. P formed 16 Delaware subsidiaries, one subsidiary for each tax specialty (e.g., M&A, HRC, SALT, International, Accounting Methods & Periods, Passthrough Entities, etc.), and one subsidiary to develop the needed technology.
>
> P was a big success. The feedback was that this was an excellent way to obtain second opinions or document research at a reasonable fee. However, the technology costs were expensive. The P consolidated group had a $10 million consolidated net operating loss (CNOL) for Year 1, all of which was attributable to its Technology Subsidiary. At the end of Year 1, P1 expressed an interest in acquiring part or all of P. P1 was owned by Public P1. P1 saw

---

[9] Reg. § 1.382-5(c).

[10] Code Sec. 382(b)(2).

[11] Reg. § 1.382-5(d).

[12] Code Sec. 382(h)(1)(B).

[13] Code Sec. 382(h)(1)(A).

[14] Code Sec. 382(b)(3).

[15] Code Sec. 382(l)(1). The legislative history to this provision indicates, however, that it should not be interpreted as broadly as the statute would suggest. See H.R. Conf. Rep. No. 841, at 189 (1986).

[16] Code Sec. 382(l)(2).

[17] Code Sec. 382(l)(3).

[18] Code Sec. 382(l)(4).

[19] Code Sec. 382(l)(5).

[20] Reg. § 1.382-4(d).

[21] Under Reg. § 1.1502-93(d)(1), a loss subgroup is treated as a single entity for purposes of determining whether it satisfies the continuity of business enterprise requirement of Code Sec. 382(c)(1). Under that provision, if the new loss corporation does not continue the business enterprise of the old loss corporation at all times during the two-year period after the ownership change, the Code Sec. 382 limitation is generally zero.

¶615.02

opportunities even P had not considered. It planned to expand the online tax service to include foreign countries and sell it to other markets.

What would the Code Sec. 382 limitation be on Technology Subsidiary's $10 million NOL carryover (assume the long-term tax-exempt rate used to compute a Code Sec. 382 limitation is 5 percent) if one of the following alternative taxable transactions occurred on December 31, Year 1:

    a. P1 purchased the stock of Technology Subsidiary from P for $30 million in cash?

    b. P1 purchased the stock of P from the P shareholders for $100 million in cash?

    c. P1 purchased the stock of M&A Subsidiary from P for $50 million in cash and the stock of Technology Subsidiary from P for $30 million in cash?

P1's purchase of the stock of Technology Subsidiary in Example 1(a) would be an ownership change of a "new loss member." A corporation is a new loss member if it:

- Carries over a NOL that arose (or is treated under Reg. § 1.1502-21(c) as arising) in a SRLY with respect to the current group and that is not described in Reg. § 1.1502-91(d)(1) [an NOL carryover of a loss subgroup]; or

- Has a net unrealized built-in loss (determined under Reg. § 1.1502-94(c) immediately before it becomes a member of the current group by treating that day as a change date) that is not taken into account under Reg. § 1.1502-91(d)(2) in determining whether two or more corporations compose a loss subgroup.[22]

Code Sec. 382 and the regulations thereunder apply to a new loss member to determine, on a separate-entity basis, whether and to what extent a Code Sec. 382 limitation applies to limit the amount of consolidated taxable income that may be offset by the new loss member's NOL carryover.[23]

Accordingly, because Public P1, a 5-percent shareholder, increases its ownership in Technology Subsidiary by more than 50 percentage points over the lowest percentage of stock of Technology Subsidiary owned by it during the testing period described in Code Sec. 382(i)(3), there is an ownership change. The Code Sec. 382 limitation is 5 percent of $30 million, or $1.5 million.[24] (As explained in Example 2 at the end of this paragraph, ¶ 615.02, the SRLY limitation does not apply. Thus, the P1 consolidated group can use up to $1.5 million of Technology Subsidiary's $10 million NOL carryover against consolidated taxable income, without regard to

---

[22] Reg. § 1.1502-94(a)(1).

[23] Reg. § 1.1502-94(b)(1).

[24] Code Sec. 382(l)(1) provides an anti-stuffing rule that would generally require reduction of the value of Technology Subsidiary for a contribution to capital made to it during the two-year period ending on the change date. However, the legislative history of this provision indicates that it was not intended to apply to certain capital infusions, including, as here, capital contributions received on the formation of the loss corporation (not accompanied by the incorporation of assets with a net unrealized built-in loss) where an ownership change occurs within two years of incorporation (H.R. CONF. REP. No. 841, at 189 (1986). This is true in several of the examples in this Chapter and, for convenience, is not repeated in each explanation.

¶615.02

which corporation earns the taxable income. Accordingly, assuming the P1 group has sufficient taxable income, it could absorb the NOL carryover in seven years.)

P1's purchase of the stock of P in Example 1(b) would be an ownership change of a "loss subgroup." Two or more corporations that become members of a consolidated group (the current group) compose a loss subgroup if:

- They were affiliated with each other in another group (the former group), whether or not the group was a consolidated group;

- They bear the relationship described in Code Sec. 1504(a)(1) to each other through a loss subgroup parent immediately after they become members of the current group (or are deemed to bear that relationship as a result of an election described in Reg. § 1.1502-91(d)(4)); and

- At least one of the members carries over a NOL that did not arise (and is not treated under Reg. § 1.1502-21(c) as arising) in a SRLY with respect to the former group.[25]

A loss subgroup has an ownership change if the "loss subgroup parent" has an ownership change under Code Sec. 382 and the regulations thereunder.[26] Solely for purposes of determining whether the loss subgroup parent has an ownership change:

- The losses described in Reg. § 1.1502-91(d) are treated as NOLs (or a net unrealized built-in loss) of the loss subgroup parent;

- The day that the members of the loss subgroup become members of the group (or a loss subgroup) is treated as a testing date within the meaning of Reg. § 1.382-2(a)(4); and

- The loss subgroup parent determines the earliest day that its testing period can begin under Reg. § 1.382-2T(d)(3) by reference to only the attributes that make the members a loss subgroup under Reg. § 1.1502-91(d).[27]

P is the loss subgroup parent.[28] Public P1, a 5-percent shareholder, has increased its ownership interest in P by more than 50 percentage points over the lowest percentage of stock of P owned by it at any time during the testing period described in Code Sec. 382(i)(3). Thus, there is an ownership change.[29] As a result, the "subgroup Code Sec. 382 limitation" is the value of the loss subgroup multiplied by the long-term tax-exempt rate that applies with respect to the ownership change.[30] Here, P1 could use $5 million (5 percent of $100 million) of Technology Subsidiary's $10 million NOL carryover each year. (As explained in Example 2 at the end of this paragraph, ¶ 615.02, the SRLY limitation does not apply. Thus, the P1 consolidated group can use up to $5 million of Technology Subsidiary's $10 million NOL carryover against consolidated taxable income annually, without regard to which corporation earns the taxable income. Accordingly, assuming that

---

[25] Reg. § 1.1502-91(d)(1).

[26] Reg. § 1.1502-92(b)(1)(ii).

[27] Reg. § 1.1502-92(b)(1)(ii).

[28] Reg. § 1.1502-91(d)(3) defines the loss subgroup parent as the corporation that bears the same relationship to

the other members of the loss subgroup as a common parent bears to the members of the group.

[29] Code Sec. 382(g)(1) and Code Sec. 382(i)(3).

[30] Reg. § 1.1502-93(a)(1) and Reg. § 1.1502-93(b)(1).

¶615.02

the P1 group has sufficient taxable income, it could absorb the NOL carryover in two years.)

P1's purchase of brother-sister corporations M&A Subsidiary and Technology Subsidiary in Example 1(c), above, presents a trap for the unwary (the proposed transaction where P1 purchased the stock of M&A Subsidiary from P for $50 million in cash and the stock of Technology Subsidiary from P for $30 million in cash). Because P, the loss subgroup parent, is not acquired, Technology Subsidiary is simply a "new loss member." Thus, the Code Sec. 382 limitation for the $10 million NOL carryover of Technology Subsidiary generally would be only $1.5 million (5 percent of $30 million), rather than 5 percent of $80 million. However, an election can be made to treat the loss subgroup parent requirement of a loss subgroup as being met.[31] If the election is made, the subgroup Code Sec. 382 limitation would be $4 million (5 percent of $80 million).[32] Equally important, as explained in Example 2 at the end of this paragraph, ¶ 615.02, the subgroup parent election is necessary to cause an overlap of the Code Sec. 382 and SRLY events that would prevent the SRLY limitation from applying.

SRLY rules. Under Reg. § 1.1502-21(c), the aggregate of the NOL carryovers and carrybacks of a member arising in separate return limitation years (SRLYs), as defined in Reg. § 1.1502-1(f),[33] that are included in consolidated NOL deductions generally may not exceed the consolidated taxable income for all consolidated return years of the consolidated group determined by reference to only the member's taxable income. If previously affiliated members join the consolidated group at the same time as the member with an NOL carryover, the loss member and the joining members generally constitute a SRLY subgroup, and the SRLY limitation applies to the entire SRLY subgroup.[34] Similar rules apply to an NOL carryback. See ¶ 635, Example 6.

Regulations issued in 1999 generally eliminate the SRLY limitation for tax years for which the due date (without extensions) of the consolidated return is after June 25, 1999, where there is an overlap with the Code Sec. 382 limitation (even if the loss member or loss subgroup was acquired earlier than the SRLY effective date).

> *Caution:* However, the overlap rule only applies to a Code Sec. 382 loss subgroup if every member of the group is a member of the SRLY subgroup, and vice versa. For example, if brother and sister corporations of one consolidated group are acquired from another consolidated group, and one or both

---

[31] Reg. § 1.1502-91(d)(4); *see* Reg. § 1.1502-96 for the time and manner of making the election.

[32] *See* Reg. § 1.1502-94 (definition of a new loss member and application of Code Sec. 382 to a new loss member); Reg. § 1.1502-91(d)(4) (election to treat loss subgroup parent requirement of a loss subgroup as satisfied).

[33] *See* Reg. § 1.1502-1(f) for the definition of a SRLY. In general, it includes any separate return year of a member or a predecessor of a member (including a separate return of another consolidated group). Exceptions are provided, for example, for the separate return year of the common parent of the consolidated group (the so-called

"lonely parent rule") and a separate return year of a member of an affiliated group that later elects to become a consolidated group, provided that the member with the NOL carryover was a member of the group every day of the separate return year. NOL carryovers from those years are not subject to the SRLY limitation. Also, in a "reverse acquisition" described in Reg. § 1.1502-75(d)(3), the target corporation's consolidated group continues in existence with the acquiring corporation becoming the common parent of the target consolidated group. In that event, the acquiring group's, rather than the target's, NOL carryovers are generally subject to the SRLY rules.

[34] Reg. § 1.1502-21(c)(2).

¶615.02

corporations have an NOL carryover, the SRLY limitation is eliminated only if an election is made under the consolidated Code Sec. 382 regulations to treat the brother and sister corporations as a Code Sec. 382 loss subgroup.[35]

Example 2: As to the overlap of Code Sec. 382 event and SRLY event: Assuming the same facts as in Example 1, above, would there be a SRLY limitation after any of the transactions?

There would be no SRLY limitation if either the stock of Technology Subsidiary or P were purchased because the SRLY limitation is eliminated when the "SRLY event" occurs within six months of a "Code Sec. 382 event."[36] For this overlap to occur, the members of any Code Sec. 382 loss subgroup and any SRLY subgroup must be coextensive. The overlap requirement would be met here if either the stock of Technology Subsidiary or the stock of P were purchased.[37]

However, the acquisition of brother-sister corporations like the M&A and Technology Subsidiaries requires close attention. There would be no SRLY limitation only if the election is made to treat the loss subgroup parent requirement as met for Code Sec. 382 purposes. In that event, the members of the Code Sec. 382 "loss subgroup" and "SRLY subgroup" would be coextensive. If the election is not made, the SRLY limitation applies to the SRLY subgroup consisting of M&A Subsidiary and Technology Subsidiary in addition to the Code Sec. 382 limitation. That is, subject to the $1.5 million new loss member Code Sec. 382 limitation, Technology Subsidiary's $10 million Year 1 NOL carryover could be used only against the cumulative taxable income of M&A Subsidiary and Technology Subsidiary after they join the P1 consolidated group.[38]

¶ 625 Successive Ownership Changes and Restructuring of Loss Subgroup

A number of situations need to be considered when there are successive ownership changes and a restructuring of loss subgroup, such as a new loss member, a loss subgroup, and the fold-in rule.

.01 New Loss Member

Reg. § 1.1502-94(b)(1) generally provides that Code Sec. 382 and the regulations thereunder apply to a new loss member to determine, on a separate-entity basis, whether and to what extent a Code Sec. 382 limitation applies to limit the amount of consolidated taxable income that may be offset by the new loss member's pre-change separate attributes. This incorporates Reg. § 1.382-5(d)(1), which provides rules for successive ownership changes and absorption of a Code Sec. 382 limitation.

---

[35] Reg. § 1.1502-21(g)(5), Example 6.

[36] *See* Reg. § 1.1502-21(g) (the overlap rule).

[37] Compare Reg. § 1.1502-91(d) (Code Sec. 382 loss subgroup) with Reg. § 1.1502-21(c)(2) (SRLY subgroup).

[38] *See* Reg. § 1.1502-21(g) (the overlap rule), Reg. § 1.1502-21(g)(5), Example 6 (brother-sister corporation acquisition fails to provide overlap where Reg. § 1.1502-91(d)(4) election not made) and Reg. § 1.1502-21(c)(2)(ii) (SRLY subgroup limitation).

Specifically, the regulation generally provides that if a loss corporation has two (or more) ownership changes, any losses attributable to the period preceding the earlier ownership change are treated as pre-change losses with respect to both ownership changes. Thus, the later ownership change may result in a lesser (but never in a greater) Code Sec. 382 limitation with respect to all such pre-change losses. In any case, the amount of taxable income for any post-change year that can be offset by pre-change losses may not exceed the Code Sec. 382 limitation for such ownership change, reduced by the amount of taxable income offset by pre-change losses subject to any earlier ownership change.

.02 Loss Subgroup

Reg. § 1.1502-95(b)(2)(iv) provides that, consistent with Code Sec. 382, an ownership change of the former member that occurs on or after the day it ceases to be a member of a loss group may result in an additional, lesser limitation amount with respect to such losses. Further, Reg. § 1.1502-95(a)(1) provides that, as the context requires, a reference in Reg. § 1.1502-95 to a loss group, a member, or a corporation also includes a reference to a loss subgroup. As a result, the successive ownership rules of Reg. § 1.382-5(d)(1) also must be taken into account when a loss member of a loss subgroup is acquired in a second ownership change.

Reg. § 1.1502-95(b)(2)(ii) provides that if a loss group has had an ownership change before a corporation ceases to be a member of a consolidated group, the Code Sec. 382 limitation with respect to such pre-change attribute is zero, unless the common parent apportions to the former member all or part of the consolidated Code Sec. 382 limitation for such attribute. Reg. § 1.1502-95(a)(1) extends the same rules to a loss subgroup and the subgroup Code Sec. 382 limitation "as the context requires."

> **Caution:** This means that after an ownership change of a loss subgroup upon joining a consolidated group, if one or more (but not all) of the members of the loss subgroup are acquired subsequently by another consolidated group, and the departing member(s) carry over the NOL limited by the first ownership change, the first subgroup Code Sec. 382 limitation related to the departing member(s) will be zero, unless the common parent of the first group apportions part or all of the first subgroup Code Sec. 382 limitation to it (or them). This is illustrated in Reg. § 1.1502-95(b)(4), Example 2 (similar rule for member leaving a loss group).

Further, if two or more former members are included in the same loss subgroup immediately after they cease to be members of a consolidated group, the principles of Reg. § 1.1502-95(b) apply to the loss subgroup.[39] Therefore, an apportionment by the common parent is made to the loss subgroup rather than separately to its members. If the common parent of the consolidated group apportions all or part of a Code Sec. 382 limitation separately to one or more former members that are included in a loss subgroup because the common parent of the acquiring group makes an election under Reg. § 1.1502-94(d)(4) with respect to those mem-

---

[39] Reg. § 1.1502-95(b)(3).

bers, the aggregate of those separate amounts is treated as the amount apportioned to the loss subgroup.

The apportionment rules are set forth in Reg. § 1.1502-95(c). Any apportionment consists of (1) a "value element" (relating to value multiplied by the long-term tax-exempt rate) without regard to adjustments, and (2) an "adjustment element." The adjustment element is so much (if any) of the limitation for the tax year during which the former member(s) ceases to be a member of the consolidated group that is attributable to a carryover of unused limitation under Code Sec. 382(b)(2) or to recognized built-in gains under Code Sec. 382(h). For examples illustrating these apportionment rules, see Reg § 1.1502-95(c)(7).

Reg. § 1.1502-95(d) provides special rules for determining whether a member ceases to be a member of a loss subgroup. Some of those rules are illustrated in Example 2.

.03 Fold-in Rule

Finally, after an ownership change of a new loss member or loss subgroup upon entering a consolidated group, the NOL carryovers are treated as non-SRLY NOL carryovers of the acquiring group for certain purposes.[40] This is important so that, upon a subsequent acquisition of, for example, P1 by P2, P1 would be considered a loss subgroup with respect to the Technology Subsidiary NOL carryover. As a result, there would be an overlap of Code Sec. 382 and SRLY events, and the SRLY limitation would not apply.[41]

> **Example 3:** An example of *successive* ownership changes: P, a Delaware corporation, was formed in Year 1 to provide online tax advice and is owned by 100 individuals, each of whom hold 1 percent of the outstanding stock. They are unrelated and have owned the stock since P was formed. P formed 16 Delaware subsidiaries, one subsidiary for each tax specialty (e.g., M&A, HRC, SALT, International, Accounting Methods & Periods, Passthrough Entities, etc.), and one subsidiary to develop the needed technology.
>
> P was a big success. The feedback was that this was an excellent way to obtain second opinions or document research at a reasonable fee. However, the technology costs were expensive. The P consolidated group had a $10 million consolidated net operating loss (CNOL) for Year 1, all of which was attributable to its Technology Subsidiary. At the end of Year 1, P1 expressed an interest in acquiring part or all of P. P1 was owned by Public P1. P1 saw

---

[40] *See* Reg. § 1.1502-96.

[41] If, as is generally the case, the fold-in rule applies to cause a new loss member's or loss subgroup's NOL carryover to be treated as a non-SRLY NOL of the acquiring group for certain purposes, the fold-in rule could accelerate a second ownership change with respect to the loss carryover that the new loss member or loss subgroup brings into the consolidated group. For example, if, before P1 acquired Technology Subsidiary, P1 had an NOL carryover and was "partially pregnant" with an ownership change, the fold-in rule could accelerate a second ownership change with respect to Technology Subsidiary's NOL carryover. To make the example more con-

crete, assume that P1 had an NOL carryover and that there had been a 40-percent increase in the ownership of P1 by its 5-percent shareholders before P1 acquired Technology Subsidiary. Assume further that there was another 11-percent increase in the ownership of P1 by its 5-percent shareholders after P1 acquired Technology Subsidiary, but during the same three-year testing period as the 40-percent increase. In this case, there would be a second ownership change with respect to Technology Subsidiary's net operating loss carryover (even though there was only an 11-percent increase in the ownership of P1 by its 5-percent shareholders during the period for which Technology Subsidiary was a member of the P1 group).

opportunities even P had not considered. It planned to expand the online tax service to include foreign countries and sell it to other markets.

P1 purchased the stock of Technology Subsidiary for $30 million, or P1 purchased the stock of P, which owns 16 subsidiaries, for $100 million. In Year 2, the P1 consolidated group absorbed the maximum amount of Technology Subsidiary's $10 million NOL carryover from Year 1 allowed by Code Sec. 382. Because the online tax service was a smashing success, P2 became interested in acquiring part or all of P1. P2 was owned by Public P2.

What would the Code Sec. 382 limitation and SRLY limitation be on Technology Subsidiary's remaining NOL carryover (assume the long-term tax-exempt rate used to compute a Code Sec. 382 limitation is 5 percent) if one of the following alternative taxable transactions occurred on December 31, Year 2:

1. After P1's purchase of the stock of Technology Subsidiary on December 31, Year 1 for $30 million, P2 purchased the stock of P1 from Public P1 on December 31, Year 2 for $20 billion?

2. After P1's purchase of the stock of P on December 31, Year 1 for $100 million, P2 purchased the stock of Technology Subsidiary from P for $40 million in cash (resulting in a gain to P1)?

Where P2 purchased P1 for $20 billion after P1 purchased Technology Subsidiary for $30 million, the first Code Sec. 382 limitation would still be $1.5 million (5 percent of $30 million). Because P1's acquisition of Technology Subsidiary resulted in an ownership change, Technology Subsidiary's unused Year 1 NOL carryover is treated as a non-SRLY NOL carryover of the P1 group.[42] As a result, P2's acquisition of P1 is the acquisition of a loss subgroup for which the subgroup Code Sec. 382 limitation is $1 billion (5 percent of $20 billion). However, as a result of successive ownership changes, the lesser ($1.5 million) Code Sec. 382 limitation applies.[43]

There is no SRLY limitation because the members of the Code Sec. 382 "loss subgroup" (i.e., all the members of the P1 group) are coextensive with the members of the SRLY subgroup.[44]

If P2 purchased Technology Subsidiary for $40 million after P1 purchased P for $100 million, Technology Subsidiary ceases to be a member of the P loss subgroup and is a new loss member of the P2 consolidated group. The first Code Sec. 382 limitation with respect to the Year 1 NOL carryover is zero for Technology Subsidiary, unless P1 apportions to Technology Subsidiary all or part of the subgroup Code Sec. 382 limitation.[45] Assume $5 million of the subgroup Code Sec. 382 limitation is so apportioned. Technology Subsidiary is a new loss member upon its acquisition by P2, which results in an ownership change and a second, lesser Code Sec. 382 limitation of $2 million (5 percent of $40 million).[46] Thus, P2's annual limitation on the use of Technology's unused $5 million Year 1 carryover is $2 million.

---

[42] *See* Reg. § 1.1502-96(a).
[43] *See* Reg. § 1.1502-95(b)(2)(iv) and Reg. § 1.382-5(d).
[44] *See* Reg. § 1.1502-96 and Reg. § 1.1502-21(g).

[45] *See* Reg. § 1.1502-95.
[46] *See* Reg. § 1.1502-95.

¶625.03

There is no SRLY limitation because P2's purchase of Technology Subsidiary is an ownership change of a new loss member and a SRLY event. As a result of the overlap of the Code Sec. 382 event and SRLY event, there is no SRLY limitation to the P2 consolidated group.[47]

> **Example 4:** As an example of restructuring loss subgroup: The facts are the same as in ¶ 615, Example 1(a) (P1 purchased the stock of P for $100 million). P, a Delaware corporation, was formed in Year 1 to provide online tax advice and is owned by 100 individuals, each of whom hold 1 percent of the outstanding stock. They are unrelated and have owned the stock since P was formed. P formed 16 Delaware subsidiaries, one subsidiary for each tax specialty (e.g., M&A, HRC, SALT, International, Accounting Methods & Periods, Passthrough Entities, etc.), and one subsidiary to develop the needed technology.
>
> P was a big success. The feedback was that this was an excellent way to obtain second opinions or document research at a reasonable fee. However, the technology costs were expensive. The P consolidated group had a $10 million consolidated net operating loss (CNOL) for Year 1, all of which was attributable to its Technology Subsidiary. At the end of Year 1, P1 expressed an interest in acquiring part or all of P. P1 was owned by Public P1. P1 saw opportunities even P had not considered. It planned to expand the online tax service to include foreign countries and sell it to other markets.
>
> Recall that, under certain circumstances, Reg. § 1.1502-95 causes a subsidiary with an NOL carryover allocable to it to have a zero prior Code Sec. 382 limitation if it ceases to be a member of the loss subgroup and part or all of the prior Code Sec. 382 limitation is not apportioned to it.

What effect, if any, would the following restructuring have on the subgroup Code Sec. 382 limitation if P distributes the stock of Technology Subsidiary to P1, and P1 distributes the stock of Technology to its shareholders? The distribution to P1 would have no effect on the subgroup Code Sec. 382 limitation.[48]

> **Caution:** However, upon the distribution of Technology Subsidiary to P1's shareholders, Technology Subsidiary takes its NOL carryover with it, and it would take a zero first Code Sec. 382 limitation unless P1 apportions part or all of the $5 million limitation to Technology.[49] Thus, without an apportionment, Technology Subsidiary's NOL carryover would have no value after it is distributed outside the P1 group.

What effect would the following restructuring have on the subgroup Code Sec. 382 limiation if Technology Subsidiary merges into M&A Subsidiary in a reorganization under Code Sec. 368(a)(1)(D)?[50] The merger would have no effect on the subgroup Code Sec. 382 limitation.[51]

---

[47] *See* Reg. § 1.1502-96 and Reg. § 1.1502-21(g).

[48] *See* Reg. § 1.1502-95(d)(3), Example 3.

[49] *See* Reg. § 1.1502-95.

[50] Most tax practitioners believe that where a corporation's NOL carryover is not limited by the SRLY rules,

Code Sec. 381(c)(1)(B) should not limit the consolidated group's use of the NOL carryover for the year that includes the Code Sec. 381(a) event if the event is between two members of the consolidated group.

[51] *See* Reg. § 1.1502-95(d)(2)(ii).

¶625.03

¶ 635 Miscellaneous Consolidated Return Net Operating Loss (NOL) Utilization Rules

A number of miscellaneous consolidated return NOL utilization rules must be kept in mind such as an acquisition of a new loss member or a loss subgroup parent in a tax-free A or C reorganization; Code Sec. 381(c)(1)(B) and Code Sec. 382 limitations for short tax years; built-in gains and losses; ordering rules for absorption of NOLs; reattribution of Code Sec. 382 limitation for an NOL carryover reattributed under Reg. § 1.1502-20(g); limitation on use of departing member's NOL under Reg. § 1.1502-11(b); and NOL carrybacks.

.01 Acquisition of a New Loss Member or Loss Subgroup Parent in a Tax-Free A or C Reorganization

Code Sec. 382(l)(8) provides that, except as provided in regulations, any entity and any predecessor or successor entities of such entity shall be treated as one entity. Numerous provisions must be considered regarding the application of the consolidated Code Sec. 382 rules and SRLY rules to the acquisition of a new loss member or loss subgroup parent in a tax-free reorganization under Code Sec. 368(a)(1)(A) or Code Sec. 368(a)(1)(C). For acquisitions that result in an ownership change of a new loss member or loss subgroup by a consolidated group, it is particularly instructive to note the following points:

1. Notwithstanding that a loss corporation ceases to exist under state law, if its NOL carryovers are succeeded to and taken into account by an acquiring corporation in a transaction described in Code Sec. 381(a), such loss corporation is treated as continuing in existence until any pre-change losses are fully utilized or expire.[52] Following a Code Sec. 381(a) transaction, the stock of the acquiring corporation is treated as the stock of the loss corporation for purposes of determining whether an ownership change occurs with respect to the pre-change losses that may be treated as pre-change losses of the transferor corporation.[53]

   An example in the regulations illustrates how a change in ownership is determined for a reorganization under Code Sec. 368(a)(1)(A) where the acquiring corporation and acquired loss corporation do not file a consolidated return:[54] A owns all of the stock of L, and B owns all the stock of P. On October 13, 1988, L merges into P in a reorganization described in Code Sec. 368(a)(1)(A). As a result of the merger, A and B own 25 and 75 percent, respectively, of the stock of P. The merger is an equity structure shift (see Code Sec. 382(g)(3)(A)) and, because it affects the percentage of L stock owned by 5-percent shareholders, it also constitutes an owner shift. On the October 13, 1988, testing date, B is a 5-percent shareholder whose stock ownership in the loss corporation following the merger has increased by 75 percentage points over his lowest percentage of stock ownership in L at any time during the testing period (0 percent prior to the merger). Accordingly, an ownership change occurs as a result of the

---

[52] Reg. § 1.382-2(a)(1)(ii).
[53] Reg. § 1.382-2(a)(1)(ii).

[54] Reg. § 1.382-2T(e)(2)(iv), Example 1.

¶635.01

merger. P is thus a new loss corporation and L's pre-change losses are subject to limitation under Code Sec. 382.

2. In determining an ownership change, all stock owned by shareholders of a corporation who are not 5-percent shareholders of such corporation is treated as stock owned by one 5-percent shareholder of such corporation.[55] This rule is applied separately with respect to each group of shareholders (immediately before an "equity structure shift," defined by Code Code Sec. 382(g)(3) to include acquisitive tax-free reorganizations other than F reorganizations) of each corporation that was a party to the reorganization.[56] To this end, "segregation rules" of Reg. § 1.382-2T(j)(2) apply to acquisitive asset reorganizations described in Code Sec. 381(a)(2) and in which a loss corporation is a party to the reorganization. In general, each direct public group that exists immediately after such transaction must be segregated so that each direct public group that existed immediately before the transaction is treated separately from the direct public group that acquires stock of the loss corporation. The direct public group that acquires stock of the loss corporation is presumed not to include any members of any direct public group that existed before the transaction. For this purpose, a person is treated as acquiring stock of the loss corporation as the result of the person's ownership interest in another corporation that succeeds to the loss corporation's pre-change losses in a transaction to which Code Sec. 381(a)(2) applies. For situations where this presumption will not apply, see Reg. § 1.382-2T(j)(2)(iii)(A).

3. A "new loss member" includes any successor to a corporation that has an NOL arising in a separate return limitation year (SRLY) and that is treated as remaining in existence under Reg. § 1.382-2(a)(1)(ii).[57]

4. A reference in Reg. § 1.1502-91 through Reg. § 1.1502-99 to a corporation, member, common parent, loss subgroup parent, or subsidiary includes, as the context may require, a reference to a predecessor or successor corporation as defined in Reg. § 1.1502-1(f)(4).[58] The latter regulation provides that the term *predecessor* includes a transferor or distributor of assets to a member (successor) in a transaction to which Code Sec. 381(a) applies.

5. For purposes of the SRLY rules, any reference to a corporation, member, common parent, or subsidiary includes, as the context may require, a reference to a successor or predecessor as defined in Reg. § 1.1502-1(f)(4).[59] Other special rules apply that are not invoked by the examples below.

Example 5: As an example of an acquisition of a new loss member in a tax-free reorganization: P, a Delaware corporation, was formed in Year 1 and is owned by 100 individuals, each of whom own 1 percent of the P stock. They are unrelated and have owned the stock since P was formed. P was formed to

---

[55] Code Sec. 382(g)(4)(A).
[56] Code Sec. 382(g)(4)(B)(i).
[57] Reg. § 1.1502-94(a)(2).

[58] Reg. § 1.1502-91(j).
[59] Reg. § 1.1502-21(f)(1).

¶635.01

provide online tax advice. P formed 16 Delaware subsidiaries, one subsidiary for each specialty (e.g., M&A, HRC, SALT, International, Accounting Methods and Periods, and Passthrough Entities, etc.), and one subsidiary to develop the technology needed to accomplish its goals.

P was a big success. The feedback was that this was an excellent way to obtain second opinions or document research at a reasonable fee. However, the technology costs were expensive. The P consolidated group had a $10 million consolidated net operating loss (CNOL) for Year 1, all of which was attributable to its Technology Subsidiary. At the end of Year 1, P1 expressed an interest in acquiring part or all of P. P1 was owned by Public P1. P1 saw opportunities even P had not considered and planned to expand the online tax service to include foreign countries and sell it to other markets.

What would the Code Sec. 382 limitation and SRLY limitation be on Technology Subsidiary's $10 million NOL carryover (assume that the long-term tax-exempt rate used to compute a Code Sec. 382 limitation is 5 percent) if Technology Subsidiary merged into P1's existing Marketing Subsidiary on December 31, Year 1? Assume that the transaction qualifies as a reorganization under Code Sec. 368(a)(2)(D), and P would receive stock of P1 with a total value of $30 million (less than 1 percent of the total P1 stock).

P1's acquisition of Technology Subsidiary for $30 million of stock would be an ownership change of a "new loss member." A corporation is a new loss member if it (a) carries over an NOL that arose (or is treated under Reg. § 1.1502-21(c)) as arising in a SRLY with respect to the current group and that is not described in Reg. § 1.1502-91(d)(1) [an NOL carryover of a loss subgroup]; or (b) has a net unrealized built-in loss (determined under Reg. § 1.1502-21(c) immediately before it becomes a member of the current group by treating that day as a change date) that is not taken into account under Reg. § 1.1502-91(d)(2) in determining whether two or more corporations compose a loss subgroup.[60]

Under Reg. § 1.1502-94(a)(2), a "new loss member" includes any successor to a corporation that has an NOL arising in a SRLY and that is treated as remaining in existence under Reg. § 1.382-2(a)(1)(ii).

Code Sec. 382 and the regulations thereunder apply to a new loss member to determine, on a separate-entity basis, whether and to what extent a Code Sec. 382 limitation applies to limit the amount of consolidated taxable income that may be offset by the new loss member's NOL carryover.[61]

Marketing Subsidiary is a new loss member because it is a successor to Technology Subsidiary. Because Public P1, a 5-percent shareholder, increases its ownership in the successor to Technology Subsidiary by more than 50 percentage points over the lowest percentage of stock of Technology Subsidiary owned by it during the testing period described in Code Sec. 382(i)(3), there is an ownership change. The Code Sec. 382 limitation is 5 percent of $30 million, or $1.5 million.

---

[60] Reg. § 1.1502-94(a)(1).

[61] Reg. § 1.1502-94(b)(1).

There should be no SRLY limitation on P1's use of Technology Subsidiary's NOL carryover. This is because, applying the successor rules described above, there is an overlap between the Code Sec. 382 event and the SRLY event.[62]

> *Example 6:* As an example of acquisition of loss subgroup parent in a tax-free reorganization: The facts are the same as in Example 5, immediately above, except that P merged into Marketing Subsidiary. The transaction qualifies as a reorganization under Code Sec. 368(a)(2)(D), and the former P shareholders would receive stock of P1 worth $100 million (less than 5 percent of the P1 stock).

P1's acquisition of P should be an ownership change of a "loss subgroup." Two or more corporations that become members of a consolidated group (the current group) compose a loss subgroup if:

- They were affiliated with each other in another group (the former group), whether or not the group was a consolidated group;

- They bear the relationship described in Code Sec. 1504(a)(1) to each other through a loss subgroup parent immediately after they become members of the current group (or are deemed to bear that relationship as a result of an election described in Reg. § 1.1502-91(d)(4)); and

- At least one of the members carries over a NOL that did not arise (and is not treated under Reg. § 1.1502-21(c) as arising) in a SRLY with respect to the former group.[63]

P literally meets the first and third requirements of a "loss subgroup." As indicated above, a reference in Reg. § 1.1502-91 through Reg. § 1.1502-99 to a loss subgroup parent includes, as the context may require, a reference to a predecessor or successor corporation as defined in Reg. § 1.1502-1(f)(4), including the acquiring corporation in a Code Sec. 381(a) transaction. The context should require that Marketing Subsidiary be treated as the successor to P, so that the second requirement of a loss subgroup should be met.

Because Public P1, a 5-percent shareholder, has increased its ownership interest in P by more than 50 percentage points over the lowest percentage of stock of P owned by it at any time during the testing period described in Code Sec. 382(i)(3), there is an ownership change. As a result, the "subgroup Code Sec. 382 limitation" is the value of the loss subgroup multiplied by the long-term tax-exempt rate that applies with respect to the ownership change. Here, P1 could use $5 million (5 percent of $100 million) of Technology Subsidiary's $10 million NOL carryover each year.

There should be no SRLY limitation on P1's use of Technology Subsidiary's NOL carryover. This is because, applying the successor rules described above, there is an overlap between the Code Sec. 382 event and the SRLY event (i.e., the members of the Code Sec. 382 "loss subgroup" are coextensive with the members of the SRLY subgroup).[64]

---

[62] *See* Reg. § 1.1502-21(g).
[63] Reg. § 1.1502-91(d)(1).

[64] *See* Reg. § 1.1502-21(g) (overlap rule); Reg. § 1.1502-91(d)(1) (definition of Code Sec. § 382 loss sub-

¶635.01

.02 Code Sec. 381(c)(1)(B) and Code Sec. 382 Limitations for Short Tax Years

Two other limitations come into play if, as is normally the case, the new loss member or loss subgroup parent's first tax year after joining the consolidated group is a short tax year. First, if the corporation is acquired in a Code Sec. 381(a) transaction, Code Sec. 381(c)(1)(B) limits the amount of the acquiring corporation's taxable income that can offset the acquired corporation's NOL carryover during the acquiring consolidated group's tax year that includes the Code Sec. 381(a) transaction. Specifically, during the acquiring consolidated group's year that includes the Code Sec. 381(a) transaction, the acquired corporation's NOL carryover can be offset with a *pro rata* portion of the acquiring corporation's taxable income for the portion of its year after the date of acquisition.[65] Second, if there is an ownership change of the new loss member or loss subgroup parent resulting in a Code Sec. 382 limitation or subgroup Code Sec. 382 limitation, the limitation for any short tax year is prorated under Reg. § 1.382-5(c), based on the proportion the number of days in the short year bears to 365.

> ***Example 7:*** As an example of prorated Code Sec. 382 limitation for taxable stock acquisition: the facts are the same as in the P and P1 example in ¶ 515, Example 1(a), except that P1 purchases the stock of Technology Subsidiary for $30 million on November 30, Year 1, instead of on December 31, Year 1.
>
> P, a Delaware corporation, was formed in Year 1 to provide online tax advice and is owned by 100 individuals, each of whom hold 1 percent of the outstanding stock. They are unrelated and have owned the stock since P was formed. P formed 16 Delaware subsidiaries, one subsidiary for each tax specialty (e.g., M&A, HRC, SALT, International, Accounting Methods & Periods, Passthrough Entities, etc.), and one subsidiary to develop the needed technology.
>
> P was a big success. The feedback was that this was an excellent way to obtain second opinions or document research at a reasonable fee. However, the technology costs were expensive. The P consolidated group had a $10 million consolidated net operating loss (CNOL) for Year 1, all of which was attributable to its Technology Subsidiary. At the end of Year 1, P1 expressed an interest in acquiring part or all of P. P1 was owned by Public P1. P1 saw opportunities even P had not considered. It planned to expand the online tax service to include foreign countries and sell it to other markets.
>
> Technology Subsidiary enters the P1 consolidated group on December 1, Year 1 and joins in the P consolidated return for the period January 1, Year 1 through November 30, Year 1.[66] For the short period Technology Subsidiary is

---

(Footnote Continued)

group); Reg. § 1.1502-21(c)(2)(i) (definition of SRLY subgroup).

[65] Without regulations providing otherwise, the acquiring consolidated group does not appear to be required to apply this limitation to the consolidated taxable income of the whole group; rather, the statute only applies to the acquiring corporation.

[66] For a discussion of subsidiaries joining the consolidated group, *see* ¶ 901 *et seq.*

in the P1 consolidated group (December 1 through December 31, Year 1), P1's Code Sec. 382 limitation on use of Technology Subsidiary's $10 million NOL carryover would be 31/365ths of 5 percent, multiplied by $30 million. (This assumes that the P group did not absorb any of the $10 million NOL carryover during the remaining month of its tax year.)

Example 8: As an example of Code Sec. 381(c)(1)(B) limitation and prorated Code Sec. 382 limitation for tax-free asset acquisition: The facts are the same as in Example 7, above, except that Technology Subsidiary merges into P1's Marketing Subsidiary in a Code Sec. 368(a)(2)(D) reorganization on November 30, Year 1. The acquisition consideration is $30 million worth of P1 stock. In addition to a prorated Code Sec. 382 limitation for use of the $10 million NOL carryover (31/365ths of 5 percent, multiplied by $30 million), the amount of taxable income of Marketing Subsidiary that could be used to absorb the NOL carryover for P1's Year 1 tax year would be limited by Code Sec. 381(c)(1)(B) to 31/365ths of Marketing Subsidiary's taxable income for Year 1. However, this may not be a significant limitation because the statute does not limit the amount of taxable income of other members of the P1 consolidated group that could be used to absorb the NOL carryover. (Again, this example assumes the P group did not absorb any of the $10 million NOL carryover during the remaining month of its tax year.)

.03 Built-in Gains and Losses—Separate Return Code Sec. 382 Built-in Gain or Loss Rules

If a loss corporation has a "net unrealized built-in loss" at the time of its ownership change, the "recognized built-in loss" for any tax year of which any portion is in the 5-year period beginning on the date of the ownership change (a "recognition period tax year") is subject to limitation under Code Sec. 382 in the same manner as an NOL carryover.[67] However, recognized built-in losses for any recognition period tax year are subject to limitation under Code Sec. 382 only to the extent that such losses do not exceed (a) the net unrealized built-in loss, reduced by (b) recognized built-in losses for prior tax years ending in the 5-year period beginning on the date of the ownership change.[68] A "net unrealized built-in loss" generally means the amount by which the aggregate adjusted basis of the assets of the corporation immediately before an ownership change exceeds the fair market value of such assets at such time.[69] However, the net unrealized built-in loss is considered to be zero unless it exceeds a threshold amount. The threshold amount generally is the lesser of 15 percent of the fair market value of the corporation's assets immediately before an ownership change, or $10 million.[70] In making this threshold computation, any cash or cash item or any marketable security that does not substantially differ from basis is not taken into account.[71]

A "recognized built-in loss" is any loss recognized during the 5-year period beginning on the date of the ownership change, except to the extent that the loss

---

[67] Code Sec.382(h)(1)(B), Code Sec. 382(h)(7), and Code Sec. 382(j).

[68] Code Sec. 382(h)(1)(B)(ii).

[69] Code Sec. 382(h)(3)(A)(i).

[70] Code Sec. 382(h)(3)(B)(i).

[71] Code Sec. 382(h)(3)(B)(ii).

corporation establishes that such asset was not held by it immediately before the ownership change, or such loss exceeds the net unrealized built-in loss of such asset on the date of the ownership change.[72] Any amount allowable as depreciation, amortization, or depletion during the 5-year period referred to above is generally treated as recognized built-in loss.

Any amount which is allowable as a deduction during the 5-year period beginning on the date of the ownership change, but which is attributable to periods before the ownership change date, is treated as a recognized built-in loss for the tax year for which it is allowable as a deduction.[73]

Under similar rules, recognized built-in gains and built-in income items taken into account during the 5-year period beginning on the date of the ownership change increase the Code Sec. 382 limitation for the tax year they are taken into account if the loss corporation has a "net unrealized built-in gain" on the date of the ownership change.[74]

> *Caution:* To increase the loss corporation's Code Sec. 382 limitation, the loss corporation must establish that (a) the built-in gain asset was held by the loss corporation immediately before the change date, and (b) the recognized built-in gain does not exceed the unrealized built-in gain of such asset on the change date.[75]

.04 Consolidated Return Code Sec. 382 Built-in Gain or Loss Rules

Again, focusing only on loss subgroups and new loss members that join a consolidated group, and ignoring loss groups, a few general principles are discussed here.

1. Two or more corporations that become members of a consolidated group compose a loss subgroup because they have a net unrealized built-in loss only if, among other requirements, they have been continuously affiliated with each other for the five-consecutive-year period ending immediately before they become members of the group.[76]

2. If a loss subgroup has a net unrealized built-in gain, any recognized built-in gain of the loss subgroup is taken into account under Code Sec. 382(h) in determining the subgroup Code Sec. 382 limitation.[77]

3. The determination of whether a loss subgroup has a net unrealized built-in gain or loss is based on the aggregate amount of the separately computed net unrealized built-in gains or losses of each member that is included in the loss subgroup, including items of built-in income and deduction.[78] The threshold requirement under Code Sec. 382(h)(3)(B) applies on an aggregate basis and not on a member-by-member basis.[79] The separately computed amount of a member included in a loss subgroup does not include

---

[72] Code Sec. 382(h)(2)(B).

[73] Code Sec. 382(h)(6)(B).

[74] Code Sec. 382(h).

[75] Code Sec. 382(h)(2)(A).

[76] Reg. § 1.1502-91(d)(2)(i).

[77] Reg. § 1.1502-93(c)(1).

[78] Reg. § 1.1502-91(g)(1). For example, amounts deferred under Code Sec. 267 or under Reg. § 1.1502-13 (other than amounts deferred with respect to the stock of a member or an intercompany obligation) included in the loss group under Reg. § 1.1502-91(g)(2) are built-in items.

[79] Reg. § 1.1502-91(g)(1).

any unrealized built-in gain or loss on stock of another member included in the loss subgroup (or an intercompany obligation).[80]

4. A loss subgroup might have recognized built-in gains that increase the amount of consolidated taxable income that may be offset by its pre-change NOL carryovers that are not treated as arising in a SRLY, and also may have recognized built-in losses of which the absorption is limited.[81] This is because of a combination of the following two rules:

   a. The members included in the determination of whether an NOL loss subgroup has a net unrealized built-in gain are all members of the loss subgroup on the day the determination is made.[82]

   b. The members included in the determination of whether a subgroup has a net unrealized built-in loss are those members that have been continuously affiliated with each other for the five-consecutive-year period ending immediately before they become members of the group, and bear the relationship described in Code Sec. 1504(a)(1) to each other through a loss subgroup parent immediately after they become members of the current group (or are deemed to bear that relationship as a result of an election described in Reg. § 1.1502-91(d)(4)).[83]

5. Gain or loss recognized by a member on the disposition of stock of another member is treated as a recognized gain or loss for purposes of Code Sec. 382(h)(2) (unless disallowed under the loss disallowance rules or otherwise), even though gain or loss on such stock was not included in the determination of a net unrealized built-in gain or loss.[84] Gain or loss recognized by a member with respect to an intercompany obligation is treated as recognized gain or loss only to the extent (if any) that the transaction gives rise to aggregate income or loss within the consolidated group.[85]

6. Reg.§ 1.1502-95 includes complex apportionment rules regarding built-in gains and losses that must be considered when a member ceases to be a member of a loss subgroup.

7. "As the context may require," the principles of Reg. § 1.1502-91(g) and Reg. § 1.1502-91(h) apply to a new loss member on a separate-entity basis.[86]

SRLY rules for built-in losses. Except where there is an overlap between the Code Sec. 382 event and the SRLY event, Reg. § 1.1502-15 generally requires built-in losses to be subject to the SRLY limitation under Reg. § 1.1502-21(c) (NOL carryovers) and Reg. § 1.1502-22(c) (net capital losses) (see ¶ 645) as if they were a NOL carryover or net capital loss carryover.[87] If a corporation has a net unrealized built-in loss under Code Sec. 382(h)(3) on the day it becomes a member of the group (whether or not it is a consolidated group), its deductions and losses are

---

[80] Reg. § 1.1502-91(g)(1).
[81] Reg. § 1.1502-91(g)(2)(iv).
[82] Reg. § 1.1502-91(d)(2)(iii).
[83] Reg. § 1.1502-91(d)(2).

[84] Reg. § 1.1502-91(h)(2).
[85] Reg. § 1.1502-91(h)(2).
[86] Reg. § 1.1502-94(c).
[87] Reg. § 1.1502-15(a).

¶635.04

built-in losses to the extent that they are treated as recognized under Code Sec. 382(h)(2)(B).[88]

In the case of a subgroup, these principles apply to the subgroup and not separately to its members.[89] Thus, the net unrealized built-in loss and recognized built-in loss are based on the aggregate amounts for each member of the subgroup. A subgroup is composed of those members that have been continuously affiliated with each other for the 60-consecutive-month period ending immediately before they become members of the group in which the loss is recognized.[90] Numerous special rules apply.

As in the case of an NOL carryover, the SRLY limitations provided by Reg. § 1.1502-21(c) and Reg. § 1.1502-22(c) do not apply to recognized built-in losses or to loss carryovers or carrybacks attributable to recognized built-in losses when the application of the SRLY rules overlaps with the application of Code Sec. 382.[91] Such an overlap with respect to built-in losses occurs if a corporation becomes a member of a consolidated group (the SRLY event) within six months of the change date of an ownership change giving rise to a Code Sec. 382 limitation that would apply with respect to the corporation's recognized built-in losses (the Code Sec. 382 event).[92] Like the counterpart NOL overlap rules, the built-in loss overlap principles generally apply to the SRLY subgroup and not separately to its members.[93] Thus, the SRLY limitation is eliminated only if all members of the SRLY subgroup with respect to built-in losses are also included in a Code Sec. 382 loss subgroup, and all members of the Code Sec. 382 loss subgroup are also members of the SRLY subgroup with respect to those built-in losses.

.05 Ordering Rules for Absorption of NOLs

Net operating loss carryovers and carrybacks to a tax year are determined under the principles of Code Sec. 172 and Reg. § 1.1502-21.[94] Thus, NOLs permitted to be absorbed in a consolidated return year generally are absorbed in the order of the tax years in which they arose. Net operating losses carried from tax years ending on the same date, and which are available to offset consolidated taxable income for the year, are generally absorbed on a *pro rata* basis. Additional rules provided under the Code or regulations also apply. For example, Code Sec. 382(l)(2)(B) provides that if losses are carried from the same tax year, losses subject to limitation under Code Sec. 382 are absorbed before losses that are not so limited. Further, Reg. § 1.1502-15(a) provides that to the extent that a built-in loss is allowed as a deduction in the year it is recognized, it offsets any consolidated taxable income for the year before any loss carryovers or carrybacks are allowed.

.06 Reattribution of Code Sec. 382 Limitation for an NOL Carryover Reattributed Under Reg. § 1.1502-20(g)

Under Reg. § 1.1502-20(g), if a member disposes of stock of a subsidiary and the member's loss would be disallowed under Reg. § 1.1502-20(a)(1), the common

---

[88] Reg. § 1.1502-15(a).
[89] Reg. § 1.1502-15(c)(1).
[90] Reg. § 1.1502-15(c)(2).
[91] Reg. § 1.1502-15(g)(1).

[92] Reg. § 1.1502-15(g)(2)(ii).
[93] Reg. § 1.1502-15(g)(4).
[94] Reg. § 1.1502-21(b)(1).

parent may make an election to reattribute to itself any portion of the NOL carryovers and net capital loss carryovers attributable to the subsidiary (and any lower-tier subsidiary) without regard to the order in which they were incurred. The amount reattributed may not exceed the amount of loss that would be disallowed if no election were made. The common parent succeeds to the reattributed losses as if the losses were succeeded to in a transaction described in Code Sec. 381(a). (If the loss carryover was subject to the SRLY limitation, see the Code Sec. 381(c)(1)(B) limitation discussed above, which is illustrated in a different context in Rev. Rul. 75-378, 1975-2 CB 355.)

Any owner shift of the subsidiary is not taken into account under Code Sec. 382 with respect to the reattributed losses. However, if the reattributed NOL carryover was subject to a prior Code Sec. 382 limitation, the common parent will need to reattribute to itself part or all of the Code Sec. 382 limitation. Otherwise the common parent's Code Sec. 382 limitation will be zero. The rules requiring the reattribution of the Code Sec. 382 limitation and an illustration of how they apply to a Reg. § 1.1502-20(g) reattribution of an NOL carryover can be found in Reg. § 1.1502-96(d). (The regulations also require the common parent to satisfy the continuity of business enterprise requirement if the two-year period specified by Code Sec. 382(c)(1) has not expired.)

.07 Reg. § 1.1502-11(b) Limitation on Use of Departing Member's NOL

See ¶ 335 for a discussion and illustration of rules that limit the ability of a consolidated group to use a departing member's NOL carryover to offset gain on the disposition of the departing member's stock. The limitation prevents a "circular basis" problem and results in the departing member leaving the group with its NOL carryover.

.08 NOL Carrybacks in General [95]

If any CNOL that is attributable to a member may be carried back to a separate return year of the member, the amount of the CNOL that is attributable to the member is apportioned to the member (apportioned loss) and carried back to the separate return year.[96] If carried back to a separate return year, the apportioned loss may not be carried back to an equivalent, or earlier, consolidated return year of the group; if carried over to a separate return year, the apportioned loss may not be carried over to an equivalent, or later, consolidated return year of the group.[97]

> **Example 9:** As an example of NOL carryback of acquired member: The P group was formed in Year 0. During Year 1 and Year 2, the P group has taxable income. At the end of Year 2, P purchases the stock of L. L has had an NOL in every year of its existence. In Year 3, the P group has a CNOL. The Year 3

---

[95] The acquiring corporation in a Code Sec. 381(a) transaction is precluded by Code Sec. 381(b)(3) from carrying back an NOL or net capital loss for a tax year ending after the date of the Code Sec. 381(a) transaction to a tax year of the acquired corporation.

[96] Reg. § 1.1502-21(b)(2). For a special "Offspring Rule" where a member has been a member of the consolidated

group since its organization, *see* Reg. § 1.1502-21(b)(2)(ii)(B). The Offspring Rule permits the CNOL attributable to the member to be included in the carrybacks to consolidated return years before the member's existence.

[97] Reg. § 1.1502-21(b)(2).

CNOL attributable to L cannot be carried back to the P group's equivalent year. Instead, the CNOL is carried forward to Year 4 of the P group.

SRLY rules. The following example illustrates the application of the SRLY rules to an NOL carryback.

> ***Example 10:*** As an example of SRLY limitation for NOL carrybacks: P sells the stock of S (which in turn owned the stock of T) to P1 on December 31, Year 1. For Year 3, the P1/S/T consolidated group generates a CNOL. The P1/S/T consolidated group does not waive the carryback period.[98] Consequently, if S and/or T generates a loss during Year 3, each will carry back its loss (if any) to the P consolidated return years Year 1 and Year 2 (both years in which the P consolidated group generated income.)[99]

Will the SRLY rules limit the P group's use of the carried back losses?[100] Code Sec. 382 does not apply to NOL carrybacks, but the SRLY rules generally do limit NOL carrybacks to consolidated groups. Because there is no overlap of these limitations, the regulations do not eliminate the SRLY limitation for NOL carrybacks from separate return limitation years. Thus, the SRLY subgroup limitation will limit the P group's use of the carried-back losses.[101]

¶ 645 Net Capital Loss and Credit Utilization System

Rules for separate return Code Sec. 383, consolidated return Code Sec. 383, and separate return limitation year (SRLY) should be addressed at this point.

.01 Separate Return Code Sec. 383 Rules

Code Sec. 383 provides that, under regulations, if an ownership change occurs with respect to a corporation, the amount of any excess credit (foreign tax credit, general business credit and/or minimum tax credit) available in any post-change year is limited to an amount determined on the basis of the tax liability attributable to so much of the taxable income as does not exceed the limitation for such post-change year, to the extent available after the application of the Code Sec. 382 limitation to net operating loss (NOL) and net capital loss carryovers.

The regulations provide as follows:[102] If an ownership change occurs with respect to a loss corporation, the Code Sec. 382 limitation and the Code Sec. 383 credit limitation for a post-change year limit the amount of taxable income and regular tax liability, respectively, that can be offset by pre-change capital losses and

---

[98] If a member of a consolidated group becomes a member of another consolidated group, the acquiring group may make an irrevocable election to relinquish, with respect to all CNOL attributable to the member, the portion of the carryback period for which the corporation was a member of another group, provided that any other corporation joining the acquiring group that was affiliated with the member immediately before it joined the acquiring group is also included in the election (*see* Reg. § 1.1502-21(b)(3)(B)). The form for the election is set forth in the regulations and must be filed with the acquiring group's original income tax return for the year the corporation(s) became a member.

[99] *See* Reg. § 1.1502-21(b)(2) (apportionment of CNOL and carry back of apportioned loss to separate return

years) and Code Sec. 172. See Code Sec. 172(b)(1)(H) for a five-year carryback period for NOLs incurred in any tax year ending in 2001 or 2002.

[100] The applicable loss and credit utilization regulations for a carryback are those in effect for the year to which an item is carried back.

[101] *See* Reg. § 1.1502-1(f) (definition of "separate return limitation year"), Reg. § 1.1502-21(c)(1) (application of SRLY limitation generally), Reg. § 1.1502-21(c)(2) (application of SRLY limitation to SRLY subgroups) and Reg. § 1.1502-21(c)(2)(ii) (definition of SRLY subgroup in the case of a loss carryback).

[102] Reg. § 1.383-1(b).

pre-change credits of the loss corporation. The amount of taxable income of a new loss corporation for any post-change year that may be offset by pre-change losses (as defined in Reg. § 1.383-1(b)(4), including pre-change capital losses) may not exceed the Code Sec. 382 limitation for the post-change year.[103] The amount of regular tax liability of a new loss corporation for any post-change year that may be offset by pre-change credits may not exceed the Code Sec. 383 credit limitation for the post-change year.[104]

Ordinarily, the "Code Sec. 383 credit limitation" after an ownership change for a corporation with a pre-change credit but no pre-change losses will be 35 percent of the Code Sec. 382 limitation. If the corporation also has a NOL carryover, the "Code Sec. 383 credit limitation" ordinarily will be 35 percent of the remainder of the Code Sec. 382 limitation left after absorption of any allowable NOL carryover.[105]

Rules for determining the order in which pre-change losses and pre-change credits absorb the "Code Sec. 382 limitation" and "Code Sec. 383 credit limitation" are provided by Reg. § 1.383-1(d)(2).

Reg. § 1.383-3(e) contains other rules for determining the carryforward of unused Code Sec. 382 limitation.

A final note: For an acquisition year only, see Code Sec. 381(c)(24) and the regulations thereunder for a limitation on use of a business credit carryover acquired in a Code Sec. 381(a) transaction where the acquisition does not occur on the last day of the acquiring corporation's tax year. The limitation is the counterpart of the Code Sec. 381(c)(1)(B) limitation for NOL carryovers.

.02 Consolidated Return Code Sec. 383 and Separate Return Limitation Year (SRLY) Rules

Under Reg. § 1.1502-98, the rules contained in Reg. § 1.1502-91 through Reg. § 1.1502-96 also apply for purposes of Code Sec. 383, with "appropriate adjustments" to reflect that Code Sec. 383 applies to net capital losses and credits.

This means that if the counterpart of a new loss member or loss subgroup joins a consolidated group in a transaction that results in an ownership change, and there are pre-change credits but no pre-change losses, the "Code Sec. 383 credit limitation" ordinarily will be 35 percent of the Code Sec. 382 limitation or subgroup Code Sec. 382 limitation, as the case may be.

The successive ownership and apportionment of subgroup Code Sec. 382 principles that are applicable to NOL utilization also apply to net capital loss and credit utilization.

Reg. § 1.1502-22 provides SRLY rules for net capital loss carryovers similar to those for NOLs. For example, the SRLY limitation generally does not apply to net capital loss carryovers when the application of the SRLY rules results in an overlap with the application of Code Sec. 383.

---

[103] Reg. § 1.383-1(d)(1).
[104] Reg. § 1.383-1(d)(1).
[105] Reg. § 1.383-1(c)(6).

Temporary Reg. § 1.1502-3T(c) and Reg. § 1.1502-55T provided a SRLY limitation, including a subgrouping concept, for business credit carryovers and minimum tax credit carryovers. These temporary regulations generally were effective for consolidated return years for which the due date of the return (without extensions) was after March 13, 1998. And Temporary Reg. § 1.1502-4T eliminated the SRLY limitation for excess foreign tax credit carryovers for consolidated return years for which the due date of the return (without extensions) was after March 13, 1998.

With few modifications, the rules set forth in the above temporary regulations were adopted in final regulations (Reg. § 1.1502-3 (consolidated tax credits), Reg. § 1.1502-4 (consolidated foreign tax credit) and Reg. § 1.1502-55 (consolidated minimum tax credit)) issued in May 2000. The final regulations generally apply to consolidated return years for which the due date (without extensions) was after March 13, 1998.[106] The principal modification to the temporary regulations is that, for consolidated return years for which the return was due (without extensions) after May 25, 2000, the overlap principles of Reg. § 1.1502-21(g) are extended to the business credit and minimum tax credit carryovers.[107] Thus, the SRLY limitation will be eliminated with respect to most credit carryovers for a calendar year consolidated group effective in 2000. Numerous other special effective dates also must be considered.

¶ 655 Conclusions

The most common Code Sec. 382 limitations come into play for consolidated groups when one member of a consolidated group acquires one or more members of another consolidated group with an NOL carryover. Then the issue is whether there is an ownership change of a "loss subgroup" or a "new loss member." If a loss subgroup is acquired, single-entity concepts are used to determine whether there is an ownership change and the amount of the Code Sec. 382 limitation. If a new loss member is acquired, separate-entity concepts are applied.

When the SRLY limitation applies to an NOL, the aggregate of the NOL carryovers and carrybacks of a member arising in separate return limitation years that are included in consolidated NOL deductions may not exceed the consolidated taxable income for all consolidated return years of the consolidated group determined by reference to only the member's taxable income. If previously affiliated members join the consolidated group at the same time as the member with an NOL carryover, the loss corporation and the joining members may constitute an SRLY subgroup, and the SRLY limitation applies to the SRLY subgroup. Similar rules apply to an NOL carryback.

The SRLY limitation, however, generally is eliminated where there is an overlap with the Code Sec. 382 limitation. However, there are traps for the unwary, because the overlap rule only applies if the members of any Code Sec. 382 loss subgroup are members of the SRLY subgroup and vice versa.

---

[106] Reg. § 1.1502-3 (d) (3) (i) and Reg. § 1.1502-55 (h) (4) (iii) (C).

[107] Reg. § 1.1502-3 (d) (2) (iv) and Reg. § 1.1502-55 (h) (4) (iii) (B) (5).

In general, the consolidated Code Sec. 382 NOL limitation rules apply for purposes of Code Sec. 383 with "appropriate adjustments" to reflect that Code Sec. 383 applies to net capital losses and credits. Ordinarily, this means that if the counterpart of a new loss member or a loss subgroup joins a consolidated group in a transaction that results in a change in ownership, and there are pre-change credits but no pre-change losses, the Code Sec. 383 credit limitation will be 35 percent of the Code Sec. 382 limitation.

SRLY rules for net capital losses correspond to the SRLY rules for net operating losses. SRLY limitations also are imposed for business credit carryovers and for minimum tax credit carryovers. However, the overlap principles for NOL carryovers are adopted for Code Sec. 383 purposes; this generally eliminates the SRLY limitation. Finally, the SRLY restriction has been eliminated for foreign tax credit carryovers without regard to an overlap with Code Sec. 383.

¶ 665 Frequently Asked Questions

Question

What is the consolidated Code Sec. 382 limitation?

Answer

The separate return Code Sec. 382 limitation is the value of the acquired loss corporation's stock immediately before a defined "ownership change," multiplied by the long-term tax-exempt rate in effect at the time of the change (as published in the Internal Revenue Bulletin). A purchaser of a loss corporation thus may only use the loss corporation's pre-change NOL carryover to the extent of the income that the loss corporation would have had if its assets were sold and the proceeds invested in long-term tax-exempt bonds. The consolidated Code Sec. 382 limitation generally comes into play when a consolidated group purchases a new loss member (to which a separate entity Code Sec. 382 limitation calculation is made) or a loss subgroup (to which a single entity Code Sec. 382 limitation calculation is made) with an NOL carryover.

Question

What is the consolidated Code Sec. 383 limitation?

Answer

Code Sec. 383 provides that if an ownership change occurs with respect to a corporation, the amount of any excess credit (foreign tax credit, general business credit, and/or minimum tax credit) available in any post-change year is limited to an amount determined on the basis of the tax liability attributable to so much of the taxable income as does not exceed the limitation for such post-change year, to the extent available after the application of the Code Sec. 382 limitation to NOL and net capital loss carryovers. Ordinarily, the Code Sec. 383 limitation after an ownership change for a corporation with a pre-change credit but no pre-change losses will be 35 percent of the Code Sec. 382 limitation. If the corporation also has an NOL carryover, the Code Sec. 383 limitation ordinarily will be 35 percent of the remainder of the Code Sec. 382 limitation left after absorption of any allowable NOL carryover. As with the consolidated Code Sec. 382 limitation, the consolidated Code Sec. 383 limitation generally comes into play when a consolidated group purchases a new loss member (to which a separate entity Code Sec. 383 limitation calculation is made) or a loss subgroup (to which a single entity Code Sec. 383 limitation calculation is made) with a credit carryover.

Question

Does the SRLY limitation apply under current law?

Answer

In most situations, the SRLY limitation is eliminated, provided there is an overlap with Code Sec. 382 or Code Sec. 383, as the case may be.

Chapter 7

Earnings and Profits System

¶ 701 Overview—Earnings and Profits System

The consolidated return earnings and profits rules are found in Reg. § 1.1502-33 and Reg. § 1.1552-1 and reflect single-entity thinking. The heart of this system consists of rules for tiering up the earnings and profits of consolidated subsidiaries, and eliminating those earnings and profits when the subsidiary leaves the group. Other rules address earnings and profits stock basis, allocation of federal income tax liability, a change in structure of the group, and other miscellaneous matters.

.01 Tiering-Up of Earnings and Profits

Reg. § 1.1502-33(b) provides rules for adjusting the earnings and profits of a subsidiary (S) and any member (P) owning S's stock (see ¶ 725). These rules adjust P's earnings and profits to reflect S's earnings and profits for the period that S is a member of the consolidated group. They duplicate the earnings and profits of lower-tier members in the earnings and profits of higher-tier members, rather than elevate them to the common parent level without duplication at the lower-tiers.

.02 Earnings and Profits Stock Basis

For the same reasons that P makes investment adjustments to its stock basis (i.e., to prevent the duplication of gain or loss on the sale of S), P maintains an earnings and profits stock basis that is explained at ¶ 735.

.03 *Allocation of Federal Income Tax Liability*

The allocation of federal income tax liability for earnings and profits purposes is a complex subject involving both a basic method and, if the consolidated group elects, a complementary method that takes into account the compensation of members for the absorption of their tax attributes. These rules, their effects, and the election procedures for allocation of federal income tax liability are explained at ¶ 745.

.04 *Changes in the Structure of the Group*

The common theme running through these earnings and profits rules is to duplicate the earnings and profits of S in P for the period S is a member of the consolidated group. In the same vein, adjustments are made to preserve the duplication of earnings and profits of lower-tier members in higher-tier members following Code Sec. 351 transfers, reverse acquisitions, and certain other changes in structure of the consolidated group (see ¶ 755).

.05 *Elimination of Earnings and Profits upon Deconsolidation*

Without special rules, "dividend-stripping" abuses could occur if either S were deconsolidated from P, but P retained S stock, or if the P group were deconsolidated. Separate return dividend distributions from S to P out of earnings and profits accumulated in consolidated return years (which generally would have increased P's S stock basis) generally would not reduce P's S stock basis (except to the extent that Code Sec. 1059 applies). Thus, S's consolidated return year earnings and profits could be distributed, reducing the value of S without a stock basis reduction, thereby creating an artificial loss if the S stock were sold. As explained at ¶ 765, to prevent this abuse, S's consolidated return year earnings and profits are eliminated upon deconsolidation.

.06 *Other Rules*

Finally, intercompany transaction, recordkeeping, anti-avoidance, predecessor and successor, and retroactive effective date rules are described (see ¶ 775).

.07 *Earnings and Profits in General*

Before discussing these rules, a brief refresher is provided on calculation of earnings and profits in general (see ¶ 715).

¶ 715 Earnings and Profits in General

Earnings and profits is an economic concept used by the tax law "to approximate a corporation's power to make distributions which are more than just a return of investment."[1] Although neither the Code nor the regulations define "earnings and profits," Code Sec. 312 and the regulations take taxable income as the starting point and adjust it for certain items that increase or decrease the ability of a corporation to pay a dividend. Most professionals who provide comments to the IRS

---

[1] *Henry C. Beck Co.*, 52 TC 1, 6, CCH Dec. 29,516 (1969), aff'd per curiam, CA-5, 70-2 USTC ¶ 9657, 433 F2d 309.

agree that the following adjustments, among others, should be made to taxable income to arrive at earnings and profits:[2]

1. Add: certain items excluded from taxable income
   a. tax-exempt proceeds of life insurance
   b. tax-exempt interest on state and municipal obligations
   c. tax-exempt compensation for injuries or sickness

2. Add: certain items deducted in computing taxable income
   a. dividends-received deduction
   b. net operating loss deduction (it is a carryback or carryover of losses that reduced earnings and profits in the year they occurred)
   c. capital loss carryback or carryover
   d. depreciation in excess of straight-line (Code Sec. 312(k))

3. Subtract: certain items not deducted in computing taxable income
   a. federal income taxes
   b. expenses and interest incurred in earning tax-exempt interest
   c. excess charitable contributions
   d. premiums on term life insurance that are disallowed in computing taxable income
   e. recognized but disallowed losses

¶ 725 Tiering-Up of Earnings and Profits

P and S are treated as a single entity by reflecting the earnings and profits of lower-tier members in the earnings and profits of higher-tier members and consolidating the group's earnings and profits in the common parent. Specifically, P's earnings and profits are adjusted under Reg. § 1.1502-33(b)(1) to reflect changes in S's earnings and profits in accordance with the principles of Reg. § 1.1502-32 (see Chapter 3), consistently applied, and an adjustment to P's earnings and profits for a tax year under the regulations is treated as earnings and profits of P for the tax year in which the adjustment arises.[3] However, modifications to the principles include:[4]

- The amount of P's adjustment is determined by reference to S's earnings and profits, rather than S's taxable income and tax-exempt items (and therefore, for example, the deferral of a negative adjustment for S's unabsorbed losses does not apply); and

- The tax-sharing rules under Reg. § 1.1502-33(d) apply, rather than those of the investment adjustment rules.

Once the earnings and profits of S are tiered up to P, P's earnings and profits do not change when S distributes a dividend to P.

---

[2] *See* B. BITTKER & J. EUSTICE, FEDERAL INCOME TAXATION OF CORPORATIONS AND SHAREHOLDERS, ¶ 803 (7th Ed. 2001).

[3] Reg. § 1.1502-33(b).

[4] For special rules when S distributes earnings and profits accumulated in separate return years of S that are not separate return limitation years, *see* Reg. § 1.1502-33(b)(2) and Reg. § 1.1502-33(b)(3), Example 1(d).

Example 1: As an example of the tier-up and distribution of earnings and profits:[5] P forms S in Year 1 with a $100 contribution. S has $100 of earnings and profits for Year 1 and no earnings and profits for Year 2. During Year 2, S declares and distributes a $50 dividend to P. S's $100 of earnings and profits for Year 1 increases P's earnings and profits for Year 1. P has no additional earnings and profits for Year 2 as a result of the $50 distribution in Year 2, because there is a $50 increase in P's earnings and profits as a result of the receipt of the dividend and a corresponding $50 decrease in S's earnings and profits under Code Sec. 312(a) that is reflected in P's earnings and profits.

Example 2: As an example of the distribution of current earnings and profits:[6] The facts are the same as in Example 1, except that S distributes the $50 dividend at the end of Year 1, rather than during Year 2. P's earnings and profits are increased by $100 (S's $50 of undistributed earnings and profits, plus P's receipt of the $50 distribution). Thus, S's earnings and profits increase by $50, and P's earnings and profits increase by $100.

Example 3: As an example of an earnings and profits deficit:[7] Assume instead that after P forms S in Year 1 with a $100 contribution, S borrows additional funds and has a $150 deficit in earnings and profits for Year 1. The corresponding loss for tax purposes is not absorbed in Year 1 and is included in the group's consolidated net operating loss carried forward to Year 2. S's $150 deficit in earnings and profits decreases P's earnings and profits for Year 1 by $150. (Absorption of the loss in a later tax year has no effect on the earnings and profits of P and S.)

Earnings and profits are not tiered up to the extent that they are attributable to stock owned by nonmembers. For example, if P owns 80 percent of S, only 80 percent (not 100 percent) of S's earnings and profits tier up to P.[8]

Note that these rules do not elevate the earnings and profits of S to P. Instead, the earnings and profits of S are duplicated by P. This has the effect of consolidating the group's consolidated return year earnings and profits in the group's common parent, without reducing the earnings and profits of the subsidiaries. As discussed below, the earnings and profits of S are eliminated upon its deconsolidation, but the earnings and profits previously tiered up to P and higher-tier members are not eliminated.

Finally, Reg. § 1.1502-33(a)(2) includes an antiduplication rule.[9] P's earnings and profits must not be adjusted under the consolidated return rules and other rules of law in a manner that has the effect of duplicating an adjustment. The example cited by the regulations is where S's earnings and profits are tiered up to P and S subsequently liquidates into P under Code Sec. 332. Without the antiduplication rule, S's earnings and profits would carry over to P under Code Sec. 381 and duplicate the tiered-up earnings and profits.

---

[5] *See* Reg. § 1.1502-33(b)(3), Example 1(a)–(b).
[6] Reg. § 1.1502-33(b)(3), Example 1(c).
[7] *See* Reg. § 1.1502-33(b)(3), Example 1(e).

[8] *See* Reg. § 1.1502-33(b)(3), Example 3.
[9] Reg. § 1.1502-33(a)(2).

¶ 735   Earnings and Profits Stock Basis

For purposes of determining P's earnings and profits from the disposition of S's stock, P's basis in S's stock is adjusted to reflect S's earnings and profits determined under the rules discussed at ¶ 725, rather than under Reg. § 1.1502-32.[10] For example, P's earnings and profits basis in S's stock is increased by positive earnings and profits and decreased by deficits in earnings and profits.

> ***Example 4:*** As an example of adjustments to stock basis:[11] P forms S in Year 1 with a $100 contribution. For Year 1, S has $75 of taxable income and $100 of earnings and profits. For Year 2, S has no taxable income or earnings and profits, and S declares and distributes a $50 dividend to P. P sells all of S's stock for $150 at the end of Year 2. P's earnings and profits basis in its S stock immediately before the sale is $150 (the $100 initial basis, plus S's $100 of earnings and profits for Year 1, minus the $50 distribution of earnings and profits in Year 2). Thus, P recognizes no gain or loss from the sale of S's stock for earnings and profits purposes.

P may have a negative earnings and profits basis in S's stock for earnings and profits purposes (whether or not there is an excess loss account under Reg. § 1.1502-32), and the negative basis is determined, adjusted, and taken into account in accordance with the principles of Reg. § 1.1502-19 and Reg. § 1.1502-32.[12]

¶ 745   Allocation of Federal Income Tax Liability

Code Sec. 1552 authorizes the election of any one of three specified basic methods (or any other method approved by the IRS) for allocating consolidated federal income tax liability of the group among its members for purposes of determining each member's earnings and profits. (An allocation of federal income taxes reduces earnings and profits, and a payment for use of tax attributes increases earnings and profits.) Each member, however, is severally liable for federal income taxes.[13]

.01   First Basic Method

Code Sec. 1552(a)(1) provides that under the first basic method, the federal income tax liability may be apportioned among the members of the consolidated group in accordance with the ratio in which that portion of the consolidated taxable income attributable to the member of the group having taxable income relates to the consolidated taxable income. More precisely, under Reg. § 1.1552-1(a)(1), the first basic method allocates the consolidated group's tax liability as follows: the group's tax liability is multiplied by a fraction, of which the numerator is the separate taxable income of such member (but not less than zero), and of which the denominator is the sum of the separate taxable incomes of all members.[14] The taxable income of a member for this purpose is the separate taxable income determined under Reg. § 1.1502-12, adjusted for the following items taken into account in the computation of consolidated taxable income:

---

[10] Reg. § 1.1502-33(d)(1).
[11] *See* Reg. § 1.1502-33(c)(1), Examples (a)–(b).
[12] Reg. § 1.1502-33(c)(1).

[13] Reg. § 1.1502-6.
[14] Other rules apply to consolidated return years beginning before December 31, 1965.

- The member's portion of the consolidated net operating loss deduction;
- The member's portion of the consolidated charitable contributions deduction;
- The member's portion of the consolidated dividends-received deduction,
- The member's portion of the consolidated Code Sec. 247 deduction;
- The member's capital gain net income (determined without regard to any net capital loss carryover attributable to the member);
- The member's net capital loss and Code Sec. 1231 net loss, reduced by the portion of any consolidated net capital loss attributable to the member; and
- The portion of any consolidated net capital loss carryover attributable to the member, which is absorbed in the tax year.

Note that the first basic method does not give effect to tax credits attributable to a member and does not compensate a member for losses and credits that are absorbed by the consolidated group.

.02 Second Basic Method

Under Code Sec. 1552(a)(2), the tax liability of the group may be allocated to the several members of the consolidated group on the basis of the percentage of the total federal income tax of each member, if computed on a separate return, would bear to the total amount of the taxes for all members of the group so computed (the second basic method). For this purpose, the separate return tax liability of a member is its tax liability as if it filed a separate return for the year. The exception is that it cannot be less than zero, and the following consolidation adjustments are made:

- Gains and losses on intercompany transactions must be taken into account as provided in Reg. § 1.1502-13 as if a consolidated return had been filed;
- Gains and losses relating to inventory adjustments must be taken into account as provided in Reg. § 1.1502-18 as if a consolidated return had been filed for the year;
- Transactions with respect to stock, bonds, or other obligations of members shall be reflected as provided in Reg. § 1.1502-13(f) and Reg. § 1.1502-13(g) as if a consolidated return had been filed for the year;
- Excess losses must be included in income as provided in Reg. § 1.1502-19 as if a consolidated return had been filed for the year;
- In computing the depreciation deduction under Code Sec. 167, property does not lose its character as new property as a result of a transfer from one member to another member during the year;
- A dividend distributed by one member to another member during the year is not taken into account in computing the deductions with respect to dividends received and dividends paid;
- Basis must be determined under Reg. § 1.1502-31 and Reg. § 1.1502-32, and earnings and profits must be determined under Reg. § 1.1502-33;

¶745.02

- Investment credit recapture must be determined under Reg. § 1.1502-33 (f) (2); and

- The amount of the graduated rate brackets of a member is the amount of the graduated brackets allowed on the consolidated return divided by the number of members (or the portion of the consolidated graduated rate brackets apportioned to the member pursuant to a schedule attached to the consolidated return for the tax year).[15]

Note that the second basic method, unlike the first basic method, takes into account credits and penalties. However, like all the basic methods, the second basic method does not compensate a member for the use of its tax attributes.

.03 Third Basic Method

Code Sec. 1552(a)(3) provides a third basic method under which the tax liability of the consolidated group (excluding tax increases arising from consolidation) must be allocated on the basis of the contribution of each member of the group to the consolidated taxable income of the group. Any tax increases arising from the consolidation must be allocated to the several members in direct proportion to the reduction in tax liability resulting to the members from the filing of the consolidated return, as measured by the difference between their tax liabilities determined on a separate return basis and their tax liabilities based on their contributions to the consolidated taxable income. Under Reg. § 1.1552-1(a)(3), the tax liability of the consolidated group is initially allocated on the basis of the contribution of each member of the group to consolidated taxable income, as under the first basic method. Any tax increases of a member arising from consolidation are then distributed to the members in direct proportion to the reduction in tax liability resulting to such members from the filing of the consolidated return, as measured by the difference between their tax liabilities determined on a separate return basis and their tax liabilities based on their contributions to the consolidated taxable income.

The regulations provide the detailed steps necessary to use this method. However, this method reflects tax detriments that were eliminated in the 1960s, and it is now rarely used.

.04 Additional Basic Methods

The tax liability of the consolidated group may be allocated in accordance with any other method selected by the group with the approval of the IRS.[16] No method of allocation may be approved that could result in the allocation of a positive tax liability for a tax year (among the members who are allocated a positive tax liability for such year) in a total amount that is more or less than the tax liability of the group for such year.

> **Example 5:** As an example of the first and second basic methods: P owns all the stock of S1, S2, and S3. For Year 1, P generates $600,000 ordinary income for the year and a $400,000 Code Sec. 1231 loss; S1 generates $200,000 ordinary income and a $30,000 business credit; S2 generates a $200,000 capital

---

[15] Reg. § 1.1552-1(a)(2).

[16] Reg. § 1.1552-1(a)(4).

gain and a $400,000 Code Sec. 1231 gain; and S3 generates a $200,000 ordinary loss and a $400,000 capital loss. Assume a flat 35-percent federal income tax rate. Consolidated taxable income was $600,000, and consolidated tax liability was $180,000. In summary, the separate and consolidated federal income tax liabilities would be as illustrated here:

	P	S1	S2	S3	Consolidated Group
Ordinary Income	$600,000	$200,000	$0	($200,000)	$600,000
Capital Gain (Loss)	0	0	200,000	(400,000)	($200,000)
Code Sec. 1231 Gain (Loss)	(400,000)	0	400,000	0	$0
Taxable Income (Loss)	200,000	200,000	600,000	(200,000)	$600,000
Separate Tax Liability	70,000	40,000 (net of $30,000 business credit)	210,000	0	
Consolidated Tax Liability Before Credits					$210,000
Business Credit					$30,000
Consolidate Tax Liability					$180,000

Under the first basic method, the $180,000 consolidated tax liability is allocated in proportion to the members' separate taxable incomes, including capital and Code Sec. 1231 gains and losses, with no member being treated as having less than zero separate taxable income.

P = 20% ($200,000 ÷ $1,000,000), or $36,000

S1 = 20% ($200,000 ÷ $1,000,000), or $36,000

S2 = 60% ($600,000 ÷ $1,000,000), or $108,000

S3 = 0% ($0 ÷ $1,000,000), or $0

Under the second basic method, the $180,000 consolidated tax liability is allocated in proportion to the relative hypothetical separate tax liabilities of the members, with no member being treated as having less than zero separate tax liability.

$P = 22\%$ ($70,000 ÷ $320,000), or $39,600

$S1 = 13\%$ ($40,000 ÷ $320,000), or $23,400

$S2 = 65\%$ ($210,000 ÷ $320,000), or $117,000

$S3 = 0\%$ ($0 ÷ $320,000), or $0

.05 Complementary Methods to Compensate for Use of Tax Attributes[17]

The basic allocation methods, however, do not reflect the absorption of another member's losses or credits. For example, if P's $100 of income is offset by S's $100 of deductions, consolidated tax liability is zero, and no amount is allocated under the Code Sec. 1552 rules.

Reg. § 1.1502-33(d) generally authorizes the election of either of two specified complementary methods (or any other complementary method approved by the IRS) to the group's basic allocation method, to cause the profit members of the group to compensate any other members for the use of their tax attributes.

.06 Percentage Complementary Method

The percentage complementary method[18] allocates tax liability based on the absorption of tax attributes, without taking into account the ability of any member to subsequently absorb its own tax attributes. The allocation under this method is in addition to the allocation under Code Sec. 1552.

Two specific rules apply to the percentage complementary method:

1. *Decreased earnings and profits.* A member's allocation under Code Sec. 1552 for any year is increased, thereby decreasing its earnings and profits, by a fixed percentage (not to exceed 100 percent) of the excess, if any, of:

   a. The member's separate return tax liability for the consolidated return year as determined under Reg. § 1.1552-1(a)(2)(ii); over

   b. the amount allocated to the member under Code Sec. 1552.

2. *Increased earnings and profits.* An amount equal to the total decrease in earnings and profits under (1) above (including amounts allocated as a result of a carryback) increases the earnings and profits of the members whose attributes are absorbed, and is allocated among them in a manner that reasonably reflects the absorption of the tax attributes.

Because of its simplicity, the percentage complementary method is most commonly used. Also, the investment adjustment rules mandate that the percentage complementary method be used in determining the allocation of federal income tax liability for stock basis purposes. Accordingly, an election to use the percentage

---

[17] Other rules apply to consolidated return years beginning before December 31, 1965.

[18] Reg. § 1.1502-33(d)(3).

complementary method for earnings and profits purposes eliminates the need for the consolidated group to make two different tax allocation computations.

Example 6: As an example of the percentage complementary method: The facts are the same as in Example 5 at ¶ 745.04, and the consolidated group has elected the first basic method and the percentage complementary method with a percentage of 100 percent. The changes in the allocation of the $180,000 federal income tax liability are as follows:

	P	S1	S2	S3
Separate Return Tax.........	$70,000	$40,000	$210,000	$0
Less: Basic Method Allocation .	36,000	36,000	108,000	0
Excess	$34,000	$4,000	$102,000	$0

The $140,000 tax benefit for use of S3's $200,000 ordinary loss and $200,000 capital loss is allocated to S3. Thus, P, S1, and S2 are treated as owing S3, $34,000, $4,000, and $102,000, respectively. Consequently, under the first basic method and percentage complementary method, the total allocation of federal income tax liability for Year 1 is:

	P	S1	S2	S3
First Basic Method	$36,000	$36,000	$108,000	$0
Add: Percentage Complementary Method ...	34,000	4,000	102,000	(140,000)
Total	$70,000	$40,000	$210,000	($140,000)

.07 Wait-and-See Complementary Method

Under the wait-and-see complementary method,[19] in the year that a member's tax attribute is absorbed, the consolidated group's consolidated tax liability is allocated in accordance with the group's method under Code Sec. 1552. When, in effect, the member with the tax attribute could have absorbed the attribute on a separate return basis in a later year, a portion of the group's consolidated tax liability for the later year that is otherwise allocated to the members under Code Sec. 1552 is reallocated. The reallocation takes into account all consolidated return years to which this method applies (the computation period), and is determined by comparing the tax allocated to a member during the computational period with the member's tax liability as if it had filed separate returns during the computation period.

Three additional rules apply to the wait-and-see complementary method:

1. *Cap on allocation under Code Sec. 1552.* A member's allocation under Code Sec. 1552 for a tax year may not exceed the excess, if any, of:

    a. The total of the tax liabilities of the member for the computation period (including under the current year), determined as if the member had filed separate returns; over

---

[19] Reg. § 1.1502-33(d)(2).

b. The total amount allocated to the member under Code Sec. 1552 and this wait and see method for the computation period (except the current year).

2. *Reallocation of capped amounts.* To the extent that the amount allocated to a member under Code Sec. 1552 exceeds the limitation under 1, the excess is allocated among the remaining members in proportion to (but not to exceed the amount of) each member's excess, if any, of:

a. The total of the tax liabilities of the member for the computation period (including the current year), determined as if the member had filed separate returns; over

b. The total amount allocated to the member under Code Sec. 1552 and this method for the computation period (including, for the current year only, the amount allocated under Code Sec. 1552).

3. *Reallocation of excess capped amounts.* If the reductions under the Code Sec. 1552 cap on allocation rule exceed the amounts allocable under the reallocation of capped amounts rule, the excess is allocated among the members in accordance with the group's method under Code Sec. 1552, without taking the reallocation of capped amounts rule into account.

Reg. § 1.1502-33(d)(6), Example 1 illustrates the wait-and-see complementary method.

.08 Additional Complementary Methods

The absorption by one member of the tax attributes of another member may be reflected under any other method approved in writing by the IRS.[20]

.09 Effect of Tax Allocations

The amount of tax liability allocated to a corporation as its share of the tax liability of the group pursuant to a basic method will (1) result in a decrease in the earnings and profits of such corporation, and (2) be treated as a liability for such amount.

If the full amount of such liability is not paid by such corporation, pursuant to a tax-sharing agreement or otherwise, the amount that is not paid will generally be treated as a distribution with respect to stock, a contribution to capital, or a combination thereof, as the case may be.[21] Likewise, the amounts allocated under the complementary methods are treated as allocations of tax liability for this purpose. For example, if P's taxable income is offset by S's loss, and tax liability is allocated under the percentage complementary method, P's earnings and profits are reduced as if its income were subject to tax, P is treated as liable to S for the amount of the tax, and corresponding adjustments are made to S's earnings and profits. If the liability of one member to another is not paid, the amount not paid is generally treated as a distribution, contribution, or both, depending on the relationship between the members.[22]

---

[20] Reg. § 1.1502-33(d)(4).
[21] Reg. § 1.1552-1(b)(2).

[22] Reg. § 1.1502-33(d)(1)(ii).

Thus, regardless of the basic and/or complementary method used, the amount of federal income tax ultimately paid often will be determined under tax-sharing agreements that nullify the effect of the basic and/or complementary method. For this reason, unless the basic and/or complementary method affects ratemaking, minority shareholders, or some other commercial purpose, most consolidated groups choose the earnings and profits methods that are easiest to administer (the first or second basic method, and the percentage complementary method). And, because the percentage complementary method with a 100-percent percentage must be used for investment adjustment purposes, administrative ease would suggest using that method for earnings and profits purposes as well.

> ***Example 7:*** As an example of the effect of tax allocation: The facts are the same as in Example 6 at ¶ 745.06 (i.e., the group uses the first basic method and the percentage complementary method), except that pursuant to a tax-sharing agreement, the parties allocate tax liabilities under the first basic method without compensating members for the use of their tax attributes under the percentage complementary method. Assume each subsidiary has sufficient earnings and profits that any distribution would be a dividend. The earnings and profits of the group would be determined as calculated in Example 6. However, adjustments must be made to reflect the failure of P, S1, and S2 to pay S3 for the use of its losses. For example, S3 would be viewed as paying a dividend to P of $34,000. S3 would be viewed as distributing the amounts owed by S1 and S2 to S3, $4,000 and $102,000, respectively, to P and then P would be treated as contributing the amounts to S1 and S2.

.10 Election of Method Procedures—First Return

According to the regulations,[23] the election of the first basic method, the second basic method, or the third basic method must be made not later than the time prescribed by law for filing the first consolidated return of the group (including extensions thereof).

A statement must be attached to the return that states which method is elected. Such statement must be made by the common parent corporation and is binding upon all members of the group. If another approved basic method is desired, approval of such method must be obtained from the IRS within the time prescribed above. The default method if no election is made is the first basic method.[24]

The regulations also state that tax liability may be allocated under one of the complementary methods only if an election is filed with the group's first return.[25] The election must:

- Be made in a separate statement entitled "Election to Allocate Tax Liability Under § 1.1502-33(d)";

- State the allocation method elected under Reg. § 1.1502-33(d) and under Code Sec. 1552;

---

[23] Reg. § 1.1552-1(c).
[24] Reg. § 1.1552-1(d).

[25] Reg. § 1.1502-33(d)(5).

¶745.10

- If the percentage method is elected, state the percentage (not to exceed 100 percent) to be used; and

- If an another complementary method has been approved by the IRS, attach evidence of its approval.

.11 Electing or Changing Methods

An election of a basic method or a complementary method once made is irrevocable and is binding on the group, unless the IRS authorizes a change to another method prior to the time prescribed by law for filing the return for the year in which the change is to be effective.

The IRS, however, has provided a revenue procedure to obtain consent, without filing an advance ruling request, to elect or to change the consolidated group's method of allocating federal income tax liability to members of the consolidated group for earnings and profits purposes.[26] This revenue procedure applies to a consolidated group if (1) it is not filing its first consolidated return, (2) it has not changed its basic method or complementary method within the five previous tax years, and (3) it is not requesting another basic method or another complementary method.

The manner of effecting the election or change is set forth in Rev. Proc. 90-39 at § 4. The common parent of the group must attach a statement to its consolidated return (timely filed, taking into account any extensions). The statement must contain the following information and representations:

- The name of the common parent corporation of the consolidated group, its Employer Identification Number (EIN) and its address, the name and EIN of all the members of the affiliated group, and the district office that has jurisdiction over the consolidated return;

- A complete description of the present method of allocating the consolidated federal income tax liability. If the present method is not the method that was used for the first filing of a consolidated return, the statement must indicate the date permission to change the group's allocation method was granted and the tax year for which the change was effective. If the group previously used this revenue procedure to elect or to change its method of allocating the consolidated federal income tax liability, a copy of the earlier statement, including the date such statement was filed and the tax year of the consolidated return with which it was filed, must be attached to this statement;

- A complete description of the group's proposed method of allocating consolidated federal income tax liability. If the percentage complementary method is to be employed, the fixed percentage must be stated; and

- A representation that adoption of the proposed method of allocation will not change the taxable status of distributions made during the year of change or in any foreseeable future year to shareholders who are not members of the affiliated group.

---

[26] Rev. Proc. 90-39, 1990-2 CB 365, clarified by Rev. Proc. 90-39A, 1990-2 CB 365.

¶745.11

If Rev. Proc. 90-39 does not apply to an affiliated group for one of the specified reasons, the group needs the IRS's consent to elect or to change its method by filing a request with the IRS as required by the regulations.[27]

¶ 755 Changes in the Structure of the Group

The common theme running through the consolidated return earnings and profits rules is that the earnings and profits of a lower-tier subsidiary should be duplicated by a higher-tier member for the period that the lower-tier member is a member of the group. The regulations extend this concept if the location of a member within the group changes. Specifically, if the location of a member changes, appropriate adjustments must be made to the earnings and profits of the members to prevent the earnings and profits from being eliminated.[28] For example, if P transfers all of S's stock to another member in a transaction to which Code Sec. 351 and Reg. § 1.1502-13 apply, the transferee's earnings and profits are adjusted immediately after the transfer to reflect S's earnings and profits immediately before the transfer from consolidated return years. On the other hand, if the transferee purchases S's stock from P, the transferee's earnings and profits are not adjusted.[29]

In the same vein, if P succeeds another corporation under the principles of Reg. § 1.1502-75(d)(2) or Reg. § 1.1502-75(d)(3) as the common parent of a consolidated group, the earnings and profits of P are adjusted to reflect the earnings and profits of the former common parent immediately before the former common parent ceased to be the common parent.[30] The adjustment is made as if P succeeds to the earnings and profits of the former common parent in a transaction described in Code Sec. 381(a). For example, if P acquires all the stock of X in a reverse acquisition in which the X group is treated as remaining in existence with P as its new common parent, X's earnings and profits are duplicated by P.

¶ 765 Elimination of Earnings and Profits upon Deconsolidation

Without special rules, "dividend-stripping" abuses could occur if either S were deconsolidated from P, but P retained S stock, or the P group were deconsolidated. Separate return dividend distributions from S to P out of earnings and profits accumulated in consolidated return years (which generally would have increased P's S stock basis) generally would not reduce P's S stock basis (except to the extent that Code Sec. 1059 applies). Thus, if prior positive investment adjustments for S's consolidated return year after-tax income were left intact and S could distribute such earnings without a stock basis adjustment:

- S could distribute consolidated return earnings and profits to P at a small tax cost because of the dividends-received deduction of Code Sec. 243; and

- P could sell S, after S has distributed value to P without a corresponding reduction in P's S stock basis, at an artificial loss.

---

[27] Reg. § 1.152-1(c)(1) and Reg. § 1.1502-33(d)(5).
[28] Reg. § 1.1502-33(f)(2).

[29] For an illustration of the effects on earnings and profits of an intragroup spinoff under Code Sec. 355, *see* Reg. § 1.1502-33(b)(3), Example 2.
[30] Reg. § 1.1502-33(f)(1).

To prevent such dividend stripping, immediately before it becomes a nonmember, S's earnings and profits are generally eliminated to the extent that they were taken into account by any member under Reg. § 1.1502-33.[31] This prevents S from paying a dividend out of such earnings and profits.

.01 Exception for Acquisition of Group by Another Group

If S is acquired in an acquisition of the group described in Reg. § 1.1502-33(e)(2), however, S's prior consolidated return year earnings and profits are not so eliminated, provided that the surviving group is a consolidated group. In that situation, dividend stripping is not an issue because a distribution by S to P will reduce P's S stock basis under investment adjustment rules.

¶ 775 Other Rules

Other rules deal with intercompany transactions, record-keeping, avoidance transactions, predecessors and successors, and effective dates.

.01 Intercompany Transactions

Intercompany items and corresponding items are not reflected in earnings and profits before they are taken into account under the intercompany transaction regulations.[32]

.02 Recordkeeping

Any allocation of federal income tax liability under a complementary method must be reflected annually on permanent records (including working papers).[33]

.03 Anti-Avoidance Rule

If any person acts with a principal purpose contrary to the purposes of Reg. § 1.1502-33, to avoid the effect of its rules or apply its rules to avoid the effect of any other provision of the consolidated return regulations, adjustments must be made as necessary to carry out the purposes of Reg. § 1.1502-33.[34]

.04 Predecessors and Successors

Any reference in the earnings and profits rules to a corporation or to a share includes a reference to a successor or predecessor as the context may require.[35] A corporation is a successor if its earnings and profits are determined, directly or indirectly, in whole or in part, by reference to the earnings and profits of another corporation (the predecessor). A share is a successor if its basis is determined, directly or indirectly, in whole or in part, by reference to the basis of another share (the predecessor).

.05 Effective Dates

In general, Reg. § 1.1502-33 applies to determinations of the earnings and profits of a member (e.g., for purposes of characterizing a distribution to which Code Sec. 301 applies) in consolidated return years on or after January 1, 1995.[36] If

---

[31] Reg. § 1.1502-33(e)(1).
[32] Reg. § 1.1502-33(c)(2).
[33] Reg. § 1.1502-33(d)(1)(i).
[34] Reg. § 1.1502-33(g).
[35] Reg. § 1.1502-33(h).
[36] Reg. § 1.1502-33(j)(1).

it applies, earnings and profits must be determined or redetermined as if Reg. § 1.1502-33 were in effect for all years.

If, however, P disposes of stock of S in a consolidated return year before January 1, 1995, the amount of P's earnings and profits with respect to S are not redetermined under the general rule described above.[37]

As further exceptions to the general rule, the earnings and profits elimination rule for deconsolidations and the group structure change rules apply only to deconsolidations and group structure changes occurring in consolidated return years beginning on or after January 1, 1995.[38]

Finally, if there was a deemed distribution and recontribution pursuant to the prior regulations in a consolidated return year beginning before January 1, 1995, the deemed distribution and contribution under the election are treated as an actual distribution by S and recontribution by P, as provided under the election.[39]

¶ 785 Conclusions

The consolidated return earnings and profits rules adjust P's earnings and profits to reflect S's earnings and profits for the period that S is a member of the consolidated group. They duplicate the earnings and profits of lower-tier members in the earnings and profits of higher-tier members rather than elevate them to the common parent level without duplication at the lower tiers.

The allocation of federal income tax liability for earnings and profits purposes is a complex subject involving both a basic method and, if the consolidated group elects, a complementary method that takes into account the compensation of members for the absorption of their tax attributes.

Adjustments are made to preserve the duplication and profits of lower-tier members in higher-tier members following Code Sec. 351 transfers, reverse acquisitions, and certain other changes in the consolidated group.

To prevent dividend-stripping abuses that could occur if either S were deconsolidated from P, but P retained S stock, or if the P group were deconsolidated, S's consolidated return earnings and profits are eliminated upon deconsolidation.

¶ 795 Frequently Asked Questions

Question

How is the tiering-up of earnings and profits achieved?

Answer

P's earnings and profits are adjusted to reflect changes in S's earnings and profits in accordance with the principles of Reg. § 1.1502-32, consistently applied, and an adjustment to P's earnings and profits for a tax year under the regulations is treated as earnings and profits of P for the tax year in which the adjustment arises. However, modifications to the principles include:

---

[37] Reg. § 1.1502-33 (j) (2).
[38] Reg. § 1.1502-33 (j) (3) (i).

[39] Reg. § 1.1502-33 (j) (4).

- The amount of P's adjustment is determined by reference to S's earnings and profits, rather than S's taxable income and tax-exempt items; and

- The tax-sharing rules under Reg. § 1.1502-33(d) apply, rather than those of the investment adjustment rules.

Once the earnings and profits of S are tiered up to P, P's earnings and profits do not change when S distributes a dividend to P.

Question

What happens to S's earnings and profits when it leaves the consolidated group?

Answer

To prevent dividend-stripping abuses, S's consolidated return earnings and profits are eliminated upon deconsolidation.

¶795

Chapter 8

Continuation of the Consolidated Group

¶ 801 Overview—Continuation of the Consolidated Group

Continuation of the consolidated group is important for determining when an intercompany transaction or excess loss account is taken into account, when tax liability of a group continues, and other matters. This chapter briefly reviews when, under Reg. § 1.1502-75 or related substance-over-form principles, a consolidated group continues.

.01 Continued Filing Requirement and Election to Discontinue

Although filing a consolidated return for a consolidated group's first tax year is elective, thereafter it is not. If a group wants to discontinue filing a consolidated return after its first tax year, it must obtain the approval of the IRS (see ¶ 815).

.02 When a Group Remains in Existence

As a general rule, a group remains in existence for a tax year if the common parent remains as the common parent and at least one subsidiary that was affiliated with it at the end of the prior year remains affiliated with it at the beginning of the year, whether or not one or more subsidiaries have ceased to be subsidiaries at any time after the group was formed. This general rule and exceptions for a mere change in identity of the common parent and for the common parent's transfer of assets to a subsidiary are discussed at ¶ 825.

¶801.02

.03 Substance over Form

Applying substance over form, in Rev. Rul. 82-152,[1] the IRS ruled that a group remained in existence when a common parent became a subsidiary of the group, even though the transaction did not literally qualify under the downstream transaction rules of Reg. § 1.1502-75(d)(2). This ruling indicates that the IRS will apply the group continuation rules in accordance with their single-entity purpose, rather than by their literal language (see ¶ 835).

.04 Reverse Acquisitions

The consolidated return regulations provide a unique rule for reversing the form of an acquisition of a group where a smaller group acquires a larger group and uses stock as part of its acquisition consideration (see ¶ 845).

.05 Creation of a Holding Company Without Terminating the Group

The IRS's substance-over-form ruling raises the question of how a holding company common parent can be created without terminating the group (see ¶ 855).

¶ 815 Continued Filing Requirement and Election to Discontinue

A group that filed (or was required to file) a consolidated return for the immediately preceding tax year is required to file a consolidated return for the tax year, unless it has an election to discontinue filing consolidated returns.[2] Notwithstanding that a consolidated return is required for a tax year, upon application by the common parent the IRS may, for good cause shown, grant permission to a group to discontinue filing consolidated returns.[3] Ordinarily, the IRS will grant a group permission to discontinue filing consolidated returns if the net result of all amendments to the Code or regulations with effective dates commencing within the tax year has a substantial adverse effect on the consolidated tax liability of the group for such year, relative to what the aggregate tax liability would be if the members of the group filed separate returns for such year.[4] In addition, the IRS will take into account other factors in determining whether good cause exists for granting permission to discontinue filing consolidated returns, including the factors described in Reg. § 1.1502-75(c)(1)(iii). These factors include changes in the Code or regulations that are effective prior to the tax year but that first have a substantial adverse effect on the filing of a consolidated return relative to the filing of separate returns by members of the group in such year.[5] Also, the IRS in its discretion may grant all groups permission to discontinue filing consolidated returns if any provision of the Code or regulations has been amended and such amendment is of the type that could have a substantial adverse effect on the filing of consolidated returns by substantially all groups, relative to the filing of separate returns.[6] A similar rule authorizes the IRS to grant a particular class of groups permission to discontinue filing consolidated returns if any provision of the Code or regulations

---

[1] Rev. Rul. 82-152, 1982-2 CB 205.
[2] Reg. § 1.1502-75(a)(2).
[3] Reg. § 1.1502-75(c)(1)(i).
[4] Reg. § 1.1502-75(c)(1)(ii).
[5] Reg. § 1.1502-75(c)(1)(iii).
[6] Reg. § 1.1502-75(c)(2)(i).

has been amended and such amendment is of the type that could have a substantial adverse effect on the filing of consolidated returns by substantially all such groups relative to the filing of separate returns.[7]

¶ 825 When a Group Remains in Existence

As a general rule, a group remains in existence for a tax year if the common parent remains as the common parent and at least one subsidiary that was affiliated with it at the end of the prior year remains affiliated with it at the beginning of the year, whether or not one or more subsidiaries have ceased to be subsidiaries at any time after the group was formed.[8]

> *Example 1:* As an example of when the last subsidiary leaves the group: P and S file a consolidated return on a calendar-year basis. On July 31, Year 1, P1 purchases all the stock of S from P. The P group ends on December 31, Year 1 unless P acquires another subsidiary before the end of the year.

> *Example 2:* As an example of when the common parent leaves the group: The facts are the same as in Example 1, except that instead of S being acquired on July 31, Year 1, P is acquired by P1 on that date. The P group ends immediately on July 31, Year 1, because the common parent is no longer in existence.

.01 Mere Change in Identity of Common Parent

As a general rule, the common parent is treated as remaining in existence irrespective of a mere change in identity, form, or place of organization as a result of an F reorganization.[9]

.02 Transfer of Assets to Subsidiary

The group is treated as remaining in existence, notwithstanding that the common parent is no longer in existence, if the members of the affiliated group succeed to and become the owners of substantially all of the assets of such former parent and there remains one or more chains of includible corporations connected through stock ownership with a common parent corporation that is an includible corporation and that was a member of the group prior to the date such former parent ceased to exist.[10]

> *Example 3:* As an example of downstream merger of a common parent into its subsidiary: P owns all the stock of S, and S owns all the stock of S1. P merges into S in a tax-free reorganization described in Code Sec. 368(a)(1)(A) and Code Sec. 368(a)(1)(D). The consolidated group is considered as remaining in existence, notwithstanding that P is no longer in existence.

¶ 835 Substance over Form

In Rev. Rul. 82-152[11] the merger of a second-tier subsidiary into the common parent of a consolidated group was ruled not to cause the termination of the group, even though the transaction was not a downstream transaction described in Reg.

---

[7] Reg. § 1.1502-75(c)(2)(ii).
[8] Reg. § 1.1502-75(d)(1).
[9] Reg. § 1.1502-75(d)(2)(i).

[10] Reg. § 1.1502-75(d)(2)(ii).
[11] Rev. Rul. 82-152, 1982-2 CB 205.

§ 1.1502-75(d)(2)(ii). In the ruling, the P group included P, S, a wholly owned subsidiary of P, and T, a wholly owned subsidiary of S. T was merged into P, with P surviving the merger, and the former P shareholders exchanged all of their P stock for S stock. As a result of this transaction, P became a first-tier subsidiary of S.

According to the IRS, the function of Reg. § 1.1502-75(d)(2)(ii) is to recognize the continuity of an affiliated group after a transaction that, even though formally restructuring the group, did not effect any substantial change in the composition of the group (judged by reference to the underlying assets of the group). The IRS reasoned that in the single-economic-entity theory underlying the consolidated return regulations, it is implicit that the group ought to continue in existence after such a transaction.

For purposes of determining the continuity of the P group, there is no significant difference, other than in form, between a transaction in which T would be the survivor and one in which P survives. If T had been the survivor, Reg. § 1.1502-75(d)(2)(ii) would be applicable. Because the transaction in the present situation is indistinguishable in substance from the transaction described in Reg. § 1.1502-75(d)(2)(ii), the transaction in the present situation should not result in a termination of the group. The P group will be treated as remaining in existence after consummation of the transaction, with S becoming the common parent of the affiliated group.

Based on this revenue ruling, the IRS can be expected to rule on continuity of group issues based on their single-entity purpose, rather than the literal language of the regulations.

¶ 845 Reverse Acquisitions

The consolidated return regulations reverse the form of certain transactions where the minnow group swallows the whale group and uses stock as its bait. Specifically, if a corporation (the first corporation) or any member of a group of which the first corporation is the common parent acquires:

- Stock of another corporation (the second corporation), the result of which the second corporation becomes (or would become but for the application of this rule) a member of a group in which the first corporation is the common parent, or

- Substantially all the assets of the second corporation, in exchange (in whole or in part) for stock of the first corporation, and the stockholders (immediately before the acquisition) of the second corporation, as a result of owning stock of the second corporation, own (immediately after the acquisition) more than 50 percent of the fair market value of the outstanding stock of the first corporation, *then* any group of which the first corporation was the common parent immediately before the acquisition, and any group of which the second corporation was the common parent immediately before the acquisition, is treated as remaining in existence (with the first corporation becoming the common parent of the group).[12] In applying this rule, any

---

[12] Reg. § 1.1502-75(d)(3)(i).

acquisitions or redemptions of the stock of either corporation are taken into account if they are pursuant to a plan of acquisition described in Reg. § 1.1502-75(d)(3)(i)(a) or Reg. § 1.1502-75(d)(3)(i)(b).[13]

Example 4: As an example of reverse acquisition: P and S comprise group PS with P being the common parent. P was merged into P1, the common parent of group P1. The shareholders of P immediately before the merger, as a result of owning stock in P, own 90 percent of the fair market value of P1's stock immediately after the merger.

The group in which P was the common parent is treated as continuing in existence with P1 and its subsidiaries being added as members of the group, and P1 taking the place of P as the common parent.

¶ 855 Creating a Holding Company Without Terminating the Group

A common consolidated group question is how to create a holding company without terminating the group.

Example 5: As an example of formation of holding company: P, the common parent of a consolidated group, is an operating company. The consolidated group files its returns on the basis of a calendar year end. Following is a discussion of three possible methods of creating the holding company without terminating the consolidated group.

1. *Shareholders form Holding and exchange P stock for Holding stock in a Code Sec. 351 transaction.* First, the shareholders of P incorporate a holding company (Holding), then exchange their P stock for Holding stock in a Code Sec. 351 transaction.

   The Code Sec. 351 exchange of P stock for Holding stock qualifies as a reverse acquisition under Reg. § 1.1502-75(d)(3). For example, Holding is the first corporation referred to in the regulations, and P is the second corporation. Holding will acquire the stock of P (in exchange for Holding stock) in the Code Sec. 351 transaction, and the former P shareholders will own more than 50 percent (i.e., because they will own 100 percent) of the Holding stock after the acquisition. Consequently, the P group should be treated as remaining in existence, with Holding as the new common parent.

2. *P forms Holding; Holding forms S; P merges into S.* Under this alternative, P will form Holding in a Code Sec. 351 exchange, and Holding will form S in a Code Sec. 351 exchange. (In each case, the transferor will transfer just enough cash to satisfy capitalization requirements.) P will then merge into S, and the P shareholders will surrender their P stock in exchange for Holding stock. P's merger into S should qualify as a reorganization under Code Sec. 368(a)(2)(D).[14] Moreover, the P group should continue in existence, notwithstanding that P ceases to exist. This is because the transaction satisfies the requirements of

---

[13] Reg. § 1.1502-75(d)(3)(i).

[14] Rev. Rul. 77-428, 1977-2 CB 117 (situation 1).

Reg. § 1.1502-75(d)(2)(ii). For example, S (a member of the affiliated group) succeeds to substantially all of P's assets, including P's stock ownership in the other subsidiaries. After the transaction, the members of the consolidated group are connected through stock ownership with Holding, the new common parent corporation. Thus, the consolidated group should be deemed to continue, with Holding as the new common parent.

The IRS has ruled favorably upon this sort of transaction.[15] In that ruling, Target, a federal mutual savings bank, formed Parent, and Parent formed Sub. Target merged into Sub, and Target's "interest holders" exchanged their equity interests in Target for equity interests in Parent. (Because Target was a mutual savings bank, Target had no authorized capital stock.) Citing Rev. Rul. 77-428 (and other authorities), the IRS ruled that the merger qualified as reorganization under Code Sec. 368(a)(1)(A) and Code Sec. 368(a)(2)(D). The IRS also ruled that the merger of Target into Sub was a "transfer to a subsidiary" under Reg. § 1.1502-75(d)(2), with Parent becoming the common parent.

3. *P forms Holding; Holding forms S; S merges into P.* The transaction is the same as the transaction described in (2) above, except that S merges into P (instead of P merging into S). The shareholders will exchange their P stock for Holding stock, and the S stock held by Holding will be converted into P stock. The shareholders will own Holding, and Holding will own P after the transaction. The transaction should qualify as a Code Sec. 368(a)(2)(E) reorganization.[16]

The reorganization does not satisfy the literal requirements of Reg. § 1.1502-75(d)(2)(ii) because P does not cease to exist in the transaction. Moreover, the IRS's position is that the transaction does not satisfy the literal requirements of a reverse acquisition under Reg. § 1.1502-75(d)(3) because P and Holding were affiliated before the transaction.[17] Nevertheless, in Rev. Rul. 82-152, the IRS ruled that a consolidated group continued in existence after a restructuring in which a second-tier subsidiary (T) merged into the parent (P), with the former shareholders of the parent becoming shareholders of the first-tier subsidiary. In reaching its determination, the IRS noted that the transaction would satisfy the literal requirements of Reg. § 1.1502-75(d)(2)(ii) if the parent had merged into the second-tier subsidiary (see discussion of situation 2 in footnote 17). Because the transaction in the present situation is indistinguishable in substance from the transaction described in Reg. § 1.1502-75(d)(2)(ii), the trans-

---

[15] IRS Letter Ruling 9125036 (March 27, 1991).

[16] Rev. Rul. 77-428, 1977-2 CB 117 (situation 2); the merger of S into P has the effect of a corporate inversion transaction as described in Notice 94-93, 1994-2 CB 563. Accordingly, P should ensure that, as a result of the transaction, there will not be a reduction in the amount a third party would pay for the stock of P or Holding.

Otherwise, regulations might require recognition of gain at the time of the inversion transaction or a reduction in the basis (or increase in gain on sale or other disposition) of the stock of one or more of the corporations involved in the inversion transaction.

[17] *See* Rev. Rul. 82-152, 1982-2 CB 205.

action in the present situation should not result in a termination of the P group. Accordingly, the P group was treated as remaining in existence, with the first-tier subsidiary as the common parent.

Based upon Rev. Rul. 82-152, the P consolidated group should remain in existence (with Holding as the new common parent) if S merges into Parent.

¶ 865 Consolidated Groups

This chapter relates to continuation of a consolidated group.

If a consolidated group wants to discontinue filing a consolidated return after its first tax year, it must obtain the approval of the IRS.

As a general rule, a group remains in existence for a tax year if the common parent remains as the common parent and at least one subsidiary that was affiliated with it at the end of the prior year remains affiliated with it at the beginning of the year, whether or not one or more subsidiaries have ceased to be subsidiaries at any time after the group was formed. This general rule and exceptions for a mere change in identity of the common parent and for the common parent's transfer of assets to a subsidiary are discussed at ¶ 825.

The IRS has applied the group continuation rules in accordance with their single-entity purpose, rather than by their literal language. Specifically, in Rev. Rul. 82-152, the IRS ruled that a group remained in existence when a common parent became a subsidiary of the group, even though the transaction did not meet the literal down-stream transaction rules of the regulations.

The consolidated return regulations provide a unique rule for reversing the form of an acquisition of a group where a smaller group acquires a larger group and uses stock as part of its acquisition consideration.

The IRS's substance-over-form ruling raises the question of how a holding company common parent can be created without terminating the group (see ¶ 855).

¶ 875 Frequently Asked Questions

Question

What turns on whether a consolidated group remains in existence?

Answer

When an intercompany transaction or excess loss account is taken into account, when tax liability of a group continues, and other matters turn on whether a consolidated group remains in existence.

Question

Which consolidated group is treated as continuing where a smaller group acquires a larger group and uses stock as part of its acquisition consideration?

Answer

Under "reverse acquisition" rules unique to consolidated returns, the larger group continues in existence.

¶875

Chapter 9

Subsidiary Joining or Leaving the Consolidated Group

¶ 901   Overview—Subsidiary Joining or Leaving the Consolidated Group
¶ 915   Basic Accounting
¶ 925   Examples

¶ 901 Overview—Subsidiary Joining or Leaving the Consolidated Group

Depending on the form of the transaction and the particular facts, countless consolidated return issues may arise when a subsidiary joins or leaves a consolidated group. There follows a selective sample of examples that illustrate consolidated return rules commonly encountered. The examples are aimed at providing a review of concepts discussed throughout the volume. Before discussing these selected situations, the reader is provided some background on the basic accounting for a subsidiary joining or leaving a consolidated group.

.01 Basic Accounting

Basic accounting elements that need to be considered include items included in the consolidated return, the due date for filing a member's separate return, allocation of disposition year items, and the next day rule for date of acquisition items (see ¶ 915).

.02 Examples

A number of examples illustrate situations where there is a taxable sale of subsidiary stock, a taxable sale of subsidiary assets, a tax-free disposition of subsidiary stock or assets, and a tax-free spinoff of subsidiary stock (see ¶ 925).

¶ 915 Basic Accounting

Basic accounting issues that need to be considered include items included in the consolidated return, separate return required for joining or departing member, due date for filing a member's separate return, allocation of disposition year items, and the next day rule for date of acquisition items.

.01 Items Included in Consolidated Return and Separate Return Required for Joining or Departing Member

What items are to be included in the consolidated return? What returns are required for a corporation that becomes or ceases to be a member of the consolidated group during the corporation's "natural" tax year?

The consolidated return must include the common parent's items of income, gain, deduction, loss, and credit for the entire consolidated return year, and each subsidiary's items for the portion of the year for which it is a member.[1]

If a corporation becomes or ceases to be a member of a consolidated group, the corporation becomes or ceases to be a member at the end of the day on which its status as a member changes, and its tax year ends for all federal income tax purposes at the end of that day.[2] The consolidated return will include the corporation's items for the portion of the consolidated return year during which the corporation is a member.[3] The corporation must file a separate return including the corporation's items for the portion of the corporation's "natural" tax year that is not included in the consolidated return.[4] A separate return includes the consolidated return of another group.

> **Example 1:** As an example of items included in the consolidated return: P and its subsidiary, S, file a consolidated return on the basis of a calendar year. T files its return on the basis of a calendar year. On July 31, 2006, P acquires the T stock. The P consolidated return for the year ending December 31, 2006 must include P's items for the entire consolidated return year. Because S was a member of the consolidated group for the entire consolidated return year, the consolidated return must also include S's items for the entire consolidated return year. T becomes a member of the P group at the end of the day on July 31, 2006, and T's tax year ends for all federal income tax purposes at the end of that day.[5] T must join in the consolidated return for the period August 1, 2006–December 31, 2006. T must file a separate return covering the period January 1, 2006–July 31, 2006. The result is the same if T is the common parent of a consolidated group before P acquires T. T's separate return is the final T consolidated return.

.02 Due Date for Joining Member's Separate Return

If a corporation joins a consolidated group during the year, what is the due date of the corporation's separate return? Except as otherwise provided, the following general discussion assumes that T (a corporation joining a consolidated group during the year) is a C corporation, that T is not acquired in a stock acquisition for which a Code Sec. 338 election is made, and that P's acquisition of T does not constitute a "reverse acquisition" described in Reg. § 1.1502-75(d)(3). In general, a corporate taxpayer must file its return on or before the 15th day of the third month following the end of the tax year.[6] If the corporation files an extension (Form 7004)

---

[1] Reg. § 1.1502-76(b)(1)(i).
[2] Reg. § 1.1502-76(b)(1)(ii)(A)(1).
[3] Reg. § 1.1502-76(b)(1)(i).
[4] Reg. § 1.1502-76(b)(1)(i).
[5] Reg. § 1.1502-76(b)(1)(ii)(A)(1).
[6] Code Sec. 6072(b).

¶915.01

on or before the due date of its return, the corporation is automatically granted a six-month filing extension.[7]

As described above, if a corporation (T) joins a consolidated group (P) during the year, T is required to file a short-year, separate return covering the period from the beginning of its tax year through the date of its acquisition by P.[8] (If T is the parent of a group filing a consolidated return, a "separate" return includes a final consolidated return of the T group.)

A two-part rule generally determines the due date of T's separate return.

1. If the P consolidated group *has filed* a consolidated return on or before the due date of T's separate return, including the extension of time to file but not including any change in T's tax year caused by T's need to adopt P's year end as a result of joining the P group, then T's separate return is due on the date that the P consolidated return is due (including extensions of time to file).[9]

2. If the P consolidated group *has not filed* a consolidated return on or before the due date of T's separate return, including the extension of time to file but not including any change in T's tax year caused by T's need to adopt P's year end as a result of joining the P group, then T's separate return is due on the due date for its separate return.[10]

In applying the two-part rule above, T should ignore a year end caused solely by Reg. § 1.1502-76(a)(1) (i.e., a year end caused by the acquisition).[11]

Example 2: As an example of P and T having calendar tax years: P is the common parent of a consolidated group. The P group files its consolidated return on the basis of a calendar year end. P purchases 100 percent of the outstanding stock of T for cash on October 31, 2006. T is the common parent of a consolidated group. The T group files its consolidated returns on the basis of a calendar year end. P and T both file extensions of time to file returns. The P group consolidated return for the year ending December 31, 2006 includes T's items for the period November 1, 2006–December 31, 2006. T must file a separate return covering the period January 1, 2006–October 31, 2006. With an extension, P's consolidated return is due September 15, 2007. Similarly, with an extension, Target's separate return is due September 15, 2007. Thus, Target's separate return is due September 15, 2007.

Example 3: As an example of T having a fiscal year: The facts are the same as in Example 2 above, except that T has a March 31 fiscal year end. With an extension, the due date for Target's separate return is December 15, 2007. With an extension, the due date for P's consolidated return is September 15, 2007. Thus, assuming that both P and T file an extension, T's separate return is due September 15, 2007. If T does not file an extension, T's separate return is due June 15, 2007.

---

[7] *See* Code Sec. 6081(a) and Reg. § 1.6081-1.
[8] Reg. § 1.1502-76(b)(1)(i).
[9] Reg. § 1.1502-76(c)(1).

[10] Reg. § 1.1502-76(c)(2).
[11] Reg. § 1.1502-76(c)(2).

¶915.02

.03 Allocation of Disposition Year Items

How does a corporation that joins or leaves a consolidated group during the year allocate items of income, deduction, loss, and credit for its "natural" tax year between the consolidated return and the corporation's separate return? As discussed below, there are three methods for allocating a corporation's items between the consolidated and separate return years. These methods are generally outlined at Reg. § 1.1502-76(b)(2).

1. *General Code rules—closing of the books.* The consolidated return regulations provide that the "closing of the books" method is the general "default" method for allocating the corporation's items between its separate and consolidated return years.[12] (The regulations refer to the closing of the books method as the general method for allocating items between short periods under the Code.) Under the closing of the books method, the corporation allocates items between the consolidated return year and the separate return year by closing its books as if it ceased to exist on becoming a member (or first existed on becoming a nonmember). The corporation is not required to annualize income under Code Sec. 443 solely because it has a short year as a result of joining the consolidated group.[13]

2. *Ratable allocation based upon days.* The second allocation method is an elective ratable allocation method, whereby the corporation's items are ratably allocated between its separate return year and the consolidated return year based on the number of days in each year.[14] However, this method is available only if the corporation is not required to change either its accounting method or its accounting period as a result of its change in status.[15] Also, "extraordinary items" cannot be allocated under this method; rather, each extraordinary item must be allocated to the day upon which it is taken into account.[16] See Reg. § 1.1502-76(b)(2)(ii)(C) for a list of extraordinary items.

   One of the principal benefits of the ratable allocation election is that the corporation's two short periods resulting from its change in status are treated as a single tax year for purposes of determining the timing, location, character, and source of items to be allocated between the two periods.[17] However, the short years resulting from the corporation's change in status are treated as different tax years (and as short periods) with respect to any item carried to or from these years (e.g., a net operating loss carried under Code Sec. 172) and with respect to the application of Code Sec. 481.[18]

   As noted, this method is elective. To make the election, a statement must be signed by both the corporation and its common parent (as well as the corporation's former common parent, if applicable). The statement is

---

[12] Reg. § 1.1502-76(b)(2)(i).
[13] Reg. § 1.1502-76(b)(2)(i).
[14] Reg. § 1.1502-76(b)(2)(ii).
[15] Reg. § 1.1502-76(b)(2)(ii).

[16] Reg. § 1.1502-76(b)(2)(ii).
[17] Reg. § 1.1502-76(b)(2)(ii)(B)(2).
[18] Reg. § 1.1502-76(b)(2)(ii)(B)(2).

attached to each member's return (i.e., the consolidated return, and the corporation's separate return). For details on making the election, see Reg. § 1.1502-76(b)(2)(ii)(D).

3. *Ratable allocation of a month's items.* The third method is a variation of the second daily allocation method and is available if the second method is not (or cannot be) elected. In this instance, the corporation ratably allocates items that it takes into account in the *month* it changes its status (i.e., the month it joins or leaves the consolidated group).[19] Any reasonable method may be employed in determining the corporation's items for the month. For example, the corporation may close its books both at the end of the preceding month and at the end of the month in which the acquisition occurs.[20]

.04 Next Day Rule for Date of Acquisition Items

If a consolidated group acquires a C corporation (T) and disposes of its appreciated property on the date of acquisition, will the gain be reportable on T's short-period return?

Reg. § 1.1502-76(b)(1)(ii)(B)'s "next day" rule was designed to prevent this. If, on the day of T's change in status as a member, a transaction occurs that is properly allocable to the portion of T's day after the event resulting in the change, T and all persons related to T under Code Sec. 267(b) immediately after the event must treat the transaction for all federal income tax purposes as occurring at the beginning of the following day (i.e., on the consolidated return of the acquiring group).[21] A determination whether a transaction is properly allocable to the portion of T's day after the event will be respected if it is reasonable and consistently applied by all affected persons. In determining whether an allocation is reasonable, the following factors are among those to be considered:

- Whether income, gain, deduction, loss, and credit are allocated inconsistently (e.g., to maximize a seller's stock basis adjustments under Reg. § 1.1502-32);

- If the item is from a transaction with respect to T stock, whether it reflects ownership of the stock before or after the event (e.g., if a member transfers encumbered land to nonmember T in exchange for additional T stock in a transaction to which Code Sec. 351 applies, and the exchange results in T becoming a member of the consolidated group, the applicability of Code Sec. 357(c) to the exchange must be determined under Reg. § 1.1502-80(d) by treating the exchange as occurring after the event; on the other hand, if T is a member but has a minority shareholder, and becomes a nonmember as a result of its redemption of stock with appreciated property, T's gain under Code Sec. 311 is treated as from a transaction occurring before the event);

---

[19] Reg. § 1.1502-76(b)(2)(iii).
[20] Reg. § 1.1502-76(b)(2)(iii).

[21] Reg. § 1.1502-76(b)(2)(iii).

- Whether the allocation is inconsistent with other requirements under the Code (e.g., if a Code Sec. 338(g) election is made in connection with a group's acquisition of T, the deemed asset sale must take place before T becomes a member, and T's gain or loss with respect to its assets must be taken into account by T as a nonmember); and

- Whether other facts exist, such as a prearranged transaction or multiple changes in T's status, indicating that the transaction is not properly allocable to the portion of T's day after the event resulting in T's change.

¶ 925 Examples

Examples of a taxable sale of subsidiary stock, a taxable sale of subsidiary assets, a tax-free disposition of subsidiary stock, a tax-free disposition of subsidiary assets, and a tax-free spinoff of subsidiary stock are examined.

.01 Taxable Sale of Subsidiary Stock

Example 4 below illustrates the concept of a taxable sale of subsidiary stock.

> ***Example 4:*** As an example of a taxable sale of stock of a member of the subgroup: P owns all the stock of S and S1, and S1 owns all the stock of S2. P previously acquired S2 when it purchased the stock of S1 from another consolidated group on December 31, Year 1. P1 has numerous subsidiaries and is negotiating with P to purchase all the stock of S2. Both the P and P1 groups have filed consolidated returns for all years on a calendar year basis, and all the corporations at issue use the accrual method. The CFOs have tentatively agreed to a purchase price of $400 million and a closing date of October 31, Year 4, subject to a discussion of the tax issues. The P group has a Year 1 net operating loss (NOL) carryover of $100 million, all of which is allocable to S2 and subject to a subgroup Code Sec. 382 limitation of $30 million. The current long-term tax-exempt bond rate is 5 percent. Before taking into account any use of the NOL carryover to offset S1's gain on the sale of the stock of S2, S1 has a $350 million basis in the stock of S2. There are no built-in gain or loss issues. What are the respective consolidated return issues that the tax departments of P and P1 should bring to the attention of their CFOs?

Stock basis computation. As discussed at ¶ 315, for purposes of determining S1's gain or loss on the sale of S2, the stock basis of S2 is adjusted to reflect taxable income or loss, tax-exempt income, noncapital, nondeductible expenses, and distributions during P group consolidated return years. Although these adjustments generally are made at the end of the tax year, they also are made immediately before the disposition of S2.[22]

Election by P1 to treat S2's NOL carryover as expired. If the P1 group is unlikely to absorb S2's NOL carryover, it should consider electing to treat part or all of the loss as having expired immediately before S2 becomes a member of the P1 group (see ¶ 315). If no such election is made, P1 will be required to make a negative basis adjustment to its S2 stock when the loss expires.

---

[22] Reg. § 1.1502-32(b).

Recapture of an excess loss account. The disposition of the stock of S2 is one of the events that requires S1 to recapture any negative S2 stock basis, called an "excess loss account." This is explained at ¶ 325. However, because S1 has a positive stock basis, the excess loss account rules are not an issue.

Anti-circular basis rule. To prevent a year-of-disposition loss or loss carry-over of S2 from being wasted, this special rule (discussed at ¶ 335) prevents the offset of such a loss or loss carryover from being taken into account in computing S1's stock gain or loss. Otherwise, the absorption of such a loss or loss carryover would decrease P's S1 stock basis, increase S1's stock gain, increase the absorption of loss, decrease stock basis, increase gain, and so on until the loss or loss carryover was fully absorbed. Thus, the net effect of this anti-circular basis rule is favorable to P1 because it preserves the carryover of S2's loss or loss carryover to the P1 group (unless it is absorbed by the income of other P group members during the rest of the disposition year).

Asset consistency rules. For the reasons explained at ¶ 355, if assets were acquired by S2 from other members of the P group during the one-year period before October 31, the consistency rules could require the P1 group to take a carryover basis in such assets. Thus, the P1 group should obtain a representation that no such intercompany transactions have occurred or will occur.

Intercompany items. S2's departure from the P group will cause the P group to accelerate any deferred gain or loss that arose in an intercompany transaction between S2 and another P group member (see ¶ 515). If S2 continues to owe P, S, or S1 any debt after P1's acquisition of S2, immediately before the acquisition, S2 is treated as satisfying the note and reissuing it. For the resulting consequences, see ¶ 565.

Carryover tax attributes and limitations thereon.[23] As explained in Chapter 5, the tax attributes S2 will bring into the P1 group and the limitations they will be subject to is a complex subject. Because the Code Sec. 382 and separate return limitation year (SRLY) events overlap for the P1 group, there will be Code Sec. 382 limitations but no SRLY limitation on these tax attributes. The P group's consolidated tax attributes attributable to S2 must be allocated as of the end of the tax year in which the subsidiary leaves the group, here December 31, Year 4. Where, as here, S2 was acquired by the P group with a loss or credit carryover that was subject to a Code Sec. 382 or Code Sec. 383 limitation, any remaining portion of the loss or credit carryover will be subject to a second limitation as a result of P1's purchase of S2. The lower of the two limitations applies. Further, where, as here, S2 was a member of a loss subgroup when it joined the P group, P1 needs to negotiate with P to elect to allocate part of the $30 million subgroup Code Sec. 382 limitation between S2 and the rest of the subgroup. (Because the second Code Sec. 382 limitation will be $20 million, P1 should negotiate to have $20 million of the subgroup limitation allocated to S2.) The risk here is on S2 because the default

---

[23] If the P1 group is expected to retain the tax benefit of any carrybacks to the P group, the parties should contractually provide for the P group to so compensate the P1 group. The parties should keep in mind that the P1 group has the flexibility to waive the carryback of a net operating loss carryback, but other carrybacks are automatic.

rule, if no election is made, is that S2 takes a zero limitation; if this were the case, S2's NOL carryover would be useless.

Elimination of earnings and profits. Upon its deconsolidation from the P group, the earnings and profits of S2 are eliminated (see ¶ 765). However, only consolidated return year earnings and profits are eliminated. P may desire to obtain a schedule of any accumulated earnings and profits of S2 that existed immediately before S2's first consolidated return year as a member of the P group.

Tax liability of S2. S2 is jointly and severally liable for any P group federal income taxes for any tax year it was a member of the P group. As a consequence, P1 should obtain representations that P will pay these liabilities and protect P1 from any unexpected consequences, such as an audit adjustment for any prior tax year.[24] In the same vein, P should obtain any tax-sharing agreement and determine whether S2 has satisfied all of its obligations thereunder.

Short tax year issues. S2 will become a member of the P1 group on November 1, and its tax year ends for all federal income tax purposes on October 30, Year 4.[25] This creation of a short tax year raises an issue of shortening the period over which a loss or credit carryover of S2 can be used by the P1 group. Also, a Code Sec. 481 adjustment could be accelerated. If this is a problem, perhaps the parties could change the closing date to December 31, Year 4. Indeed, any such loss or credit carryover of S2 is subject to absorption by the P group through December 31, even if the closing were to occur on October 30.

Allocation of acquisition date items. As discussed at ¶ 915, regulations provide that if a closing date transaction is properly allocable to the portion of S2's date after the event resulting in the change in S2's status, the transaction must be treated as occurring at the beginning of the following day.[26] A determination whether a transaction is properly allocable to the portion of S2's day after the event will be respected if it is reasonable and consistently applied by all affected persons. The regulations list some factors that will be considered in determining whether an allocation is reasonable, such as whether items are allocated consistently. Thus, the parties should agree who will report any closing date items.

Allocation of S2's items for year of disposition. As discussed at ¶ 915 where, as here, S2 is not required to change its annual accounting period as a result of its change in status (i.e., because its stock is sold between consolidated groups that have the same annual accounting periods), S2 and P and P1 may, if the appropriate statement is filed, elect to ratably allocate to each day of S2's original year (January 1 through December 31 of Year 4) an equal portion of S2's items taken into account in Year 4.[27] However, as an exception to this general ratable allocation rule, "extraordinary items" (as defined in the regulations) must be allocated to the day that they are taken into account.

If this ratable allocation is not elected, the parties may allocate only S2's items taken into account in the month of October, but only if the allocation is consistently

[24] Reg. § 1.1502-6.
[25] Reg. § 1.1502-76(b)(1)(ii)(A).
[26] Reg. § 1.1502-76(b)(1)(ii)(B).
[27] Reg. § 1.1502-76(b)(2)(i).

¶925.01

applied by all affected persons.[28] For example, S1 may close its books both at the end of October and at the end of November, and allocate only its items (other than extraordinary items) from the month of the change.

If neither the annual nor the monthly ratable allocation method is used, S2's items are allocated for the year of disposition by closing S2's books on the date of sale.

Due date of S2's final short-period return. For special rules for determining the due date of S2's final short-period return where it was not a member of a consolidated group, see a discussion of Reg. § 1.1502-76(c) at ¶ 915. Those rules do not apply here.

.02 Taxable Sale of Subsidiary Assets

A taxable sale of assets of a consolidated subsidiary (S) can be accomplished, for example, by contractually selling all the assets of the subsidiary and liquidating it under Code Sec. 332. The same consequences can be achieved via a taxable (such as all-cash) merger.[29] Code Sec. 338(h)(10) provides a third option.

General effects of a Code Sec. 338(h)(10) election. Specifically, a Code Sec. 338(h)(10) election may be made for S if P acquires stock meeting the requirements of Code Sec. 1504(a)(2) from a selling consolidated group in a qualified stock purchase.[30] The consequences to the parties making a Code Sec. 338(h)(10) election are as follows:[31]

- Old S is treated as transferring all of its assets to an unrelated person in exchange for consideration that includes the discharge of its liabilities in a single transaction at the close of the acquisition date. In general, Old S recognizes all of the gain realized on the deemed transfer of its assets in consideration for the Aggregate Deemed Sales Price (ADSP). The ADSP for Old S is determined under Reg. § 1.338-4 and allocated among the acquisition date assets under Reg. § 1.338-6 and Reg. § 1.338-7. Old S realizes the deemed sale tax consequences from the deemed asset sale before the close of the acquisition date, while Old S is a member of the selling consolidated group.

- Old S is treated as if, before the close of the acquisition date, after the deemed asset sale described above, and while Old S is a member of the selling consolidated group, it transferred all of its assets to the selling consolidated group and ceased to exist. The transfer from Old S is characterized in the same manner as if the parties had actually engaged in the transactions deemed to occur. In most cases, the transfer will be treated as a liquidating distribution to which Code Sec. 332 applies.

- Members of the selling consolidated group recognize no gain or loss on the sale or exchange of S stock included in the qualified stock purchase.

---

[28] Reg. § 1.1502-76(b)(2)(iii).
[29] *See* Rev. Rul. 69-6, 1969-1 CB 104.

[30] Reg. § 1.338(h)(10)-1(c).
[31] Reg. § 1.338(h)(10)-1(d).

- The adjusted grossed-up basis for New S's assets is determined under Reg. § 1.338-5 and is allocated among the acquisition date assets under Reg. § 1.338-6 and Reg. § 1.338-7.

Note that, in contrast to a regular Code Sec. 338(g) election,[32] there is only one level of taxation in a Code Sec. 338(h)(10) election. However, for state tax reasons, sometimes a taxable merger is preferred because the state involved does not fully recognize a Code Sec. 338(h)(10) election, and its effects for state tax purposes are the same as a regular Code Sec. 338(g) election (i.e., taxation of both the target's assets and its shareholder's stock). Thus, before making a Code Sec. 338(h)(10) election, it is prudent to consider the state ramifications as well.

> *Example 5:* As an example of a Code Sec. 338(h)(10) election for subsidiary: P and S have been filing a consolidated return for the past 4 years. S has two assets: land ($6 million fair market value; basis of $4 million) and equipment ($2 million fair market value; basis of $1 million). S also has liabilities that amount to $3 million and an NOL carryover of $1 million that will expire in two years. P's basis in S is an excess loss account of $2 million. How much gain or loss must be recognized by P and S if the parties make a Code Sec. 338(h)(10) election and agree that P1 will pay $5 million for the S stock?

> P will recognize no gain or loss on the sale of the S stock. The consolidated group will recognize gain on the deemed sale of assets of $2 million. This is a $2 million gain on the sale of the land: a $1 million gain on the sale of the equipment minus the $1 million NOL carryover. (Under other facts, any excess loss or credit carryovers would be inherited by P under Code Sec. 381.)

Qualified stock purchase by a corporate purchaser. The main issue in a Code Sec. 338(h)(10) election is whether a corporate purchaser has made a qualified stock purchase of S from a consolidated group, and whether both parties make the election. A qualified stock purchase is any transaction or series of transactions in which, during a 12-month period, P purchases sufficient stock of S to be affiliated with S under Code Sec. 1504(a).[33]

Insolvent S. Code Sec. 338 regulations issued in 2001 clarify that stock in a target may be considered purchased if, under general principles of tax law, the purchasing corporation is considered to own stock of the target meeting the requirements of Code Sec. 1504(a)(2), notwithstanding that no amount may be paid for the stock.[34]

Intercompany items. As discussed in Chapter 4, if S was the buying member in a prior intercompany transaction, the selling member must restore its remaining intercompany gain or loss. If S was the selling member in a prior intercompany transaction, its remaining intercompany gain or loss continues to be deferred and is

---

[32] A Code Sec. 338(g) election is made unilaterally by the purchaser corporation. When such an election is made, both the target corporation and its shareholders recognize gain or loss. The election was placed in the Code when most of a target's gain was not recognized under the old Code Sec. 337. Since the repeal of Code Sec. 337 in 1986, a regular Code Sec. 338(g) election is rarely made. For example, it might still be made when there is effectively only one level of taxation because the target corporation has little realized gain or it has NOLs to offset its gain.

[33] Code Sec. 338(d)(3).

[34] Preamble to T.D. 8940, 2001-15 IRB 1016.

¶925.02

inherited by its parent corporation as if there had been an actual liquidation. Any intercompany gain or loss from a prior intercompany transaction with respect to S's stock is restored as a result of the deemed liquidation unless an election is made.[35]

Tiered targets. The consistency rules would generally prohibit the election for a subsidiary without also making the election for its parent if the parent is being sold to the same purchaser.[36] Where Code Sec. 338(h)(10) elections are made for tiered entities (i.e., a parent-subsidiary chain of corporations), the parent is deemed to sell its assets before the subsidiary, but the subsidiary is deemed to liquidate before the parent.[37]

Tax liability of S. New S remains jointly and severally liable for the tax liabilities of Old S, so that the purchaser should negotiate with P to eliminate this liability.[38]

.03 Tax-Free Disposition of Subsidiary Stock

Example 6 below illustrates a tax-free disposition of subsidiary stock:

> **Example 6:** P owns all the stock of S and S1, and S1 owns all the stock of S2. P previously acquired S1 (which owned S2) when it purchased the stock of S1 from another consolidated group for $400 million on December 31, Year 1. P1 has numerous subsidiaries and is negotiating with P to acquire all the stock of S1. Both the P and P1 groups have filed consolidated returns for all years on a calendar year basis, and all the corporations at issue use the accrual method. The P group has no intercompany debt or debt with the acquiring group. The CFOs have tentatively agreed to an acquisition price of $300 million in P1 voting stock (a B reorganization) and a closing date of October 31, Year 2, subject to a discussion of the tax issues. P's adjusted basis in the stock of S1 as of the date of the reorganization will be $500 million. What are the respective consolidated return issues that the tax departments of P and P1 should bring to the attention of their CFOs?

Reverse acquisitions. Because the stock of P1 was used as part of the acquisition consideration, the transaction must be tested to determine whether it is a "reverse acquisition." As discussed at ¶ 845, if P1 issued more than 50 percent of its stock (but less than 80 percent) to P, this would be a reverse acquisition. This would cause the P1 group to terminate. P1 would become the parent of the S1 group. Because the S1 group had not previously been a group, the S1 group is not a continuing group but is a resulting new group.

Because a reverse acquisition is unusual, assume for the rest of the discussion that P1 does not issue more than 50 percent of its stock to P.

Stock basis computation and loss disallowance rules. The consolidated return investment adjustment rules are important to both P and P1 in a B reorganization. P1 carries over P's S1's stock basis under Code Sec. 362, as well as its "loss disallowance history" (see below).

---

[35] Reg. § 1.1502-13(f)(5) and Reg. § 1.1502-13 (f)(7), Example 5.

[36] Reg. § 1.338-8(a)(6).

[37] Reg. § 1.338(h)(10)-1(d)(3)(ii) and Reg. § 1.338(h)(10)-1(d)(4)(ii).

[38] Reg. § 1.1502-6.

Election by P1 to treat any S1 or S2 NOL carryover as expired. This election will be available but would result in a reduction in the S1 or S2 stock basis because this is not a "cost basis transaction" (see ¶ 315).

Loss limitation rules (LLR). As explained in Chapter 4, under the successor rules to the LLR, P is treated as deconsolidating its S1 stock before exchanging it for new P1 stock. Under the deconsolidation rules, P must reduce its basis in its P1 stock to its $300 million fair market value, except to the extent the P group can show the basis in its S1 stock is not attributable to the reorganization of built-in gain on the disposition of an asset. P1 carries over P's $500 million S1 stock basis and its "loss disallowance history" to be taken into account when P1 disposes of S1 or deconsolidates S1. Compare the successor in interest example at ¶ 415.11.

Intercompany items. S1's departure from the P group will cause the P group to accelerate any deferred gain or loss that arose in an intercompany transaction between S1 and another P group member.

Carryover tax attributes and limitations. If S1 or S2 has carryover tax attributes, see Chapter 6.

Other issues. For a discussion of short-period tax year, allocation of closing date items, allocation of items for year of disposition, elimination of earnings and profits, tax liability, and due date of final short-period return, see Example 4 at ¶ 925.01.

.04 Tax-Free Disposition of Subsidiary Assets

An example best illustrates a tax-free disposition of subsidiary assets.

> **Example 7:** P owns all the stock of S. P1 owns all the stock of S2. Both the P and P1 groups have filed consolidated returns for all years on a calendar year basis, and all the corporations at issue use the accrual method. The CFOs have tentatively agreed to merge S into S2 in exchange for $400 million worth of P1 voting stock in a tax-free forward triangular merger on July 1, subject to a discussion of the tax issues. As a result of the merger, P will become the owner of 10 percent of the P1 stock. The group has no loss carryovers or credit carryovers or debt. What are the respective consolidated return issues that the tax departments of P and P1 should bring to the attention of their CFOs?

Termination of P group. A consolidated group remains in existence for a tax year if the common parent remains as the common parent and at least one subsidiary that was affiliated with it at the end of the prior year remains affiliated with it at the beginning of the year, whether or not one or more corporations have ceased to be subsidiaries at any time after the group was formed.[39] Thus the P group will terminate on December 31 if P does not form or acquire another subsidiary before then.

Stock basis of S. The general rule for a forward triangular merger is to treat P1 for stock basis purposes as if it acquired the assets of S in a tax-free reorganization and dropped them down into a subsidiary under Code Sec. 351.[40] Thus, P1's

---

[39] Reg. § 1.1502-75(d)(1).   [40] Reg. § 1.358-6.

stock basis in S generally is increased by an amount equal to S's inside net asset basis. The main difference for consolidated return purposes is that P1 can take a negative stock basis if S has sufficient liabilities.[41]

Other issues. For a discussion of short tax year issues, allocation of closing date items, allocation of S's items for year of disposition, elimination of earnings and profits, and tax liability, see Example 4 at ¶ 925.01.

.05 Tax-Free Spinoff of Subsidiary Stock

Example 8 below illustrates the tax-free spinoff of subsidiary stock:

> **Example 8:** P owns all the stock of S and S1. P plans a tax-free spinoff of S on October 31, Year 6. The CFOs of P and S have tentatively agreed that P and S will be valued at $600 million and $400 million respectively after the spinoff. The P group has a Year 5 general business credit carryover of $20 million, all of which is allocable to S. What are the respective consolidated return issues that the tax departments of P and S should bring to the attention of their CFOs?

Recapture of excess loss account. The stock basis of P in S becomes immaterial in a tax-free spinoff. However, if P had an excess loss account in its S stock, the spinoff would be a recapture event.

Intercompany items. Whether S was the buying member or the selling member, the spinoff of S would accelerate the deferred gain or loss from prior intercompany transactions.

Carryover tax attributes and limitations. The consolidated return regulations have not been updated to provide for the allocation of the general business credit. However, most practitioners believe that, in the absence of regulations that address the general business credit, it should be allocated in the same manner as the outdated investment credit. Under those rules, here all of the general business credit carryover would be allocated to S. Because the credit carryover here was generated after S joined the P group, there is no Code Sec. 383 limitation. If the facts were like those in Example 4 at ¶ 925.01, where S joined the P group as a member of a subgroup with a change of ownership, it would be important for S to negotiate with P to have part of the Code Sec. 382 limitation allocated to it. Otherwise, there the credit carryover would lose its use.

Earnings and profits adjustments. The elimination of a subsidiary's earnings and profits rule of Reg. § 1.1502-33(e) is modified "to the extent necessary to effectuate the principles of section 312(h)."[42] Thus, P's earnings and profits, rather than S's earnings and profits, may be eliminated immediately before S becomes a nonmember. P's earnings and profits are eliminated to the extent that its earnings and profits reflect S's earnings and profits after applying Code Sec. 312(h) immediately after S becomes a nonmember (determined without taking this rule into account).[43]

---

[41] Reg. § 1.1502-30.

[42] Reg. § 1.1502-33(e)(3) and Reg. § 1.1502-33(f).

[43] *See* Bean, "Allocating E&P in a Spin-Off in Light of the Latest Consolidated Return Regulations," 84 *J. Tax'n* 69 (1996); *IU Int'l Corp.*, FedCl, 1996-1 USTC ¶ 50,121, 34 FedCl 767, *aff'd* CA-FC, 97-2 USTC ¶ 50,534, 116 F3d 1461.

Other issues. For a discussion of the short tax year issues, allocation of closing date items, allocation of items for year of spinoff, and tax liability of S, see Example 4 at ¶ 925.01.

Practice Tools

¶ 10,010 Checklist of Consolidated Return Statements and Elections

The consolidated return regulations applicable to current and future tax years provide for the key statements and elections set forth in the table below. Selected sample documents follow thereafter.

Regulation	*Statement of Election*
Reg. § 1.337(d)-2(c)(1) and (3)	Statement of allowed loss
Reg. § 1.1502-4(b)(1) and (2)	Common parent's foreign tax credit overall or per-country limitation deemed election for group, and limitation effective for subsequent years
Reg. § 1.1502-9(c)(2)(iv)	Statement of loss basket items apportioned to department member
Reg. § 1.1502-13(e), Example 5	Election out under Code Sec. 453(d)
Reg. § 1.1502-13(f)(5)(ii)	Election to recharacterize certain transactions to prevent S's items from being taken into account or to provide offsets to those items
Reg. § 1.1502-13(f)(6)(i)(C)(1)	Election to waive built-in loss on P stock

Regulation	*Statement of Election*
Temp. Reg. § 1.1502-13T	Statement for making Reg. § 1.1502-13(f)(5)(ii) and Reg. § 1.1502-13(f)(6)(i)(C)(1) elections for consolidated returns due after May 30, 2006; certain additional effective date provisions
Reg. § 1.1502-21(b)(3)	Elections to relinquish CNOL carrybacks
Reg. § 1.1502-28(b)(2)	Election under Code Sec. 108(b)(5)
Reg. § 1.1502-31(e)(1)	Election to waive loss carryovers of former common parent immediately before group structure change
Temp. Reg. § 1.1502-31T	Statement for making Reg. § 1.1502-31(e)(1) election for consolidated returns due after May 30, 2006; certain additional effective date provisions
Reg. § 1.1502-32(b)(4)	Election to waive loss carryovers from SRLY years
Temp. Reg. § 1.1502-32T	Statement for making Reg. § 1.1502-32(b)(4) election for consolidated returns due after May 30, 2006; certain additional effective date provisions
Reg. § 1.1502-33(d)(5)	Election to allocate additional amounts of federal income tax liability to reflect absorption by one member of the tax attributes of another member for earnings and profits purposes
Reg. § 1.1502-35(c)(5)(i)	Statement of allowed loss
Reg. § 1.1502-75(c)	Election to discontinue filing consolidated returns
Reg. § 1.1502-75(d)(5)(iii)(B)	Statement of delayed election to continue in existence
Reg. § 1.1502-76(b)(2)(ii)	Election to ratably allocate items within a year

¶10,010

Regulation	*Statement of Election*
Temp. Reg. § 1.1502-76T	Statement for making Reg. § 1.1502-76(b)(2)(ii) election for consolidated returns due after May 30, 2006; certain additional effective date provisions
Reg. § 1.1502-77	Statement of primary liability for the consolidated tax assigned to a successor of a member
Reg. § 1.1502-91(d)(4)	Election to treat loss subgroup parent as satisfied
Reg. § 1.1502-92(e)	Information statements required by Temp. Reg. § 1.382-11T(a)
Reg. § 1.1502-95(c)	Election to apportion consolidated section 382 limitation (or subgroup section 382 limitation) or a loss group's (or loss subgroup's) net unrealized built-in gain
Temp. Reg. § 1.1502-95T(f)	Statement for making Reg. § 1.1502-95(c) election for consolidated returns due after May 30, 2006; certain additional effective date provisions
Reg. § 1.1552-1(c)(1)	Election of basic method
Reg. § 1.1552-1(c)(5)	Election of complementary method

¶10,010

¶ 10,020 Sample Legal Document—Election to Waive Loss Carryovers from Separate Return Years (Reg. § 1.1502-32(b)(4)(iv))

If S has a loss carryover from a separate return limitation year when it becomes a member of a consolidated group, the group may make an irrevocable election to treat all or any portion of the loss carryover as expiring for all federal income tax purposes immediately before S becomes a member of the consolidated group (deemed expiration). If S was a member of another group immediately before it became a member of the consolidated group, the expiration is also treated as occurring immediately after it ceases to be a member of the prior group. If S becomes a member of the consolidated group in a qualifying cost basis transaction and an election is made, the noncapital nondeductible expense resulting from the deemed expiration does not result in a corresponding stock basis adjustment. The statement must be filed with the consolidated group's return for the year S becomes a member. A separate statement must be made for each member whose loss carryover is deemed to expire.

ELECTION TO TREAT LOSS CARRYOVER OF [INSERT NAME AND EMPLOYER IDENTIFICATION NUMBER OF S] AS EXPIRING UNDER REG. § 1.1502-32(b)(4)

[Name of the Common Parent]

[EIN of the Common Parent]

Tax year Ended [Date]

[1. The statement must identify the amount of each loss carryover deemed not to expire, with any balance of any loss carryovers being deemed to expire.]

[2. If the subsidiary did not become a member in a qualifying cost basis transaction with respect to its stock, the statement must include the basis of any stock reduced as a result of the deemed expiration, and the computation of the basis reduction.]

¶10,020

¶ 10,030 Sample Legal Document—Statement of Allowed Loss Under Reg. § 1.337(d)-2(c) (Reg. § 1.337(d)-2(c)(1) and (3))

For dispositions of stock of a consolidated subsidiary governed by Reg. § 1.337(d)-2, loss is allowed to the extent the taxpayer can establish it is not attributable to the recognition of built-in gain on an asset, provided an appropriate statement is filed with the taxpayer's return for the year of the disposition. Similar rules apply to a deconsolidation. The statement is set forth below.

REG. § 1.337(d)-2(c) STATEMENT

[Common Parent] and Subsidiaries

[EIN of Common Parent]

Tax year Ended [Date]

[1. Insert the name and EIN of the subsidiary.]

[2. State the amount of the loss not disallowed under Reg. § 1.337(d)-2 by reason of Reg. § 1.337(d)-2(c) and the amount of basis not reduced under Reg. § 1.337(d)-2(b)(1) by reason of Reg. § 1.337(d)-2(c).]

¶ 10,040 Sample Legal Document—Election of Basic Method (Reg. § 1.1552-1(c)(1))

Code Sec. 1552 provides three specific methods for allocating consolidated tax liability for earnings and profits purposes. As discussed more fully in Chapter 6, using the first basic method, the group's tax liability is apportioned based on each member's contribution to consolidated taxable income. Under the second basic method, the consolidated tax liability is apportioned based on each member's separate return tax liability. The third basic method initially allocates tax liability to each member based on the member's contribution to consolidated income as under the first basic method. Any tax increases arising from consolidation are then apportioned to those members whose liability is reduced by the consolidation. Whether a member has an increase or reduction because of consolidation is determined by comparing its allocated tax liability under the first basic method with its separate return tax liability. Code Sec. 1552 also authorizes the selection of other methods with the Commissioner's approval.

The election of one of the methods above is effective for the tax year of election and all subsequent years unless the taxpayer obtains approval from the Commissioner to change to another basic method. The election is made by attaching a statement to the consolidated return in its initial year. If a consolidated group fails to elect a specific method in its first consolidated return, the group is treated as having elected the first basic method without the complementary methods under Reg. § 1.1502-33(d).

THIS IS AN ELECTION UNDER REG. § 1.1552-1(c) TO ALLOCATE THE CONSOLIDATED TAX LIABILITY

[Common Parent] and Subsidiaries

[EIN of Common Parent]

Tax year Ended [Date]

[Name of Common Parent], as the common parent corporation, hereby elects to allocate the tax liability of the consolidated group in accordance with the method prescribed by Reg. § 1.1552-1(a) [insert (1), (2), or (3)]. [If any other method is elected under Reg. § 1.1552-1(a)(4), evidence of advance approval by the IRS must be provided.]

¶10,040

¶ 10,050 Sample Legal Document—Election of Complementary Method (Reg. § 1.1502-33(d)(5))

Reg. § 1.1502-33(d) provides two complementary methods that may be used in conjunction with the basic methods of Code Sec. 1552. Under the "wait-and-see method," a member whose tax liability is reduced by using the attribute of another member is treated as having paid that member for the use of the attribute only when the other member could have used it. On the other hand, the "percentage method" permits the group to allocate to loss and credit members the consolidated tax benefits attributable to the use of their losses and credits without taking into account the member's ability to utilize its attributes itself. Allocations under Reg. § 1.1502-33(d) must be reflected annually in the permanent records.

The election of a complementary method must be made by including the election in the consolidated return by the due date (including extensions) for the filing of the first consolidated return of the group. If a complementary method is not elected for the first consolidated return year of the group, the election may be made for a later year only with the approval of the Commissioner.

ELECTION TO ALLOCATE TAX LIABILITY UNDER REG. § 1.1502-33(d)

[Name of Common Parent]

[EIN of Common Parent]

Tax year Ended [Date]

[Name of the common parent], as the common parent of the consolidated group, hereby elects to allocate the tax liability of the consolidated group beginning with [tax year] in accordance with Reg. § 1.1502-33(d) [insert (2), (3), or (4)] in conjunction with the method described in Reg. § 1.1552-1(a) [insert (1), (2), (3), or (4)].

[If the percentage method is elected, state the percentage (not to exceed 100 percent) to be used.]

[If a method is permitted under Reg. § 1.1502-33(d)(4), attach evidence of approval of the method by the Commissioner.]

[Common Parent]

by _____

    [Title]   [Date]

¶ 10,060 Sample Legal Document—Election to Change Basic or Complementary Method (Rev. Proc. 90-39)

An election of a basic method or a complementary method once made is irrevocable and is binding on the group unless the IRS authorizes a change to another method prior to the time prescribed by law for filing the return for the year in which the change is to be effective.

The IRS, however, has provided a revenue procedure to obtain consent, without filing an advance ruling request, to elect or to change its method of allocating federal income tax liability to members of the consolidated group for earnings and profits purposes.[1] This revenue procedure applies to a consolidated group if (1) it is not filing its first consolidated return, (2) it has not changed its basic method or complementary method within the five previous tax years, and (3) it is not requesting another basic method or another complementary method.

The manner of effecting the election or change is set forth in Rev. Proc. 90-39, section 4. The common parent of the group must attach a statement to its consolidated return (filed on a timely basis, taking into account any extensions).

---

[1] Rev. Proc. 90-39, 1990-2 CB 365, clarified by Rev. Proc. 90-39A, 1990-2 CB 367.

¶10,060

ELECTION TO CHANGE METHOD OF ALLOCATING CONSOLIDATED TAX LIABILITY UNDER CODE SEC. 1552 AND REG. § 1.1502-33(d)

[Common Parent] and Subsidiaries

[EIN of Common Parent]

Tax year Ended [Date]

[1. Insert the name of the common parent corporation of the consolidated group, its Employer Identification Number (EIN) and its address, the name and EIN of all the members of the affiliated group, and the district office that has jurisdiction over the consolidated return.]

[2. Insert a complete description of the present method of allocating the consolidated federal income tax liability. If the present method is not the method that was used for the first filing of a consolidated return, the statement must indicate the date permission to change the group's allocation method was granted and the tax year for which the change was effective. If the group previously used this revenue procedure to elect or to change its method of allocating the consolidated federal income tax liability, a copy of the earlier statement, including the date such statement was filed and the tax year of the consolidated return with which it was filed, must be attached to this statement.]

[3. Insert a complete description of the group's proposed method of allocating consolidated federal income tax liability. If the percentage complementary method is to be employed, the fixed percentage must be stated.]

[4. Insert a representation that adoption of the proposed method of allocation will not change the taxable status of distributions made during the year of change or in any foreseeable future year to shareholders who are not members of the affiliated group.]

Under penalties of perjury, I declare that the representations made in this statement, including accompanying documents, are to the best of my knowledge and belief, true, correct, and complete.

[Common Parent]

by _____

    [Title]   [Date]

¶10,060

¶ 10,070 Sample Legal Document—Election to Ratably Allocate Income and Deductions of Subsidiary (Reg. § 1.1502-76(b)(2)(D))

When a corporation becomes or ceases to be a member of the consolidated group, the corporation must ordinarily treat its tax year as closing at that time, and its original year, (*i.e.,* the tax year the corporation would have had without taking into account Reg. § 1.1502-76) becomes two short, separate tax years. An irrevocable election may be made to ratably allocate certain of the corporation's nonextraordinary items between the short periods as if they were still part of the same tax year, provided the subsidiary is not required to change its annual accounting period or its method of accounting as a result of its change in status. If the first election is not made, an election may be made to ratably allocate only the corporation's nonextraordinary items for the month of its change in status.

Either election is made by submitting a separate statement signed by the corporation and the common parent of each affected group. The election must be made by the due date (including extensions) of the returns that include the items of the corporation for the years ending and beginning with the corporation's change in status.

THIS IS AN ELECTION UNDER REG. § 1.1502-76(b)(2)(ii) TO RATABLY
ALLOCATE THE YEAR'S ITEMS OF
[INSERT NAME AND EIN OF THE MEMBER]

The following disclosure is made an integral part of this election:

	Total	Included in the Separate or Consolidated Year End [Date]	Included in the Separate or Consolidated Year End [Date]
1. Extraordinary items:			
[Item 1]	[Amount]	[Amount]	[Amount]
[Item 2, etc.]	[Amount]	[Amount]	[Amount]
2. Aggregate amount to be ratably allocated for the original year	[Amount]	[Amount]	[Amount]
3. Name and EIN of Common Parent of each group that must take into account the items		[Name] [EIN]	[Name] [EIN]

An agreement as
described in Reg.
§ 1.1502-76(b)(2)(ii)(D)(2)
has been entered into.

[Name of Common Parent] [Name of Common Parent]

By _____ By _____

   [Title]   [Date]   [Title]   [Date]

Name of Sub that became/ Name of Sub that became/
ceased to be a member]   ceased to be a member]

By _____ By _____

   [Title]   [Date]   [Title]   [Date]

¶10,070

Finding Lists

Citations found in this book's text are listed below under the following categories:

Internal Revenue Code Sections, Regulations, Proposed Regulations, Temporary Regulations, Chief Counsel Advice, Field Service Advice, IRS Letter Rulings, Notices, Revenue Procedures, Revenue Rulings, and Treasury Decisions.

References are to paragraph (¶) numbers

Internal Revenue Code Sections

Regulations

References are to paragraph (¶) numbers

References are to paragraph (¶) numbers

Proposed Regulations

References are to paragraph (¶) numbers

Temporary Regulations

Chief Counsel Advice

Field Service Advice

IRS Letter Rulings

Notices

Revenue Procedures

Revenue Rulings

Treasury Decisions

Index

All references are to paragraph (¶) numbers

A

Acceleration rule for intercompany property transactions . . . 145.02

Accounting methods and periods . . . 115.01, 145.02, 201.04, 245.03
. change in . . . 255
. items included in . . . 245.02
. tax year for . . . 245.01
. timing rules as . . . 575.01

Accounting when subsidiary joins or leaves consolidated group . . . 901, 901.01, 915
. allocation of disposition year items for . . . 915.03
. due date for . . . 915.02
. items included in . . . 915.01
. next day rule for . . . 915.04

Accumulated earnings tax. *See* Tax liability

Affiliated group
. accounting . . . 201.04, 245, 245.03
. acquisition by another group . . . 325.03
. consolidated tax liability . . . 201.06, 275–275.01

Affiliated group—continued
. consolidated taxable income of members . . . 201.05, 255
. qualifications . . . 115.01, 201.01, 215
. restructuring . . . 835
. succeeding as owners of assets of former parent . . . 825.02

Aggregate deemed sales price (ADSP) . . . 925.02

Alternative minimum tax (AMT). *See* Tax liability

Appreciated notes . . . 665.01

Asset consistency rules . . . 125.05, 375
. example . . . 925.01
. in stock basis system . . . 301.04, 345

B

Basic method of allocating consolidated tax liability . . . 10,040
. changing, election . . . 745.11, 10,060
. effect of allocations . . . 745.09
. first method . . . 745.01, 745.04
. first return . . . 745.10

CON

LOS

STO

WOR